Freedom from Religion and Human Rights Law

Although human rights belong to all persons on the basis of their humanity, this book demonstrates that in the practice of international human rights law, the freedom to be non-religious or atheist does not receive the same protection as the freedom to be religious. Despite the claimed universality of freedom of religion and belief contained in article 18 of the International Covenant on Civil and Political Rights, the key assertion made is that there is a hierarchy of religion and belief, with followers of major established religions enjoying high protection and low regulation at the top, and atheists and non-believers enduring high persecution and weaker protection at the bottom. The existence of this hierarchy is proven and critiqued through three case study chapters that respectively explore the extent to which non-religious and atheist rights-holders enjoy freedom from proselytism, freedom from hate and freedom from the religions of their parents.

Marika McAdam is an independent legal consultant and adviser who has worked for the United Nations Office on Drugs and Crime, the Office of the High Commissioner of Human Rights, the International Organization for Migration and the Nexus Institute among other organisations.

Routledge Research in Human Rights Law

Available titles in this series include:

Freedom from Religion and Human Rights Law
Strengthening the Right to Freedom of Religion and Belief for Non-Religious and Atheist Rights-Holders
Marika McAdam

Freedom of Expression and Religious Hate Speech in Europe
Erica Howard

The Protection of Vulnerable Groups under International Human Rights Law
Ingrid Nifosi-Sutton

Children's Rights Law in the Global Human Rights Landscape
Isolation, Inspiration, Integration?
Edited by Eva Brems, Ellen Desmet and Wouter Vandenhole

The Istanbul Convention, Domestic Violence and Human Rights
Ronagh J.A. McQuigg

Human Rights Education and the Politics of Knowledge
Joanne Coysh

Resolving Conflicts between Human Rights
The Judge's Dilemma
Stijn Smet

The ECHR and Human Rights Theory
Reconciling the Moral and the Political Conceptions
Alain Zysset

For more information on this series visit: https://www.routledge.com/Routledge-Research-in-Human-Rights-Law/book-series/HUMRIGHTSLAW

Freedom from Religion and Human Rights Law

Strengthening the Right to Freedom of Religion and Belief for Non-Religious and Atheist Rights-Holders

Marika McAdam

Routledge
Taylor & Francis Group
LONDON AND NEW YORK

First published 2018
by Routledge

2 Park Square, Milton Park, Abingdon, Oxfordshire OX14 4RN
52 Vanderbilt Avenue, New York, NY 10017

Routledge is an imprint of the Taylor & Francis Group, an informa business

First issued in paperback 2019

British Library Cataloguing in Publication Data
A catalogue record for this book is available from the British Library

Library of Congress Cataloging-in-Publication Data
Names: McAdam, Marika, author.
Title: Freedom from religion and human rights law : strengthening the right to freedom of religion and belief for non-religious and atheist rights-holders / Marika McAdam.
Description: New York, NY : Routledge, 2017. |
Series: Routledge research in human rights law |
Includes bibliographical references and index.
Identifiers: LCCN 2017025919 | ISBN 9781138632967 (hardback)
Subjects: LCSH: Freedom of religion. | Human rights. | Atheism.
Classification: LCC K3258 .M34 2017 | DDC 342.08/522--dc23
LC record available at https://lccn.loc.gov/2017025919

ISBN: 978-1-138-63296-7 (hbk)
ISBN: 978-0-367-88667-7 (pbk)

Typeset in Galliard
by Taylor & Francis Books

Contents

Acknowledgments

Sincerest thanks to Professor Sarah Joseph of the Castan Centre for Human Rights Law at Monash University, for her unwavering intellectual commitment and support of the PhD thesis on which this book is based. Thank you also to Patrick Emerton who lent his big brain to the process in the home stretch.

As always, thank you to my ever-supportive Jo, who made it possible for me to do this work and kept at me to prioritise it. Thank you for putting up with my near-obsessive passion for this topic.

Above all, thank you to my parents, Laurie and Jennie McAdam, who took me to synagogues, mosques, churches and temples and told me I was free to believe anything I chose to, and nothing I didn't.

Introduction

The history of religion and belief is a bloody one. Even in today's globalised, pluralist 21st century, people are driven to hate, torture and murder in asserting or defending their religion or belief. And remarkably, people continue to hold beliefs and practise religions in defiance of the violence perpetrated against them because of it. Attempts by private persons, religious groups and even the state to stifle religious movements have continually failed, oftentimes fanning the flames of religious resolve. Alongside the proliferation of religion, is the parallel plight of those who refuse to profess beliefs they do not hold, or who even deign to assert atheism sometimes in the face of grave danger for doing so. Indeed, the freedom of atheists and non-theists to manifest their beliefs is a human right that many people continue to be killed in the exercise of, and yet is a right that is often overlooked in the interpretation and application of international human rights law.

The central argument of this monograph is that the human right to freedom of religion and belief of non-religious and atheistic rights holders is inadequately protected. Human rights attach to humans on the basis of their humanity, not on the basis of their religion or belief; article 18 of the International Covenant on Civil and Political Rights (ICCPR) protects "theistic, non-theistic and atheistic beliefs, as well as the right not to profess any religion or belief".[1] But in exploring interpretations of freedom of religion and belief, it becomes apparent that the religion or belief of right-holders impacts on the extent to which their freedom is respected and protected. Jurisprudence reveals a lack of protection across the spectrum of worldviews, and trepidation of the international human rights community to test the limits and boundaries of this right. Atheists have the right to *not* adhere to the religions around them, as well as a positive right to manifest their atheism, but in practice, when their rights conflict with those of their theistic counterparts, it becomes apparent that freedom *from* religion is subordinated to freedom of religion.

1 Human Rights Committee, *General Comment 22: The right to freedom of thought, conscience and religion (Article 18)*, UN Doc CCPR/C/21/Rev.1/Add.4 (27 September 1993) [2].

Chapter 1 shows that freedom of religion and belief is one of the strongest human rights contained in the ICCPR, evincing the special place that 'religion' enjoys relative to 'belief' in international law. The chapter unpacks article 18 and interrogates the ways it has been understood, applied and limited to reveal the pro-religious bias of human rights law, notwithstanding the normative pluralism that should underpin it.

Chapter 2 asserts that there is a hierarchy of religion and belief in the practice of international human rights law. By considering the high influence of monotheistic religions, and the weak regulation of them when their activities trespass on the rights and freedoms of others, major monotheistic religions are shown to occupy the highest rung of the hierarchy, with followers of newer, less established religions and atheists and non-religious rights holders below them. This contention is further explored in three case study chapters.

Chapter 3 offers proselytism as a case study to prove the hierarchy of religion and belief at play in the interpretation and administration of human rights law, and the resulting disadvantage to atheists and non-believers. Whether proselytism is protected as a manifestation of religious freedom or prohibited as a form of coercion is shown to depend on the religion and belief of its source and target. Again the advantage of adherents of major religions is proven, relative to the disadvantage of non-religious rights holders. The chapter asserts that proselytism should be limited where it undermines choice, not on the basis of the religion or belief being proselytised.

Chapter 4 explores the prohibition of hate speech that incites discrimination, hostility or violence, to find that persons who are hated *for* their religion are more likely to be protected than those who are hated *by* the religious. Again the disadvantaged position of atheists and non-religious rights-holders is revealed; while clearly targets of hate speech, their non-religion is not explicitly captured as a prohibited ground of 'religious hatred' by the ICCPR. The beliefs and hated traits of parties concerned are thus found to have more bearing on legal decisions than do considerations as to whether or not the hate speech in question incites discrimination, hostility or violence. Again the entrenched privilege of certain monotheistic religions over atheism and non-religion is revealed.

The third and final case study chapter, Chapter 5, considers the conflict between a child's right to freedom of religion and belief and the right of her parents to impose their religion or belief upon her. The religious upbringing of children is explored in this context, with ritual circumcision of infants particularly scrutinised to illustrate the pro-religious bias of international human rights law, that protects parental rights to manifest their religion on their child, above the child's own rights and freedoms.

Having established that there is a hierarchy of religion and belief at international law, the concluding chapter considers whether such a hierarchy is justified. From a rights-based perspective that values individual freedoms over ideologies, the conclusion reached is that the hierarchy is wholly indefensible and serves to entrench the vulnerability of rights holders on the basis of their religion or belief. Freedom *from* religion – entailing more than a negative right *not* to manifest religion but also a positive right to manifest atheism – is offered as the means of levelling the hierarchy at play and the true measure of freedom of religion and belief. Freedom *from* religion emerges as an inviolable asset not only for non-religious and atheist rights holders, but as a vital component of meaningful and equal enjoyment of religious and belief freedoms for those who believe in God, those who believe in many gods, and those who believe that there is no god.

1 Freedom of religion or belief

This chapter explores the meaning of both 'religion' and 'belief' in international law, to show that the rights of non-religious and atheist rights-holders are not equally protected relative to those of their religious counterparts. Distinctions between notions of atheism, non-religion and ideological indifference are considered, to understand those concepts and their locus in rights discourse. On the basis of that discussion, pluralism is pointed to as the fundamental principle that must guide interpretation and application of the human right to freedom of religion and belief.

The various components of freedom of religion or belief, as captured by article 18 of the International Covenant on Civil and Political Rights (ICCPR) are then briefly unpacked with a view to exploring the extent to which the right encompasses the spectrum of religions and beliefs, including non-religion, irreligion and atheism. Finally, permissible limitations to manifestations of religion and belief are considered to show the special position of this right above others, and the special place of religions above beliefs. This analysis concludes that article 18 of the ICCPR does not protect freedom to be non-religious or atheist as rigorously as it upholds the right to practise a major, established religion.

1. The meaning of 'religion' and 'belief' in international law

Article 18

1 Everyone shall have the right to freedom of thought, conscience and religion. This right shall include freedom to have or to adopt a religion or belief of his choice, and freedom, either individually or in community with others and in public or private, to manifest his religion or belief in worship, observance, practice and teaching.

2 No one shall be subject to coercion which would impair his freedom to have or to adopt a religion or belief of his choice.

3 Freedom to manifest one's religion or beliefs may be subject only to such limitations as are prescribed by law and are necessary to protect public safety, order, health, or morals or the fundamental rights and freedoms of others.

4 The States Parties to the present Covenant undertake to have respect for the liberty of parents and, when applicable, legal guardians to ensure the religious

and moral education of their children in conformity with their own convictions.

Article 18 of the ICCPR upholds "freedom to have or to adopt a religion or belief of his choice".[1] Both 'religion' and 'belief' remain undefined in international law, for clear reasons; "if these terms were defined, states might be tempted routinely to label as spurious all expressions of belief and practices that do not conform to the details of the definitions."[2] In the absence of agreed definitions, this section considers the extent to which atheism and other forms of non-religious or irreligious belief are captured in understandings of religion and belief for the purposes of article 18.

1.1. Defining 'religion' and 'belief'

Jeremy Gunn points to two underlying challenges involved in defining 'religion', being firstly the metaphysical assumptions about the nature of religion, and secondly the type of definition to be used in describing them.[3] In relation to the first of these points, the challenge lies in the fact that there is no single understanding of the nature of religion. It can be construed in a metaphysical sense (e.g. truth of the existence of God), as a psychological experience (e.g. feelings of believers) or as a cultural or social force (e.g. binding or dividing communities).[4] Yet notwithstanding these challenges, several attempts have been made to legally define religion at the domestic level.[5] The result is that people whose beliefs fall outside of the outcome of those attempts, may also fall outside of the scope of protection. Definitions that capture a theistic notion of a Supreme Being may exclude nontheistic or polytheistic religions like Buddhism and Hinduism, or favour some interpretations over others *within* a given religious tradition.[6] Those at particular risk of falling foul of the ambit of protection are groups or individuals with particular beliefs or practices, especially supporters of non-established religions or atheism.[7] Members of religions that are not recognised as religions may be in particularly fraught positions; some newer religions and beliefs may be

1 *International Covenant on Civil and Political Rights*, opened for signature 16 December 1966, 999 UNTS 171 (entered into force 23 March 1976).
2 Donna Sullivan, 'Advancing the Freedom of Religion or Belief through the UN Declaration on the Elimination of Religious Intolerance and Discrimination' (1988) 82 *American Journal of International Law* 487, 492.
3 Jeremy T. Gunn, 'The Complexity of Religion and the Definition of "Religion" in International Law' (2003) 189 *Harvard Human Rights Journal* 16, 193.
4 Ibid 193–194.
5 See Arif A. Jamal, 'The Impact of Definitional Issues on the Right of Freedom of Religion and Belief' in Silvio Ferrari (ed.) *Routledge Handbook of Law and Religion* (Routledge, 2015) 93–99, and Rex Ahdar and Ian Leigh, *Religious Freedom in the Liberal State* (Oxford University Press, 2013) 145–155.
6 Jamal, above n 5, 100.
7 For more on challenges in defining 'religion', see Peter Edge, *Religion and Law: An Introduction* (Ashgate, 2006) 27–30.

considered undeserving of the status of 'religion' where the same is not true for established religions.

At the international level, the question of which canons of conduct can be considered 'religious' for the purposes of article 18 has arisen before the Human Rights Committee (HRC). In the complaint of *MAB, WAT and J-AYT v Canada* the authors[8] were members of the 'Assembly of the Church of the Universe', whose beliefs and practices involved the cultivation, possession, distribution and use of marijuana.[9] The HRC found the complaint inadmissible given that "a belief consisting primarily or exclusively in the worship and distribution of a narcotic drug cannot conceivably be brought within the scope of article 18 of the Covenant."[10] However, in the more recent HRC decision of *Prince v South Africa*,[11] the status of Rastafarianism as a religion within the meaning of article 18 was not at issue, nor was its practice involving the use of a narcotic, but the HRC found that prohibitions on its practices including worship and use of a narcotic drug, constituted a justifiable limitation on the freedom to manifest the Rastafarian religion.[12] The fact that Rastafarianism was found to enjoy the status of 'religion' was appropriate given that "it is perhaps unwise…to deny such groups the status of 'religion', especially if such denial is motivated by the Committee's disapproval of a group's activities."[13] This is commensurate with what is noted by Asma Jahangir when she was Special Rapporteur on Freedom of Religion or Belief:

> Due to the problem of finding a satisfactory definition of the 'protected religion or belief', the pertinent international human rights standards provide for a broad view of these concepts. Consequently freedom of religion or belief is not limited in its application to traditional religions or to religions and beliefs with institutional characteristics or practices analogous to those of traditional religions.[14]

The substance of the protection offered by article 18 of the ICCPR applies equally to freedom of religion and freedom of belief, raising the question of whether *all* beliefs are protected.[15] Some commentators, including Natan Lerner, assert that

8 The term 'author' is used in accordance with the HRC's terminology to denote the party bringing an individual complaint before the Committee.

9 *MAB and ors v Canada, Admissibility*, Human Rights Committee, Communication No. 570/1993, UN Doc CCPR/C/50/D/570/1993 (1994).

10 Ibid [4.2].

11 *Prince v South Africa, Merits*, Human Rights Committee, Communication No. 1474/2006, UN Doc CCPR/C/91/D/1474/2006 (2007).

12 Ibid [6.5].

13 Sarah Joseph, Jenny Schultz and Melissa Castan, *The International Covenant on Civil and Political Rights: Cases, Materials, and Commentary* (Oxford University Press, 2nd ed., 2004) 503.

14 Asma Jahangir, *Report of the Special Rapporteur on freedom of religion or belief*, UN Doc A/HRC/6/5 (20 July 2007) 6 [6].

15 Some have referred to the fact that 'belief' is not mentioned in the first phrase of article 18(1), while the following phrase allows for the manifestation of both religion

the meaning of belief should be interpreted in connection with the term religion, such that

> the term *religion*, usually followed by the word *belief*, means theistic convictions, involving a transcendental view of the universe and a normative code of behaviour, as well as atheistic, agnostic, rationalistic, and other views in which both elements may be absent.[16]

Similarly, Johan D. van der Vyver considers that the meaning of 'belief' is to be drawn from the meaning of 'religion'. He asserts that not every belief is afforded protection under article 18 but rather that "the kind of beliefs that come within the protection of those instruments tend to be religious or have something in common with religious belief."[17] Hence, protected religions and beliefs have in common the "acceptance of the existence of something without the backing of sensorial observation, scientific demonstration, or rational proof; that is, convictions founded on metaphysical assumptions".[18] The implication of accepting such an understanding would be that where a religious belief *is* proven by "sensorial observation, scientific demonstration, or rational proof", it would cease to enjoy the protection of article 18 of the ICCPR. Yet contrarily, a sensorial observation of an apparition of the Virgin Mary or a blood-crying statue would likely have the affect of bolstering rather than detracting from the religiosity of the person who sees it. Similarly, it is difficult to determine whether the hallucinogenic effect of marijuana (which, according to the Rastafarianism religion, is important in the facilitation of meditation and reflection on the word of God) is based on a metaphysical assumption or scientific demonstration. Profound questions arise about whether the theory of evolution is scientifically rational enough to disprove creationism and so place the belief that God created man outside the ambit of protection. Is God's invisibility a sensorial observation that would render the atheist's 'belief' in his non-existence too rational to attract protection? Importantly, for present purposes: what protection would be afforded to atheists whose beliefs consist in denial of metaphysical assumptions? Cornelis D. de Jong offers a simpler approach, noting that the word 'belief' has been deliberately translated in French to 'conviction' in order to include non-religious beliefs.[19] Roger Trigg agrees that

and belief. See *inter alia* Malcolm Evans, *Religious Liberty and International Law in Europe* (Cambridge University Press, 1997) 203 and Carolyn Evans, *Freedom of Religion under the European Convention on Human Rights* (Oxford, 2001) 52 referring to article 9 of the European Convention on Human Rights which also refers only to "freedom of thought, conscience and religion".

16 Natan Lerner, *Religion, Secularism and Human Rights* (2nd edn, Martinus Nijhoff Publishers, 2012) 14, 49.

17 Johan D. van der Vyver, 'Limitations on Freedom of Religion or Belief: International Law Perspectives' (2005) 19 *Emory International Law Review* 499, 506.

18 Ibid.

19 Cornelis D. de Jong, *The Freedom of Thought, Conscience and Religion or Belief in the United Nations (1946–1992)* (Intersentia, 2000), School of Human Rights Research Series, Vol. 5, 23–24.

'belief' was added to capture protection of anti-religious views but finds this problematic as 'belief' will gain its salience from the meaning of 'religion' or be so stretched to any belief as to become meaningless, ultimately detracting from the special nature of 'religion' that is deeply grounded in human nature and an integral part of being human.[20]

That the ambit of international human rights protection extends to religious and non-religious beliefs is borne out in the history of the role of Special Rapporteur on Freedom of Religion or Belief.[21] In 1998, the second appointee to that position, Abdelfattah Amor, recommended that the original title of the 'Special Rapporteur on Religious Intolerance' be changed to the 'Special Rapporteur on Freedom of Religion or Belief', explicitly naming agnosticism, freethinking, atheism and rationalism as examples of the latter.[22] Subsequent Rapporteurs have followed this approach to also emphasise protection of the right to profess theistic, atheistic and non-theistic beliefs.[23] The inclusion of atheism as a belief was also stressed by Asma Jahangir in a 2007 report that highlighted that while atheists and non-theists are not as institutionalised as theists (for historical and cultural reasons, as well as the fact that they often take a more personal approach to their convictions), freedom of religion or belief applies equally to them.[24] In differentiating atheism from theism, Jahangir noted:

> Theism is the belief in the existence of one supernatural being (monotheism) or several divinities (polytheism), whereas a non-theist is someone who does not accept a theistic understanding of deity. Atheism is the critique or denial of metaphysical beliefs in spiritual beings.[25]

Cornelis D. de Jong reiterates that there is a tendency towards broadening the scope of what is meant by 'religion or belief' with the inclusion of the word "whatever" in the Declaration on the Elimination of All Forms of Intolerance and of Discrimination Based on Religion or Belief (the 1981 Declaration).[26] While the

20 Roger Trigg, *Equality, Freedom and Religion* (Oxford University Press, 2012) 14, 18–25, 156.
21 The Special Rapporteur on Freedom of Religion or Belief is an independent expert mandated to offer recommendations towards strengthening enjoyment of freedom of religion and belief.
22 See Abdelfattah Amor, Special Rapporteur, *Implementation of the Declaration on the Elimination of all forms of intolerance and of discrimination based on religion or belief*, UN Doc E.CN/4/1998/6/Add.2 (22 December 1997) [105].
23 See for instance, Asma Jahangir, *Elimination of all forms of religion intolerance: interim report of the Special Rapporteur on freedom of religion or belief*, UN Doc A/62/280 (20 August 2007) and Heiner Bielefeldt, *Report of the Special Rapporteur on freedom of religion or belief*, UN Doc A/HRC/16/53/Add.1 (14 February 2011) [97], [349].
24 Jahangir, above n 23 [75].
25 Jahangir, above n 23 [67].
26 *Declaration on the Elimination of All Forms of Intolerance and of Discrimination Based on Religion or Belief*, UN GAOR, UN Doc A/Res/36/55 (25 November 1981). Article 1 reads "Everyone shall have the right to freedom of thought, conscience and

1981 Declaration lacks the binding status of a treaty, its wording offers insight into states' positions in the decades after the 1966 ICCPR was negotiated. The 1981 Declaration is the result of agreement between delegates (with the exception of the Islamic group of states) that the scope of the Declaration included non-theistic and atheistic beliefs.[27] It was determined that any attempt to define 'religion or belief' and enumerate such beliefs (for instance, theistic, non-theistic, atheistic) would inevitably be incomplete; the word "whatever" was therefore introduced as a catchall compromise.[28]

Beyond these understandings, 'religion' and 'belief' remain undefined in human rights law, and must remain so in order to protect as broad a range of religions and beliefs as possible. Rights-holders may not neatly fit one or the other label. Non-religious belief does not start where religious belief stops or vice versa; there is a slippage between the two. Someone who considers him or herself to belong to a religion or be 'spiritual', may also identify as an atheist. Abby Day points to atheists who believe in ghosts or who are superstitious or fatalistic or simply believe in 'something' whether in the form of God, Jesus, a goddess or fairies and gnomes; or who identify as Christian for having been baptised despite their non-belief, or when bereaved, hope for an afterlife for their loved ones.[29] Day argues that the division between 'religious' and 'non-religious' is overly simplistic as 'belief' is not a single statement that neatly reflects its content but is dependent on interrelated and changing dimensions.[30] Added to this is the broad notion of what 'secular' or non-religious people can be crudely labelled, regardless of what, if anything, they label themselves. Among other concepts, Lois Lee flags free thought, non-religious humanism, scepticism, a-religion, un-religion, irreligion and non-religion, some of which, it must be noted, may also be present in a person who otherwise identifies as religious.[31]

It is clear, then, that while 'belief' ought to remain undefined, a tension remains between the need to protect all manner of spiritual and a-spiritual ideas that would not fall within religion, while also narrowing understanding so that the 'species' of beliefs at issue does not morph beyond the realm of article 18 into the territory of article 19 protecting freedom of opinion and expression. For the purpose of this monograph, 'belief' is understood to entail spiritual beliefs that may not attach to a specific religion, as well as non-religious, anti-religious or irreligious beliefs such as atheism, while beliefs having nothing to do with this ideological 'family' of beliefs (for instance, democratic opinions or environmentalist convictions) are more appropriately allocated to the domain of article 19(1). If it were not so,

religion. This right shall include freedom to have a religion or whatever belief of his choice."

27 Lerner, above n 16, 28–31.

28 de Jong, above n 19, 24 and 30–31.

29 Abby Day, *Believing in Belonging* (Oxford, 2011), 99, 103, 107–109, 115, 122, 174–190. Trigg also notes that even virulent atheists can react to their surroundings in ways that can lead them to think of supernatural agency or purpose. Trigg, above n 20, 27.

30 Day, above n 29, 159–173.

31 Lois Lee, *Recognizing the Non-Religious: Reimagining the Secular* (Oxford 2015) 21.

there would be little value in the ICCPR articulating a right to freedom of thought, religion and belief (article 18), distinct from a right to hold opinions and to express them (article 19). In this sense, Johan D. van der Vyver's explanation above, that the concept of 'religion' informs the meaning of 'belief', is instructive;[32] the 'beliefs' anticipated by article 18 hang on their religiosity (such as a new sect of an old religion or a general spirituality of no particular religion) or their non-religiosity (such as atheism), as opposed to vegetarianism which may be a manifestation of a religion or may be entirely unrelated to it; a Hindu or an atheist can be a vegetarian. By way of illustration, the answer 'I am an atheist' is a sensible response to the question 'what is your religion?' in the way that 'I am a vegetarian' or 'I am a democrat' is not.

The semantic compromise reached by adding "whatever belief" alongside "religion" in the drafting of freedom of religion and belief, ensured a broad interpretation but did not clarify that equal weight is to be given to the right to profess either.[33] The HRC's General Comment 22 on article 18 is unambiguous: "article 18 protects theistic, non-theistic and atheistic beliefs, as well as the right not to profess any religion or belief. The terms 'belief' and 'religion' are to be broadly construed."[34] It is clear then that the decision not to define religion or belief in international law is for the purpose of ensuring that protection is more inclusive than it is exclusive.[35] Indeed, human rights law cannot anticipate the range and content of religions or beliefs held across the world or which will emerge, and nor indeed is it its function to do so. Rather, drafters of human rights norms must ensure their equal applicability to all manner of religions and beliefs professed and practised by rights-holders.

This monograph proceeds on the basis that while holders of 'belief' are entitled to equal protection that 'religious' rights-holders are, they do not receive it. The relatively less attention 'belief' receives in rights discourse suggests that it is the poor cousin of supernatural 'religious' belief. This inequitable treatment gives rise to the contention to be discussed, that there is a hierarchy of religion and belief in the practice of international human rights law, with some religions favoured over others, and all religions over non-religion and atheism.

1.2. Pluralism as the guiding principle

Pluralism has been defined philosophically as "a theory or system that recognizes more than one ultimate principle".[36] In the present context it denotes not merely

32 van der Vyver, above n 17, 506.

33 Lerner, above n 16, 58–59; also see Carolyn Evans, above n 15, 60–61.

34 Human Rights Committee, *General Comment 22: The right to freedom of thought, conscience and religion (Article 18)*, UN Doc CCPR/C/21/Rev.1/Add.4 (27 September 1993) [2].

35 See however Carolyn Evans, above n 15, 51, who suggests that controversy over the definition of religion and belief calls into question that drafters had any common intention.

36 Oxford Dictionary Online, http://oxforddictionaries.com/definition/english/pluralism, accessed 22 March 2017.

the existence of several religions and beliefs, but also their entitlement to equal respect at the level of international law. As Ahdar and Leigh note, "[r]eligious pluralism is a fact of life."[37] Acknowledging this in both fact and in law requires that individuals and their multitudinous religions and beliefs be equally valued.[38] In acknowledging the diversity of worldviews, pluralism underpins the principle that rights-holders should not be discriminated against on the the basis of their religion or belief.[39] According to former Special Rapporteur on Freedom of Religion and Belief, Heiner Bielefeldt, the fact that human beings are rights-holders, follows on from this diversity of worldviews, meaning that religious and belief pluralism – including irreconcilable differences in ideas and practices – must be taken seriously. He explained this point thus:

> while some religions are based on scriptures transmitted through prophets, other religions do not have the notions of prophecy, scriptural revelation or even God. What is sacred for one community may remain rather opaque to another community. It is not least for this reason that legal recognition in the framework of human rights cannot immediately be accorded to the particular contents of religions or beliefs – such as their truth claims, scriptures or practices –, but only to human beings as the responsible agents who hold, cherish, develop and try to live in accordance with their convictions. Only by focusing on human beings as rights-holders can freedom of religion or belief do justice to the broad variety of religious and non-religious convictions, identities and practices, without singling out one specific religion or belief (or one type of religion) for privileged treatment.[40]

The "irreconcilable views" that are mentioned here extend to those that run contrary to pluralism, by preferring the dominance of one belief to the existence of many. Abdulaziz Sachedina explains that rights advocates cannot expect religious people to surrender their belief that their religious tradition is the absolute truth and sole source of human salvation. The challenge is how to allow disagreements to foster respect for different versions of the truth while still allowing for the belief that one is right and the other wrong.[41] Sachedina talks of an Islamic notion of pluralism in the form of the God-given right of a person to determine his or her spiritual destiny without coercion, as the cornerstone of inter- and intra-religious relations.[42] The Koran, he says, allows for pluralism in matters of faith and law to exist

37 Ahdar and Leigh, above n 5, 112. Also see Gozdecka's analysis of the shift in European Court of Human Rights jurisprudence from approaching pluralism as a fact, to it being a cornerstone necessary to democratic society. Dorota Anna Gozdecka, *Rights, Religious Pluralism and the Recognition of Difference* (Routledge, 2016) 25–36.

38 Here the term 'pluralism' refers to religious pluralism, in contrast to 'legal pluralism'. See *inter alia* Lerner, above n 16, 104–109.

39 See Ahdar and Leigh, above n 5, 109–112.

40 Heiner Bielefeldt, *Report of the Special Rapporteur on freedom of religion or belief*, UN Doc A/HRC/31/18, 23 December 2015 [14].

41 Abdulaziz Sachedina, *Islam and the Challenge of Human Rights* (Oxford University Press, 2009) 197–199.

42 Ibid 201.

in society; several paths to salvation have been provided for humanity that are united by pursuit of a common morality that offers the foundation for the universalism of human rights.[43] In addition to the need to identify religious morality alongside rational morality in public discourse, Sachedina stresses religious pluralism as necessary to overcome violence and extremism.[44]

Sachedina's God-centred pluralism is limited for present purposes in that it extends only to monotheist religions that can be united under the same Creator and therefore considered spiritually equal; nothing is said about polytheists or atheists beyond their innate human dignity.[45] Yet the essential point he makes is that human dignity and moral ability to determine one's spiritual path without interference are values common to Islam and international human rights law.[46] In this way, Muslim rights and duty holders can be brought within the human rights framework without losing their theological framework. Similar lines of religious reasoning may achieve the same for people professing other faiths.[47] But even if this is not the case, and some religious rights-holders cannot be convinced of the claims of other rights-holders to enjoy freedom of religion and belief equal to their own, from a rights-based viewpoint this is ultimately irrelevant. Despite the limited tolerance that exists in many parts of the world, ideological neutrality must be a non-negotiable in freedom of religion and belief; a human right that is founded on normative universalism.[48]

The type of pluralism that is offered here is one that takes a neutral approach to the nature of the religion or belief in question, and considers the sincerity of rights-holders in professing their beliefs.[49] This approach also accords with Bielefeldt's caution to err on the side of being more inclusive so as to capture the diversity of rights-holders,[50] and to guard against the risk of the human right to freedom of

43 Ibid 80, referring to *Koran* 5:48.
44 Ibid 186.
45 Ibid 206. Bielefeldt also takes issues with this "limited tolerance". See Heiner Bielefeldt, 'Misconceptions about Freedom of Religion and Belief' (2013) 35 *Human Rights Quarterly* 33, 36.
46 Sachedina, above n 41, 208. For more on compatible readings of Islam and international human rights law, see *inter alia* Ann Elizabeth Mayer 'Universal versus Islamic Human Rights; a Clash of Cultures or a Clash with a Construct?' (1994) 15 *Michigan Journal of International Law* 307; Ann Elizabeth Mayer, *Human Rights and Islam: Tradition and Politics* (Westview Press, 5th edition, 2013); Abdullahi Ahmed An-Na'im, 'Islam and Human Rights' in John Witte Jr and M. Christian Green, *Religion and Human Rights: An Introduction* (Oxford University Press, 2012); Mashood A. Baderin, 'Islam and the Realisation of Human Rights in the Muslim World: a Reflection on Two Essential Approaches and Two Divergent Perspectives' (2007) 4 *Muslim World Journal of Human Rights* 5, and Mashood Baderin, *International Human Rights and Islamic Law* (Oxford University Press, 2003) 117.
47 Rawls develops an approach to developing human rights though "overlapping consensus" of religious and belief systems. John Rawls, *Political Liberalism* (Columbia University Press, 1996).
48 Bielefeldt, above n 45, 36–37.
49 On neutrality models of the Church–state relationship, see Ahdar and Leigh, above n 5, 112–119.
50 Bielefeldt, above n 45, 40.

religion and belief becoming "lost in trivialities",[51] or as Ahdar and Leigh caution, becoming "a blank cheque for exemption from the law of the land".[52] Sincerity, or the extent to which beliefs are genuinely held, is crucial in distinguishing a religious leader of an emerging sect from a criminal whose sole motivation is financial or sexual exploitation of indoctrinated followers, while not penalising those followers for the sincerity of their beliefs. It would also serve to distinguish between a genuine practitioner of Rastafariasm for whom marijuana is a holy sacrament, and a stoner for whom marijuana is a hobby and religion an excuse.[53]

The challenge for decision-makers is how to establish this sincerity in a person whose beliefs are unfamiliar and whose actions are questionable enough to have attracted the scrutiny of the law.[54] The temptation to measure sincerity of beliefs by plausibility must be rigorously avoided to protect legal reasoning from being muddied by religious theorising.[55] Indeed, even proving the sincerity of followers of widely known, long-standing religions is a fraught task in the absence of objective measures; a Christian may not literally believe in resurrection or a Hindu in reincarnation, but these doubts should not render him any less Christian or Hindu for the purpose of protecting his religious freedom. Sincerity of belief should not be measured on objective grounds, but should be determined on the basis of the subjective religion or belief of the individual rights holder.[56]

Bielefeldt adds to the criteria of sincerity (expressed by him as "earnestness") the criteria of comprehensiveness, given that "[n]ot any opinion which I might just happen to have today can claim the status of a serious 'belief', and turning any coffee circle into a religious community would certainly go too far."[57] In elaborating what is meant by "comprehensiveness", Bielefeldt refers to guidance offered by the European Court of Human Rights, through its prescription of "a certain level of cogency, seriousness, cohesion and importance".[58] Criteria of earnestness and comprehensiveness, therefore, "can be used to ensure that the concepts of religion and

51 Ibid 39–40, referring to the 'Star Wars' religion.
52 Ahdar and Leigh, above n 5, 156.
53 See for instance *US v Kuch*, 288 F Supp 439 (1968) referred to in Ahdar and Leigh, above n 5, 142–143, in which the Court found that the desire was to use drugs for their own sake and that the organisation at issue was created for that purpose.
54 Ahdar and Leigh note domestic courts have almost always been convinced by sincerity considerations given their similarity to other judicial 'state of mind' questions. Ahdar and Leigh, above n 5, 147–148.
55 Cf. Ahdar and Leigh, above n 5, 143 and 156. Ahdar and Leigh caution that over-reliance on broad understandings of religions and subsequent limitations of manifestation, may not comprehend the internal nature of religion that for many beliefs, must be manifested externally.
56 Ahdar and Leigh note that even objective insights of an expert authority on a given religion or belief do not speak to the individual's own religion or belief. See Ahdar and Leigh, above n 5, 196.
57 Heiner Bielefeldt, 'Freedom of Religion or Belief – a Human Right Under Pressure' (2012) 1 *Oxford Journal of Law and Religion* 1, 7.
58 See Bielefeldt, above n 45, 39, referring to *Campbell and Cosans v The United Kingdom*, European Court of Human Rights, Application Nos. 7511/76, 7743/76, 13 (25 February 1982).

belief keep their basic contours relating to *people's deep and existential convictions and concomitant individual and communitarian ethical or ritualistic practices*".[59] Yet comprehensiveness may raise questions similar to those raised by sincerity; would a person lacking a comprehensive understanding of his own belief set (for instance, as a child or a poorly educated but devout adult) be entitled to less protection than someone whose beliefs are more studied and developed? Or would a more established religion be considered more comprehensive for the weight of scholarship historically attached to it, relative to a less theologised, newer one?

As with 'sincerity' then it perhaps is impossible to prescribe a definitive threshold to 'comprehensiveness', but both sketch out the nature of belief and its significance to the person concerned, irrespective of how that belief is perceived by others. Ultimately the criterion should depend on the sincerity of beliefs held, regardless of what they are, and its comprehensiveness to the holder of the beliefs, regardless of how it fares against other belief holders or other beliefs. Whether or not the substance of a belief is genuine or plausible is irrelevant in upholding the special nature of faith; what matters is that the belief is genuinely held regardless of what it is. A caution must also be issued that consideration of 'sincerity' of beliefs does not give way to invasive scrutiny. A person should not be penalised for grappling with his beliefs; inquisitiveness or doubt may both be important ways of enjoying freedom of religion and belief.

The Commission on Human Rights highlighted the rights-facilitative role that pluralism can play, reiterating

> the obligation of all states and the international community to...[p]romote a culture conducive to promoting and protecting human rights, fundamental freedoms and tolerance, inter alia through education leading to genuine pluralism, a positive acceptance of diversity of opinion and belief, and respect for the dignity of the human person.[60]

Similarly (and more succinctly), Dickson notes that "for the sake of a healthy, pluralistic society the law should go out of its way to tolerate diversity and non-conformity."[61] Indeed, not only does pluralism serve to protect individual diversity thereby strengthening the universality of human rights, but it also promotes diversity as an outcome of human freedom.[62] The notion of pluralism emerges as both a necessary means of ensuring universal religious freedom and in some contexts, an end of that freedom itself. Many scholars (including Dickson) discuss pluralism in terms of tolerating diversity. But diversity should not merely be 'tolerated'; it must be vehemently defended and actively supported through equal

59 Ibid.

60 UN Commission on Human Rights, *Tolerance and pluralism as indivisible elements in the promotion and protection of human rights*, UN Doc E/CN.4/RES/1998/21 (9 April 1998) [2(f)].

61 Brice Dickson, 'The United Nations and Freedom of Religion' (1995) 44 *International and Comparative Law Quarterly* 327, 327.

62 Rawls asserts that diversity of belief is the outcome of human freedom in Rawls, above n 47, 36.

treatment of all religious and non-religious rights-holders.[63] At the same time, fierce protection of pluralism requires that certain manifestations of religion or belief be staunchly opposed. In pluralistic states that respect religious beliefs equally and host partially or wholly incompatible doctrines, tolerance of difference may have a hierarchising effect, and in any case is only useful up to the point that violations of human rights are not tolerated.[64]

Respect for pluralism extends to the spectrum of ideological diversity spanning major established religions, through newer, less-accepted ones, to non-belief and atheism. It is a tool with which to check that decisions as to whether manifestations of religion and belief should be limited are made on the basis that the rights of others are trespassed on, rather than on the basis of the content or nature of the religion or belief. Pluralism should assist in weighing competing rights not merely because it is exists as a fact of life, but because pluralism – as the acceptance of more than one idea – is a good that should come of protecting those rights.

2. ICCPR Article 18 and the plurality of religion and belief

The essential point of article 18 is not 'religion' or 'belief', but the 'freedom' accorded to them. This freedom is considered an unrestricted internal right – the *forum internum* – of a person to think or believe what he or she will. Intervention with this right can only be considered when religions or beliefs manifest.[65] It is the outward manifestation of this right – the *forum externum* – that raises the most challenges where article 18 is concerned.

2.1. Freedom to have or adopt a religion or belief

Freedom to *change* religion is not explicitly protected in the ICCPR. The omission of the word "change" from article 18 represents a dilution over time; from explicit freedom to "change" religion or belief in the 1948 Universal Declaration of Human Rights (UDHR),[66] to freedom to "have or adopt" a religion or belief of choice in the 1966 ICCPR, to freedom simply to "have" a religion or belief of choice in the 1981 Declaration. During the drafting of the 1981 Declaration,

63 Deborah Jones Merritt & Daniel C Merritt, 'The Future of Religious Pluralism: Justice O'Connor and the Establishment Clause' (2007) 39 *Arizona State Law Journal* 895, 896–897. Also see Viet Bader, 'Religious Pluralism and Democratic Institutional Pluralism' (2003) 31 *Political Theory* 265 and Viet Bader, 'Taking Religious Pluralism Seriously, Arguing for an Institutional Turn' (2003) 6 *Religious Pluralism, Politics and the State* 3. Wendy Brown, *Regulating Aversion: Tolerance in the Age of Identity and Empire* (Princeton University Press, 2006) 186–187. Brown argues that the discourse of "tolerance" is divisive in elevating the tolerator over the toleratee on a "table of virtue".

64 Alan Gewirth, *Human Rights: Essays on Justification and Applications* (University of Chicago Press, 1982).

65 See Dickson, above n 61, 327.

66 *Universal Declaration of Human Rights*, GA Res 217A(III), UN GAOR, 3rd sess, 183rd plen mtg, UN Doc A/810 (10 December 1948) article 18.

the right to "change one's religion" was strongly opposed, as was the wording "or to adopt", which was argued to imply that "change" had occurred. Therefore, the term "have or adopt" was softened further in the 1981 Declaration by expressing the right as "freedom to have a religion or whatever belief of his choice".[67] Concern about the notion of 'change' was not owing to fears that atheists or non-believers would adopt religious beliefs, but that religious believers would surrender theirs. Opposition primarily emanated from Islamic states on two grounds: firstly the idea that providing freedom to change religion would unsettle the freedom to maintain it, and secondly, the fact that 'changing' religion was incompatible with Islamic prohibitions on heresy and apostasy.[68] The emphasis on the right to maintain one's religion over the right to change religion or belief is borne out in comments of the Afghan delegate during the process of drafting the ICCPR, who explained that:

> If an individual who had freely accepted a certain religion was told that he was free to change it, the idea was put into his mind that he was believing in something which he could change if given the right to do so. Doubt would be instilled and his belief damaged.[69]

Mere knowledge of and exposure to alternative religions and beliefs cannot be considered an interference with a person's maintenance of his or her religion. What can be gleaned from the Afghan delegate's intervention is the subjectivity of religious beliefs and the potentially insurmountable conflict between freedom to maintain a religion and freedom to change it, or between religion and religious freedom. The same delegate expressed a more ideologically blatant attitude against the right to change religion when he explained, "Moslems permitted non-Moslems to become Moslems but did not allow Moslems to leave Islam [sic]."[70] Yemen also raised concerns: where legislation was religious in origin an express right to change religion could not possibly be in compliance for "[i]t would be impossible to force a state to abandon traditional legislation which it had applied for centuries and which was known to be in conformity with the aspirations and needs of the people."[71] The Organisation of Islamic Conference (OIC) declared that it could not support the

67 1981 Declaration, article 1(1).

68 See *inter alia*, Roberta Aluffi Beck-Peccoz, 'Proselytism and the Right to Change Religion in Islam' in Silvio Ferrari and Rinaldo Cristofori, *Law and Religion in the 21st Century* (Ashgate, 2010) 253–260; Derek H. Davis, 'The Evolution of Religious Freedom as a Universal Human Right: Examining the Role of the 1981 United Nations Declaration of the Elimination of all forms of Intolerance and of Discrimination based on Religion or Belief' (2002) *Brigham Young University Law Review* 217, 229–230; Carolyn Evans, above n 15, 35–36; and Malcolm Evans, above n 15, 188.

69 UN Doc A/C.3/9/SR.565 (1954) [12–13] (Afghanistan) referred to in Paul Taylor, *Freedom of Religion: UN and European Human Rights Law and Practice* (Cambridge University Press, 2005) 30. Also see United Nations Secretary General, *Annotations on the text of the draft International Covenants on Human Rights*, UN GAOR, 10th Session, Agenda Item 28, Part II, Annexes (1 July 1955) UN Doc A/2929 [108].

70 Ibid [12] (Afghanistan).

71 UN Doc A/C.3/5/SR.289 (1950) [63] (Yemen) referred to in Taylor, above n 69, 29.

right to change religion, given that some in Islam consider changing or leaving religion to be apostasy. Indeed, although the Koran says "there is no compulsion in religion"[72] several Islamic states are guided by the Hadith, instructing that Muslims who change religion be killed.

Ultimately it was decided that the ICCPR text would not explicitly affirm an individual's right to change religion.[73] The phrase "to have or to adopt" was accepted after the alternative wording "to maintain or to change" was rejected, as were the words, "to have a religion or belief", on the basis that it could be construed as making the choice of religion or belief permanent. The words "to have or to adopt a religion or belief of his choice" were ultimately accepted. The right to change religion can be inferred therein, as the phrase allows for choices including adopting non-traditional religions, adopting religion where none was previously held, or even adopting non-religious beliefs where religion was previously held, thereby extending its ambit of concern to those who have no religion or are atheists.[74]

Despite drafting disputes and differences between the UDHR, the ICCPR and the 1981 Declaration, the point is that they "all meant precisely the same thing: that everyone has the right to leave one religion or belief and to adopt another, or to remain without any at all."[75] And indeed, the HRC considers freedom to change religion when considering state reports, and has raised concerns with several countries along these lines.[76] It has also become clear over time that human rights bodies no longer need to avoid using the word "change". In its General Comment 22, the HRC unequivocally protects the concept as "the freedom to choose a religion or belief, including the right to replace one's current religion or belief with another or to adopt atheistic views".[77] The word "change" is not used in this paragraph, but the concept is clear within this broad construction of what is entailed in the freedom to choose one's religion or belief. The Human Rights Council has also explicitly stressed that freedom of religion and belief includes the right to change one's religion or belief.[78] This being the case, the omission of the word "change" in rights provisions and the reliance on awkward and

72 *Koran*, Surah 2:256

73 During the drafting of the ICCPR, concern was also raised that freedom to change religion would encourage missionary proselytism and anti-religious propaganda; the compromise reached was that the freedom must protect a person's right to have or adopt a religion of his choice – logically including the choice of removing one's self from a particular denomination and choosing another or choosing none. Proselytism is the subject of Chapter 3.

74 Taylor, above n 69, 31; Paul M. Taylor, 'Religion and Freedom of Choice', in John Witte Jr and M. Christian Green, *Religion and Human Rights: An Introduction* (Oxford University Press, 2012) 171–172.

75 Elizabeth Odio Benito, *Elimination of all Forms of Intolerance and Discrimination based on Religion or Belief* (United Nations Centre for Human Rights, 1989) 4 [21].

76 Countries that have been questioned by the HRC with regard to protection of freedom to change religion include Algeria, Indonesia, Iran, Jordan, Kazakhstan, Libya, Malaysia, Mexico, Mauritania, Pakistan, Sudan, Tunisia and Yemen.

77 *General Comment 22*, above n 34 [5].

78 Human Rights Council, *Freedom of Religion or Belief*, UN GAOR, 16th Session, Agenda Item 3, UN Doc A/HRC/16/L.14 (18 March 2011) [1].

ambiguous phrases in its place is difficult to comprehend. From a religious perspective, the right to change religion raises questions that go to the heart of maintaining a religion or belief; as delegates of many Islamic states suggested, allowing change of religion to any other than Islam undermines the inviolable nature of Islam. But from a rights perspective, failure to explicitly protect the right to change religion undermines the nature of religious freedom. If the absence of the word "change" truly makes no practical difference to the existence of the right, it is unclear why religious agitators were appeased by its removal. Religious perspectives aside, in international law it is clear that a person can change religion or belief, adhere to a non-traditional religion, adopt atheistic or agnostic views or remain religiously indifferent. From a normative perspective, changes in any of these directions are equal as far as human rights are concerned.[79]

Yet the plight of dissenters, atheists and non-believers proves that the existence of the right to change is not tantamount to its protection. There is widespread prosecution of 'apostates', particularly in the Islamic world. In 2014, the Pew Research Centre found in 2014, that some 25 countries in the world have laws penalising apostasy, most of which are in the Middle East and North Africa.[80] Examples of these laws being implemented include the arrest of Raif Badawai in Jeddah in June of 2012 for alleged apostasy, a charge that carries the death penalty; he received 50 of the 1000 lashes he was sentenced to in 2015.[81] Also in Saudi Arabia, a Palestinian poet, Ashraf Fayadh, was sentenced to death for apostasy in 2015.[82] A blogger in Mauritania was sentenced to death in December 2014 after criticising the use of religion to marginalise groups in society.[83] In May 2014, Meriam Ibrahim was convicted of apostasy in Sudan.[84] In February of 2012, Hamza Kashgari was deported from Malaysia to Saudi Arabia to face apostasy charges for comments he had made on Twitter, and released the following year.[85] In June 2010 at a large public event in the

79 Heiner Bielefeldt, Nazila Ghanea and Michael Weiner, *Freedom of Religion and Belief: An International Law Commentary* (Oxford University Press, 2016) 64.

80 Afghanistan, Bahrain, Brunei, Comoros, Egypt, India, Iran, Iraq, Jordan, Kuwait, Malaysia, Maldives, Mauritania, Mauritius, Nigeria, Oman, Pakistan, Qatar, Saudi Arabia, Somalia, Sudan, Syria, United Arab Emirates, Western Sahara, Yemen. See Angelina E. Theodorou, *Which countries still outlaw apostasy and blasphemy?* Pew Research Centre's Forum on Religion and Public Life, 29 July 2016, accessed 22 March 2017, http://www.pewresearch.org/fact-tank/2016/07/29/which-countries-still-outlaw-apostasy-and-blasphemy/.

81 See Middle East Online, 'Saudi rights activist faces apostasy charge', 17 December 2012, http://www.middle-east-online.com/english/?id=56110 and 'Saudi blogger Raif Badawai faces further round of flogging, supporters say' *The Guardian*, 18 October 2016, https://www.theguardian.com/world/2016/oct/18/saudi-blogger-raif-badawi-faces-further-flogging both accessed 22 March 2017.

82 *World Report 2016* (Human Rights Watch, 2015) 485.

83 *Amnesty International Report 2015/16* (Amnesty International, 2016) 247.

84 *Report of the Independent Expert on the situation of human rights in the Sudan*, Mashood A. Baderin, UN Doc. A/HRC/27/69, 4 September 2014, 12 [43].

85 Human Rights Watch, 'Saudi Arabia: Writer Faces Apostasy Trial', 13 February 2012, accessed 22 March 2017, https://www.hrw.org/news/2012/02/13/saudi-arabia-writer-faces-apostasy-trial.

Maldives (where those who leave Islam may lose citizenship) Muhammad Nazim asked an Islamic preacher what Islam thought of people like himself, who tried to believe but could not. Police arrested Nazim as the crowd attempted to attack him. Nazim was given 'religious counselling' while it was determined whether he should be executed for apostasy. During his counselling, Nazim embraced Islam.[86]

Domestic apostasy cases of course do not challenge the existence of the right to change religion in international law. Notwithstanding semantic deference shown to states that would wish to deny the choice of non-religion or atheism to their citizens, it is clear that anti-apostasy provisions in criminal law violate freedom of religion and belief and the unequivocal right to change religion or belief entailed by it.[87] The lack of consensus, particularly from states that continue to dissent from normative universalism, is evidence only of the fact that international human rights law continues to be violated, not that the right in question does not exist.[88]

2.2. Freedom to manifest religion or belief

Freedom to manifest religion has been referred to as the 'active' component – the *forum externum* – of religious freedom.[89] Manifestation is the point where thoughts (which need never be limited) become actions (which sometimes have to be limited for the protection of people who are impacted by them). In 1956, Arcot Krishnaswami submitted his 'Study of Discrimination in the matter of Religious Rights and Practices' to the Subcommission on Prevention of Discrimination and Protection of Minorities of the UN Commission on Human Rights, noting that "it may be safely assumed that the intention was to embrace all possible manifestations of religion or belief within the terms 'teaching, practice, worship and observance'."[90]

Manifestation of religion or belief can also be achieved through the refusal to act in a particular way, including through conscientious objection,[91] exercising the right *not* to profess a religion or belief, *not* to attend worship, or simply not to care about religious issues.[92] The fact that there is a 'negative' aspect to manifestation

86 International Humanist and Ethical Union (IHEU), *Freedom of Thought 2012: A Global Report on Discrimination against Humanists, Atheists and the Non-Religious* (IHEU, 2012) 48.
87 Heiner Bielefeldt, *Interim report of the Special Rapporteur on freedom of religion or belief, Elimination of all forms of religious intolerance*, UN Doc A/71/269 (2 August 2016) 13 [43].
88 Also see Evans, above n 3, 221.
89 See Joseph, Schultz and Castan, above n 13, 506.
90 Arcot Krishnaswami, *Study of Discrimination in the matter of Religious Rights and Practices*, UN Doc E/CN.4/Sub.2/200/Rev.1 (1960), UN. Pub. No 60.XIV.2, 17.
91 See *Atasoy and Sartuk v Turkey*, Communication Nos 1853/2008 and 1854/2008, UN Doc CCPR/C/104/D/1853–1854/2008 (29 March 2012). The working group to draft General Comment 22 opted to replace "religious or other beliefs" with "religion or belief" to stress that "there should be no distinction between exemption from compulsory military service on account of beliefs that were not religious in nature."
92 Bielefeldt, Ghanea and Weiner, above n 79, 21, 174.

of religion or belief should not be assumed to imply that atheists or non-believers generally manifest their beliefs by simply not manifesting religion. Atheists or freethinkers are not necessary spiritually or ideologically ambivalent; they may openly refute the existence of supernatural beings and in this sense may manifest their beliefs in positive ways, including "by speaking out, or by rejecting religious requirements, or by publicly seeking to identify as non-religious".[93]

This positive manifestation of religion or belief according to article 18(1) includes worship, observance, practice and teaching: non-exhaustive, potentially overlapping components that are to be broadly construed to subsume a range of actions.[94] In relation to 'worship', the HRC has appropriately opted for an understanding that "extends to ritual and ceremonial acts giving direct expression to belief, as well as various practices integral to such acts, including the building of places of worship, the use of ritual formulae, and objects, the display of symbols, and the observance of holidays and days of rest".[95] Interferences and restrictions on these rights have been the subject of growing international concern.[96] It must be noted though that the concept of worship is arguably inherently 'religious' in nature; it is difficult to conceive of how irreligion or atheism could be manifested through 'worship'.

'Observance' is understood to include "not only ceremonial acts but also such customs as the observance of dietary regulations, the wearing of distinctive clothing or head coverings, participation in rituals associated with certain stages of life, and the use of a particular language, customarily spoken by a group".[97] 'Observance' and 'practice' are not clearly distinguished; it is unclear whether some

93 IHEU, above n 86, 9.

94 de Jong, above n 19, 79.

95 *General Comment 22*, above n 34 [4]. For more on 'worship' see Commission on Human Rights, *Resolution 2005/40 on Elimination of all forms of Intolerance and of Discrimination based on Religion or Belief*, UN Doc E/CN.4/RES/2005/40 (19 April 2005) [4(b)].

96 In *Malakhovsky and Pikul v Belarus*, Human Rights Committee, UN Doc CCPR/C/84/D/1207/2003 [7.5–7.6], the Committee found that refusal to register a religious association amounted to a violation of the right to manifest religion or belief in the absence of reasons why such interference may be necessary. Also see Abdelfattah Amor's concerns about vague registration criteria, in *Report of the Special Rapporteur on the implementation of the Declaration on the Elimination of all Forms of Intolerance and of Discrimination based on Religion or Belief*, UN Doc E/CN.4/1995/91 (22 December 1994) 114, 117 and 132.

97 *General Comment 22*, above n 34 [4]. Included in this concept is religious clothing, *Singh Bhinder v Canada*, Human Rights Committee, UN DOC CCPR/C/37/D/208/1986 (1989); *Hudoyberganova v Uzbekistan, Merits*, Human Rights Committee, UN Doc CCPR/C/82/D/931/2000 (5 November 2004); *Leyla Şahin v Turkey*, ECHR Application No. 44774/98, Judgment (10 November 2005); wearing beards (*Boodoo v Trinidad and Tobago*, UN Doc CCPR/C/74/D/721/1996), prayer and all other customs and rites of the various religions, and the practice of circumcision. Human Rights and Equal Opportunity Commission, *'Article 18 Freedom of Religion and Belief'* (Commonwealth of Australia 1998) 59. The issue of circumcision is discussed in Chapter 5. See generally Manfred Nowak, *CCPR Commentary* (NP Engel Kehl, 2nd edn, 2005) 420.

manifestations (such as wearing of religious symbols) fall within one or the other, and it may be unwise to force strict separation between them.[98] As with worship, it is also not clear how atheism would be 'observed', and the extent to which it would be protected if it were. Cornelis D. de Jong considers manifestation through observance to include: "religious as well as to non-religious beliefs, as long as there is a common set of values and precepts serving as guidance for Man's way of living, and protects the right to live up to the basic duties of one's religion or belief".[99] Manifestation through observance is also taken to mean the right to *refrain* from acts contrary to one's religion or belief.[100] The HRC has not specifically considered whether an atheist or non-religious person *refraining* from practising a religion would constitute 'observance' of his or her belief.

In relation to 'teaching' religion and belief, General Comment 22 explains that this includes "acts integral to the conduct by religious groups of their basic affairs, such as freedom to choose their religious leaders, priests and teachers, the freedom to establish seminaries or religious schools and the freedom to prepare and distribute religious texts or publications".[101] It is unclear again, how teaching of non-religion, irreligion or atheism would fare under such a construct. In short, all four forms of manifestation do not explicitly exclude manifestation of non-religion or atheism, but are framed primarily as 'religious' manifestations.

2.3. Freedom from coercion

Article 18(2) of the ICCPR states that "[n]o one shall be subject to coercion which would impair his freedom to have or to adopt a religion or belief of his choice." Article 1(2) of the 1981 Declaration omits freedom "to adopt", stating instead that "[n]o one shall be subject to coercion which would impair his freedom to have a religion or belief or his choice." The HRC in General Comment 22 does not define coercion but offers examples of it:

> Article 18(2) bars coercion that would impair the right to have or adopt a religion or belief, including the use of threat or physical force or penal sanctions to compel believers or non-believers to adhere to their religious beliefs and congregations, to recant their religion or belief or to convert. Policies or practices having the same intention or effect, such as, for example, those restricting access to education, medical care, employment or the rights guaranteed by article 25 and other provisions of the Covenant, are similarly inconsistent with article 18(2). The same protection is enjoyed by holders of all beliefs of a non-religious nature.[102]

98 Bielefeldt, Ghanea and Weiner, above n 79, 97–98.
99 Ibid.
100 Ibid 106–116.
101 *General Comment 22*, above n 34 [4]. Concepts of teaching a religion and proselytising clearly overlap; education is discussed in Chapter 5 and proselytism in Chapter 3.
102 *General Comment 22*, above n 34 [5].

From this statement, it is clear that non-religious – and atheistic – rights-holders are protected from coercion, yet as will be discussed in subsequent chapters, atheist and non-religious rights-holders do not enjoy the same level of freedom from coercion as their religious counterparts. As a prelude to that discussion, it is necessary to emphasise that coercion is not only prohibited where it emanates from the state, but also from non-state actors. Manfred Nowak posits that articles 18(1) and 18(2) require states to prevent private coercion by a person or entity of another to have or adopt a religion, belief, conscience or opinion.[103] This view is verified by the fact that most ICCPR rights have been interpreted as having some 'horizontal' application; in addition to its 'vertical' obligations to ensure that its own authorities do not interfere with a person's enjoyment of religious freedom, the state also has a positive duty to impose obligations on non-state actors not to breach the rights of others.[104] The 'freedom' entailed in freedom of religion or belief contains freedom to do certain things, and freedom to refrain from doing certain things. In other words, upholding rights extends beyond prohibition on state interference with individual freedom of religion or belief, to also require states to actively create conditions for the full enjoyment of it.[105]

3. Limitations to manifestations

Broadly construing 'religion and belief', and limiting manifestations under article 18(3) can serve to protect atheist and non-religious rights-holders alongside religious individuals. Indeed, "as the right to manifest a religion can be subjected to proportionate limitations under article 18(3), there seems to be no policy reason to deny even the most bizarre of religious fringe groups the status of 'religion'."[106] Limitations imposed on article 18 rights must be prescribed by law, and serve one of the purposes listed in article 18(3). They must also be 'necessary' for attaining that purpose, such that the interference is "proportionate to the specific need upon which it is predicated".[107] Special Rapporteurs on freedom of religion and belief, opinion and expression, assembly and association and on the situation of human rights defenders have gone further than this to also note that limitations must not "harm the principles of pluralism, tolerance and broadmindedness".[108] These considerations are common to many ICCPR rights, but a comparison of the

103 Nowak, above n 97, 411.
104 Joseph, Schultz and Castan, above n 13, 36.
105 See Dickson, above n 61, 341.
106 Sarah Joseph, 'Human Rights Committee: Recent Cases' (2001) 1 *Human Rights Law Review* 83, 94.
107 *General Comment 22*, above n 34 [8].
108 'Indonesia: "Restrictive bill threatens freedoms of association, expression and religion," warn UN rights experts', OHCHR, 14 February 2013, accessed 22 March 2017, http://newsarchive.ohchr.org/en/NewsEvents/Pages/DisplayNews.aspx?NewsID=12989 and Maina Kiai, *Report of the Special Rapporteur on the rights to freedom of peaceful assembly and of association*, UN Doc A/HRC/20/27 (21 May 2012) [84].

limitations permitted for article 18 with those allowed for other ICCPR rights reveals the privilege of religious freedoms over other freedoms.

3.1. Fewer limitations to article 18 than for other rights

A key point of difference between the limitations prescribed in article 18 and those prescribed for other ICCPR rights, is the absence of national security and *ordre public* as permissible purposes for interference.[109] The notion of *ordre public* is not a ground to limit freedom of religion and belief, but is contained in articles 12 (freedom of movement), 14 (right to a fair hearing), 19 (freedom of expression), 21 (freedom of assembly) and 22 (freedom of association). The fact that various limitations clauses in the ICCPR take the trouble to list both *ordre public* and public order makes it "unmistakably clear" to Nowak that the latter term has a different meaning in article 18(3) than in those articles, the consequence being that limitations can only be imposed narrowly to avoid disturbances to public order, rather than in the broader sense of *ordre public.*[110] The civil law concept of 'l'ordre public' is explained as

> a legal concept used principally as a basis for negating or restricting private agreements, the exercise of police power or the application of foreign law.[111]

It was decided during the drafting process that the inclusion of the term 'l'order public' in the limitations clause of article 18 could potentially "create uncertainty and might constitute a basis for far-reaching derogations from the rights guaranteed".[112] Unfortunately there is a dearth of international cases addressing the distinction between public order and *ordre public*, which implies that the difference in international human rights law in practice is negligible. A HRC case involving public order in the context of religious manifestation was *Coeriel and Aurik v The Netherlands,* in which the authors sought to change their names in accordance with Hindu requirements to enter the priesthood.[113] The authors asserted that the state's refusal to allow them to do so violated their article 18 rights. The HRC rejected that claim as inadmissible, noting that such restrictions were justified on the basis of public order,[114] though it ultimately found that the restrictions

109 Public order or *ordre public* as used in the Covenant has been defined in the Siracusa principles as "the sum of rules which ensure the functioning of society or the set of fundamental principles on which society is founded", including respect for human rights. Commission on Human Rights, *The Siracusa Principles on the Limitation and Derogation Provisions in the International Covenant on Civil and Political Rights*, UN Doc E/CN.4/1985/4 (28 September 1984) [22].

110 Nowak, above n 97, 428.

111 Marc J. Bossuyt, *Guide to the 'Travaux Préparatoires' of the International Covenant on Civil and Political Rights* (Martinus Nijhoff Publishers, 1987) 365–366.

112 Ibid 366.

113 *Coeriel et al v The Netherlands*, Human Rights Committee, UN Doc CCPR/C/52/D/453/1991 (1994).

114 Ibid [6.1].

breached the authors' rights to privacy under article 17. In this case, it must be wondered whether the same decision would have been reached by the Netherlands and the HRC if the authors had sought to enter the dominant religion of the state.

Also notable is the absence of 'national security' as a limiting purpose in article 18(3) in contrast to freedoms of expression (article 19), assembly (article 21) and association (article 22).[115] The term 'national security' in the context of freedom of religion was deemed by the General Assembly in 1949 as "not sufficiently precise to be used as a basis for the limitation of the exercise of the rights guaranteed".[116] This may be so, but this lack of precision does not account for its inclusion in other articles and its exclusion from article 18.

3.2. Limitations favour religion over non-religion

The limitations that are permitted under article 18(3) reveal some disadvantage to non-religious or atheist rights-holders, or at least, some advantage to religious rights-holders. Manifestations of religion or belief may be restricted by proportionate measures to protect 'public morals'. General Comment 22 acknowledges that "the concept of morals derives from many social, philosophical and religious traditions; consequently, limitations on the freedom to manifest a religion or belief for the purpose of protecting morals must be based on principles not deriving from a single tradition."[117] It is notable that this description does not acknowledge 'belief traditions' alongside religious traditions. This interpretation avoids the situation of morals in article 18(3) being interpreted in accordance with a state or popular religion, given that "public morality varies over time and from one culture to another."[118] Yet there is some evidence that dominant religions hold sway in practice. The HRC initially afforded a margin of discretion to states here in its statement that

> public morals differ widely. There is no universally applicable common standard. Consequently, in this respect, a certain margin of discretion must be accorded to the responsible national authorities.[119]

This statement, made in the case of *Hertzberg et al v Finland*,[120] mirrored the wide 'margin of appreciation' afforded to states parties to the ECHR in limiting

115 Article 12(3), 14(1) and 19(3) allow interferences for the protection or reason of national security, while articles 21 and 22(2) provide restrictions in the interest of national security.
116 UN Secretary General, *Annotations on the text of the draft International Covenants on Human Rights*, above n 69 [114].
117 *General Comment 22*, above n 34 [8].
118 Commission on Human Rights, *Siracusa Principles*, above n 109 [27].
119 *Hertzberg et al v Finland*, Human Rights Committee, UN Doc CCPR/C/OP/1 (2 April 1982) 124 [10.3].
120 Ibid.

freedom of expression for the purpose of protecting public morals.[121] While the notion of the margin of appreciation has since been rejected in the ICCPR context,[122] it is evident that a certain margin nonetheless applies with respect to 'morals' as a ground for limiting freedom of religion or belief. In *Delgado-Paez v Colombia*, the author was pressured to leave his teaching post as a religion and ethics teacher at a secondary school, as his advocacy of 'liberation theology' and views differed from the Apostolic Prefect of Leticia in Colombia. He argued that the state's failure to intervene amounted to a violation of several of his rights, including under article 18. The HRC found no violation of article 18 given that a state's religious authorities were permitted to circumscribe the rights of a teacher to teach religion and belief in schools in accordance with their own religions and beliefs.[123] The HRC was explicitly influenced by the "special relationship between church and state in Colombia".[124] It is presumed that the restrictions to Delgado-Paez's rights were permitted in order to protect public morals, but the HRC should have clarified its reasoning in this respect. It is clear from this case that 'public morals' vary from state to state, and that permissible limitations to rights will also differ.[125] The implications of such a decision for a non-religious or atheistic rights-holder in a religious state are acute where a state determines that morality derives from a religion, and where international law accommodates its religious peculiarities too widely.

In the later case of *Toonen v Australia*,[126] the HRC agreed with the complainant who alleged that laws criminalising private consensual sex between adult men interfered with his rights. In doing so, it rejected the state's argument that such laws were necessary to preserve public morals on the basis that "there [was] now a general Australian acceptance that no individual should be disadvantaged on the basis of his or her sexual orientation" and that "a complete prohibition on sexual activity between men [was] unnecessary to sustain the moral fabric of Australian society."[127] The implication of *Toonen* was that if the author had come from a

121 Joseph, Schultz and Castan, above n 13, 527, referring to *Handyside Case*, Series A (1979–80) 1 EHRR 737 [48].

122 Ibid, referring to *Länsman v Finland* (511/92) where the HRC rejected application of the margin of appreciation. Some scholars consider that the HRC applies a margin of appreciation despite claiming otherwise. See *inter alia*, Dominic McGoldrick, 'Multiculturalism and its discontents', (2005) 1 *Human Rights Law Review* 5, 27 at 55. Bielefeldt, Ghanea and Weiner note that HRC jurisprudence has been inconsistent in applying a margin of appreciation in Bielefeldt, Ghanea and Weiner, above n 79, 565.

123 *Delgado-Paez v Colombia*, Human Rights Committee, UN Doc CCPR/C/39/D/195/1985 (12 July 1990) [5.6].

124 Ibid [5.8].

125 Joseph, Schultz and Castan, above n 13, 529.

126 *Toonen v Australia,* Human Rights Committee, UN Doc CCPR/C/5/D/488/1992 (31 March 1994).

127 Ibid [6.7]. Also see *X v Colombia*, Human Rights Committee, UN Doc CCPR/C/89/D/1361/2005 (30 March 2007) in which the HRC found that the state was acting discriminatorily by denying a survivor's pension to the same-sex partner of the deceased.

country where there was general *in*tolerance of homosexuality, the public morals defence would have prevailed in favour of the state.[128] Limiting rights according to public morals requires reconciliation of subjective views of morality within an international human rights framework that strives for universal standards. This challenge is immense where religion comes into play given that many will claim that their particular religion or belief represents the highest moral order.[129] The same leaning towards a 'religious' worldview can be foreseen in limitation on the basis of the "fundamental rights and freedoms of others", permitted by article 18(3). Article 18 differs here from other ICCPR rights that allow for restrictions where manifestation simply interferes with "the rights and freedoms of others" generally, or in the case of freedom of expression, the "rights and reputations of others".

The strong interconnection between article 18 freedom of religion and belief and article 19 freedom of expression must be acknowledged.[130] Manifestation of religion (worship, observance, practice and teaching) can also be construed as 'expressions' falling within the ambit of article 19.[131] For atheistic and non-religious rights-holders then, manifestations that do not fall within the ambit of article 18, may be protected by article 19.[132] Some cases show that religious expression can fall within the domain of both articles.[133] In *Ross v Canada*, the assessment of whether the limitation to Ross's rights was permitted under articles 18(3) and 19 (3) was treated as involving "substantially the same" issues.[134] More telling is the fact that while article 19 rights can be limited to protect the reputations of others, reputation is not mentioned in article 18. The implication is that where a person

128 Sarah Joseph, 'Toonen v Australia: Gay Rights under the ICCPR' (1994) 13 *University of Tasmania Law Review* 392. Subsequent decisions, general comments and concluding observations confirm that international law now requires states to protect individuals from persecution on the basis of their sexual orientation. See *inter alia*, *Young v Australia*, Human Rights Committee, CCPR/C/78/D/941/2000 (6 August 2003) and *X v Colombia*, Human Rights Committee, UN Doc CCPR/C/89/D/1361/2005 (30 March 2007).

129 Manfred Nowak and Tanja Vospernik, 'Permissible Restrictions on Freedom of Religion or Belief' in T. Lindholm, W. Cole Durham and B. G. Tahzib-Lie, *Facilitating of Freedom of Religion or Belief: A Deskbook* (Martinus Nijhoff, 2004) 159. Nowak and Vospernik refer to an Austrian case in which the government of Vorarlberg was called upon to balance the Jewish and Islamic religious morality of ritual slaughter of sheep against the moral value of protecting animals from unnecessary cruelty, deciding in this case in favour of the former.

130 *Report of the Special Rapporteur on freedom of religion or belief*, UN Doc. A/HRC/31/18, 23 December 2015.

131 *General Comment 22*, above n 34 [4].

132 Freedom of expression includes expression and receipt of communications of every form of idea and opinion, regardless of frontiers, including religious discourse and expressions that may be regarded as deeply offensive. Human Rights Committee, *General Comment 34: Freedom of Opinion and Expression (Art 19)*, UN Doc CCPR/C/GC/34 (29 June 1983) [11].

133 See *Ross v Canada*, Human Rights Committee, UN Doc CCPR/C/70/D/736/1997 (18 October 2000) and *MAB and ors v Canada*, Human Rights Committee, UN Doc CCPR/C/50/D/570/1993.

134 *Ross v Canada*, ibid [11.8].

makes derogatory comments about another's sexuality that tarnishes the reputation of that person as well as the community of people of that particular sexuality, a case brought under article 19 could result in a limitation of this person's expression, where it would not if considered a manifestation of religion, pointing to greater freedom to manifest religion than non-religion.

3.3. Non-derogability of article 18

Beyond the finding that non-religious expressions are less protected than religious expressions, is the fact that article 19 can be derogated from, while article 18 cannot.[135] Article 4(1) of the ICCPR allows for derogations from obligations, "in time of public emergency which threatens the life of the nation" where such measures do not discriminate on grounds of race, colour, sex, language, religion or social origin. Of note here again, is the omission of 'belief' alongside religion, meaning that measures could discriminate against holders of non-religious beliefs, such as atheists, non-believers and others not espousing a 'religion'. Article 4(2) goes on to prohibit derogations from articles 6, 7, 8(1) and (2), 11, 15, 16 and 18, meaning that in practice, derogations from freedom of 'belief' would also not be permissible, supposing of course that non-religious belief is protected equally alongside religion, which here it is argued it is not. While it is difficult to imagine circumstances in which derogations would be required that are not already permitted by limitations of article 18(3), the material point is that limitations beyond those specified could be justified by virtue of article 4.[136] The fact that article 18 contains limitations at all is noteworthy given that with the exception of the article 6 right to life, other rights containing limitation provisions are not considered non-derogable.[137] On this point, the HRC tells us that the inclusion of article 18 "indicates that the permissibility of restrictions is independent of the issue of derogability. Even in times of most serious public emergencies, states that interfere with the freedom to manifest one's religion or belief must justify their actions by referring to the requirements specified in article 18, paragraph 3."[138] The absence of national security as a ground of limitation takes on greater significance.

One reason for the non-derogability of article 18 in so far as the internal component of the right is concerned, is that it is never necessary or practicably possible to interfere with a private, internal thought. This explanation provides no answer, however, for the non-derogability of *manifestation* of freedom of religion or belief, or for that matter, the derogability of article 19(1) that also has a passive, internal component, being the right to hold opinions. General Comment 29

135 ICCPR, article 4(2).
136 Sarah Joseph, 'Human Rights Committee: General Comment 29' (2002) 2 *Human Rights Law Review* 81, 90.
137 Article 6 of the ICCPR protects against arbitrary deprivations of life, meaning non-arbitrary deprivations (e.g. killing in proportionate self defence of one's life) are allowed. Capital punishment is allowed in some circumstances (see articles 6(2)–6(6)).
138 Human Rights Committee, *General Comment 29: Article 4: Derogations during a State of Emergency*, UN Doc CCPR/C/21/Rev.1/Add.11 (31 August 2001) [7].

justifies this particular non-derogability, not "in recognition of the peremptory nature of some fundamental rights" (as with the right to life and the prohibition of torture or cruel, inhuman or degrading punishment) but because "it can never be necessary to derogate from [it] during a state of emergency."[139] It offers freedom of religion as an example. Yet perhaps there *are* circumstances in which a state of emergency would justify interference with article 18 manifestations. Consider for instance, a state of emergency declared in a hypothetical city faced with an imminent hurricane. Would it be justifiable in this situation to repress non-religious expressions advising people to independently flee the city because of the potential failure of state evacuation services which might lead to a panicked and unruly exodus, and *not* be justifiable to curtail religious proclamations advising people to remain in the city to welcome the forthcoming disaster as the prophesised judgment day?[140]

It is interesting to speculate on why the manifestation of article 18 rights is deemed to pose less threat to national security than manifestations of article 19 rights do, particularly in an era of religiously inspired terrorism whose culprits may consider themselves to be manifesting their religion. Perhaps the answer lies in the very real danger that derogations – *particularly* in an era of terrorism that results in states of emergency being declared – will be misused by states. Former Special Rapporteur on freedom of religion or belief, Heiner Bielefeldt noted that the 'war on terror' has proven a "convenient pretext" in several states where severe controls have been imposed that trespass on freedom of religion and belief and other rights.[141] This situation might be exacerbated if freedom of religion or belief were a derogable right. Indeed, an earlier Special Rapporteur stressed its non-derogable status as implying that states "should avoid equating certain religions with terrorism as this may have adverse consequences on the right to freedom of religion or belief of all members of the concerned religious communities or communities of belief".[142] Yet while it may be dangerous to make a simple link between terrorism and religion, it is also simplistic to dismiss the possibility that such a link may exist. The Ku Klux Klan historically used biblical ideology to justify its terrorism of African Americans and others and continues to base its white supremacist ideology on its brand of Christian beliefs.[143] The 1995 sarin gas attacks in the Tokyo

139 Ibid [11]; Human Rights Committee, *General Comment 24: Issues relating to reservations made upon ratification or accession to the Covenant or the Optional Protocols thereto, or in relation to declarations under article 41 of the Covenant*, UN Doc CCPR/C/21/Rev.1/Add.6 (11 April 1994) [10] also notes that "[o]ne reason for certain rights being made non-derogable is because their suspension is irrelevant to the legitimate control of the state of national emergency."

140 *Bible*, Psalms 107:25–33, "He raiseth the stormy wind which lifted up the waves of the sea…He turns rivers into a desert, and springs of water into thirsty ground; a fruitful land into a salt waste, because of the wickedness of those who dwell in it."

141 *Elimination of all forms of religious intolerance*, UNGA, 71st session, item 69(b) of provision agenda, UN Doc A/71/269 (2 August 2016) [31].

142 Asma Jahangir, *Report of the Special Rapporteur on freedom of religion and belief*, UN Doc E/CN.4/2005/61 (20 December 2004) [60].

143 See for instance, Juan O. Sánchez, *Religion and the Ku Klux Klan: Biblical Appropriation in their literature and song* (McFarland and Company, 2016) 177–182.

subway perpetrated by members of Aum Shinrikyo, was based on doomsday teachings blending Hindu, Buddhist and Christian beliefs, preached by the group's leader, Shoko Asaraha.[144] Because of their beliefs about the evil of the world, death and the afterlife, members of the Aum believed that they could kill people in order to save them.[145] On a larger scale, a 2016 study by the Pew Research Center notes a "marked increase" in religion-related terrorism, understood as being acts carried out that use religion as a justification or motivation (including Nigerian-based Boko Haram, al-Qaida and the Islamic State) as well as acts by individuals or groups with non-religious identity that deliberately target religious groups or individuals, such as clergy.[146] Of nearly 200 countries and territories included in that study, 82 (41%) experienced religion-related terrorist activity in 2014, in contrast with 73 (37%) in 2013.[147] Some of those activities were limited to recruitment or fundraising, but injuries or deaths resulted in 60 countries (including at least 50 casualties in 28 of them), in contrast to 51 countries in 2013 and 40 in 2012.[148]

Derogations from freedom of religion and belief could indeed be misused. But this is true for all human rights from which derogation is allowed, and does not explain the privileged position of article 18.[149] There is no particular justification for singling out freedom of religion and belief as a non-derogable right. The failure of the ICCPR to allow derogation from freedom of religion or belief in states of emergency may reduce the capacity of states to protect human rights that are trespassed on by manifestations. Other rights which are derogable – including freedom of expression – cannot be argued to pose a higher risk to society and security than freedom of religion or belief; on the contrary it is submitted that the manifestation of religion or belief can pose significant threats that should be guarded against under exceptional circumstances. The risk posed by its *non*-derogable status is a counterpoint to the risk posed by derogability; that is, misuse of the privilege to the detriment of other human rights in states of emergency. The range of acts understood to constitute manifestation of religion or belief must cater to an infinite spectrum of possibilities, even encompassing some that are abhorrent. Allowing derogation from article 18 in "exceptional and temporary"[150] circumstances may be necessary to ensure similar respect for equally important rights that are subordinated to freedom of religion and belief.

In short, the fact that article 18 is non-derogable underlines the privileged nature of this right relative to others. The fact that any derogation from other

144 See for instance, 'BBC Profile: Shoko Asaraha', 27 February 2004, accessed 22 March 2017 http://news.bbc.co.uk/2/hi/asia-pacific/3504237.stm.
145 Peter Edge, *Legal Responses to Religious Difference* (Kluwer, 2002) 396–397.
146 *Trends in Global Restrictions on Religion* (Pew Research Center, 2016) 41.
147 Ibid 9.
148 Ibid.
149 The Pew Research Center study found an "overall decline in religious restrictions and hostilities despite continued rise in religion-related terrorism". *Trends in Global Restrictions on Religion*, above n 146, 5.
150 *General Comment 29*, above n 138 [2].

rights must not discriminate on the basis of religion, but can on the basis of belief – including non-religion or atheism – shows again the particular vulnerability and relative disadvantage of those rights-holders.

4. Conclusion: The limits of article 18 to protect freedom from religion

"If there were only one religion…there would be danger of despotism, if there were two, they would cut each other's throats, but there are thirty, and they live in peace and happiness."[151]

The purpose of international human rights law is not to protect religions or beliefs, but to protect the rights of individuals, humanity being the starting point and 'common denominator' across the diversity of worldviews.[152] Any definition of 'religion' could never comprehensively capture the range of what that notion entails, and protecting 'religion' over those who practise it or not, is to privilege religious rights-holders over those who hold non-religious or atheistic beliefs.[153] 'Religion' and 'belief' must remain undefined at international law in order to ensure their application to the widest range of religions and beliefs possible, regardless of how strange, implausible, 'good' or 'bad' those religions and beliefs may seem. The freedom to manifest religion or belief, that is, the point where internally held beliefs become actions that can impact on the rights of others, is construed broadly. Yet subjective interpretations of what can or cannot constitute a manifestation of religion or belief have sometimes served to construe them narrowly. The available literature reveals a bias towards 'religious' understandings of what can constitute manifestation, leaving the exercise of that freedom by non-believers or atheists much less certain. In the same way that it should be for the holder of a religion or belief to determine what that religion or belief entails, so too should that person decide how to manifest it. Manifestations of religion and belief, like the meaning of 'religion' and 'belief', should be conceived to ensure the widest possible protection for the widest spectrum of worldviews so as not to exclude what is new, unusual, indigenous, controversial or offensive. Any danger posed by such an approach would be mitigated by applying limitations across the breadth of manifestations that may emanate from such religions or beliefs.

Yet here too a pro-religious bias is evident. The limitations on freedom to manifest one's religion or belief contained in article 18(3) are narrower than those for most other rights, adding to the result that less interference is permitted with religious or belief freedoms than with other civil and political rights, including freedom of expression. This is of particular relevance for the non-religious or atheistic rights-holder whose ideological manifestations may not be interpreted as

151 Voltaire, quoted in Brian J. Grim and Roger Finke, *The Price of Freedom Denied: Religious Persecution and Conflict in the Twenty-first Century* (Cambridge University Press, 2011) 3.

152 Bielefeldt, Ghanea and Weiner, above n 79, 25, 175.

153 Winnifred Fallers Sullivan, *The Impossibility of Religious Freedom* (Oxford: Princeton University Press, 2011) 157.

falling within article 18 but instead be relegated to article 19; a right containing more grounds for limitation and that can be derogated from. This non-derogability of article 18 is curious given the derogability of analogous rights, and the fact that manifestations of religion can pose as much threat as manifestations of opinion can. Notwithstanding the supposed non-hierarchical relationship between human rights set out in the ICCPR, the failure to bring freedom of religion and belief into stronger accord with comparable human rights evinces the special nature of religion and belief. The interpretation and implementation of that right evinces the privileged nature of religion over belief. All this, it has been suggested, may give the "rather Orwellian…impression that some rights, notably freedom of *religion* (less so freedom of *belief*), might be considered 'more equal than others'."[154]

Against this background, the following chapters illustrate not only that freedom of religion and belief is itself privileged above other rights, but also that the rights of persons espousing particular religions occupy a higher place on a hierarchy of freedom of religion and belief, than the rights of those who reject religious beliefs to profess non-religion or atheism.

154 Bielefeldt, Ghanea and Weiner, above n 79, 548.

2 The hierarchy of religion and belief

The applicability of article 18 of the ICCPR to all people, regardless of their religion and belief, is essential to the universality of human rights law. The fact that neither 'religion' nor 'belief' are defined for purposes of article 18 means that protection can, in theory, stretch to include even followers of religions or beliefs that are not widely recognised. Indeed, any attempt to classify or determine the legitimacy of old, new, monotheistic, polytheistic, atheistic, traditional, revisionist, animist, indigenous, popular or unpopular beliefs, would beg the question of which group of believers would be left vulnerable next. However, in practice, justice is only partially blind where religion and belief are concerned. International human rights mechanisms and the individuals who administer them are not immune from bias in separating the rights a person has from the beliefs he or she holds.

Despite the apparent normative pluralism of article 18, it is asserted in this chapter that there is a *de facto* hierarchy of religion and belief in domestic and international adjudicative practice of international human rights law, with established mainstream religions at the top, new and therefore 'unusual' religions below them, and atheism at the bottom.

1. Established, major religions at the top of the hierarchy

Well-established religions occupy the top rung of the hierarchy of freedom of religion and belief in international law. By 'well-established' is loosely meant those religions whose establishment significantly predates living memory and whose adherents are numerous enough to be considered 'mainstream', including the three key monotheistic Abrahamic religions, Judaism, Christianity and Islam, and some offshoots thereof. A key reason certain religions enjoy a high place in the hierarchy is because they often have support of states. There are many states with Christian or Islamic traditions, a few with Buddhist or Hindu traditions and there is one Jewish state. The same is not true for less-established religions.[1] Whether a religion is established is more than a historical fact and numbers of adherents are more than a reflection of popularity; these are also political advantages. States lobby for adherents of established religions not only in implementing human rights domestically but also in representing them at the international level. The same is not true for newer or less-usual religions. It stands to political reason that states are more often called to account for treatment of followers of minority rather than majority religions as they throw the weight of their support behind demographic groups that support them.

1.1. High influence of religious non-state actors

Some religious actors exercise power that profoundly impacts on enjoyment of human rights, in both beneficial and detrimental ways. Religious actors may wield ideological influence so essential to national and spiritual identity in a given state that they shape government policy directly or indirectly by swaying public opinion. This fact underlines the need to consider the specific nature of the relationship between a given state and a given religious actor in holding the latter to account.

A particularly complicated example can be found by looking to the Holy See, a state entity comprised of the Pope and his curia that is almost inextricable from the Catholic Church it speaks for, and that is the source of its canon law.[2] Its 'statehood' has been criticised, including by Geoffrey Robertson QC who notes that it is "really a religion which has, through historical anomalies and lack of principle, been accorded the status of 'party' to many international treaties".[3] Indeed, the Holy See enjoys privileges of statehood, participates in international processes, is a permanent observer state at the UN and party to international treaties.[4] While it has a population of only 800, its influence extends well beyond its 0.44 square kilometres, particularly in states with Christian histories or tendencies. The Catholic Church has been criticised for many of its teachings and actions; labelling of homosexuality as sinful (and sometimes curable) is rife with discrimination, as are policies concerning the role of women in the Church. The Vatican's in-depth interest in the sexual and reproductive practices of its adherents

1 The Pew Forum on Religion and Public Life, 'The Global Religious Landscape; A report on the size and distribution of the world's major religious groups as of 2010', December 2012, 12. It is noted that there is no country in the world in which Baha'is, Jains, Shintoists, Sikhs, Taoists, followers of Tenrikyo, Wiccans and Zoroastrians make up the majority of the population.

2 On the distinction between the Vatican City state and the Holy See, see Ioana Cismas, *Religious Actors and International Law* (Oxford University Press, 2014) 153–238.

3 Geoffrey Robertson QC, *Crimes against Humanity* (4th edn, The New Press, 2013) 412–413.

4 Participation of the Holy See in the work of the United Nations, GA Resolution 58/314 of 1 July 2014; also see Cismas, above n 3, 155, 157, 213–218.

is well known; it has issued detailed Encyclicals on the issue, the most famed of which forbids

> any action which either before, at the moment of, or after sexual intercourse, is specifically intended to prevent procreation...[for] it is never lawful, even for the gravest reasons, to do evil that good may come of it – in other words, to intend directly something which of its very nature contradicts the moral order, and which must therefore be judged unworthy of man, even though the intention is to protect or promote the welfare of an individual, of a family or of a society in general...[5]

Some three decades later, in its 'Statement of Interpretation of the Holy See on the adoption of the Declaration of Commitment on HIV/AIDS', the Holy See "emphasise[d] that, with regard to the use of condoms as a means of preventing HIV infection, it has in no way changed its moral position".[6] Benedict XVI who succeeded Pope John Paul II in 2005 continued to uphold the Encyclical. During his Papacy, beyond implying that the work of secular inter-governmental organisations (IGOs) and non-governmental organisations (NGOs) attempting to curb the spread of AIDS is somehow immoral, the Church has also said that such efforts are ineffective. Papal spokesman Father Federico Lombardi responded to criticisms that the Church's position puts lives at risk by saying that "[t]he spread of AIDS is completely independent from the religious faith of populations and of the influence of the clergy, while policies against AIDS based on the distribution of condoms have largely failed".[7] Pope Francis, who was elected on 13 March 2013, has not directly changed the Church's position on *Humanae Vitae* but in response to a question about whether condoms could be used to prevent transmission of the Zika virus, reportedly said "avoiding pregnancy is not an absolute evil," though abortion is still considered to be.[8]

5 Pope Paul VI, 'Humanae Vitae', *Encyclical on the Regulation of Birth Control* (1968) [14].

6 'Statement of interpretation of the Holy See on the Adoption of the Declaration of Commitment on HIV/AIDS' 27 June 2001, accessed 22 March 2017, http://www.vatican.va/roman_curia/secretariat_state/documents/rc_seg-st_doc_20010627_declaration-aids_en.html. Also see Statement of the Holy See in Explanation of its Position on the Resolution 'Women, the child and HIV/AIDs' (E/CN.6/2011/L.3) 55th Session of the Commission on the Status of Women of the ECOSOC, New York, 4 March 2011, in which it explicitly prohibits use of condoms, "either as a family planning measure or in HIV/AIDS prevention programmes".

7 'Vatican rejects criticism over its anti-condom stance', *EarthTimes*, 25 July 2008, accessed 2 January 2009, www.wwrn.org.

8 See for instance, Barbara Ellen, 'If condoms are OK for Zika, why not Aids, Pope Francis?' *Guardian*, 21 February 2016, https://www.theguardian.com/commentisfree/2016/feb/21/pope-francis-zika-virus-contraception and James Carroll 'The New Morality of Pope Francis', *New Yorker*, 8 April 2016, http://www.newyorker.com/news/news-desk/new-morality-of-pope-francis-joy-of-love both accessed 22 March 2017.

Instructions issued by the Vatican and its global representatives on sexual morality and health have misled many who rely on it. Putting aside warnings issued by Cardinal Alfonso Lopez de Trujillo (the Vatican's president of the Pontifical Council for the Family) that condoms are punctured to let the AIDS virus pass through, consider less conspiratorial views such as those of Cardinal Wamala who expressed the position that a woman who dies of AIDS rather than use a condom should be considered a martyr.[9] The Holy See's position on abortion even manifested in efforts to stop NATO distributing the morning after pill to victims of rapes by Serbian militia.[10]

As a religious entity that enjoys statehood, the Catholic Church has exceptional influence. Yet there are numerous other examples of states harnessing religious precepts (most often, of the majoritarian religion) and forming allegiances with religious authorities to legitimise a political agenda or exploit repression of rights and freedoms for political gain.[11] Religious instructions concerning the 'sin' of contraception have filtered into state policy in real ways. Under the United States administration of George W. Bush, financial aid was denied to any charity or group offering advice on safe sexual practices other than abstinence, even though millions of deaths had resulted from AIDS contracted through unsafe sexual practices.[12] A related example pertains to the sexually transmitted human papilloma virus (HPV) that can lead to cervical cancer, which members of the Bush administration opposed making immunisation available for on the ground that doing so would encourage premarital sex.[13] The late Christopher Hitchens, enthusiastically critical of religion's "weird obsession with sex", believed that "[t]o accept the spread of cervical cancer in the name of god is no different, morally or intellectually, from sacrificing women on a stone altar and thanking the deity for giving us the sexual impulse and then condemning it."[14] The policy prohibiting funding to NGOs that perform or provide information about abortions was instated by the Reagan administration, rescinded by the Clinton administration, reinstated by Bush, rescinded by the Obama administration and reinstated by President Trump's executive action in January 2017; an action that if not inspired by his religious beliefs, can be considered driven by those of his supporters.[15]

9 'African family values', *BBC News* (online), 27 June 2004, accessed 22 March 2017, http://news.bbc.co.uk/2/hi/programmes/panorama/3844959.stm.

10 Robertson, above n 4, 413.

11 Manfred Nowak and Tanja Vospernik, 'Permissible Restrictions on Freedom of Religion or Belief' in T. Lindholm, W. Cole Durham and B. G. Tahzib-Lie, *Facilitating of Freedom of Religion or Belief: A Deskbook* (Martinus Nijhoff, 2004) 147.

12 See Kaci Bishop, 'Politics before Policy: The Bush Administration, International Family Planning, and Foreign Policy' (2003–2004) 29 *North Carolina Journal of International and Commercial Law Regulation* 521, 521.

13 Michael Specter, 'Political Science' *The New Yorker*, 13 March 2006, 58.

14 Christopher Hitchens, *God is not Great* (Allen & Unwin, 2007) 48.

15 Michelle Goldberg, 'Donald Trump, the Religious Right's Trojan Horse', *The New York Times,* 27 January 2017, accessed 22 March 2017, https://www.nytimes.com/2017/01/27/opinion/sunday/donald-trump-the-religious-rights-trojan-horse.html?_r=0.

Among Trump's other early actions in support of a Christian-right agenda in US policy, are his drastic funding cuts to the UN Population Fund on the basis of its reproductive health work, and his nomination of Judge Gorsuch for the Supreme Court, a judge notable for supporting the decision to recognise the religious beliefs of corporations, allowing them to object on religious grounds to providing insurance to enable employees to access contraceptives.[16]

Another example of the influence of religion on the state can be found in Moldova. Following his country visit to the Republic of Moldova in September 2011, the Special Rapporteur on Freedom of Religion and Belief noted the privileged status of the Moldovan Orthodox Church. Though he did not fault the significance of the Church, he raised concerns about some of its rights-incompatible views filtering into state policy.[17] The fact that state authorities seek approval of the Orthodox Church, effectively gives Orthodox priests *de facto* powers to veto public gatherings of religious minorities. The Special Rapporteur pointed to restrictions imposed on peaceful protests and even non-Orthodox burials, and state repression of rights of sexual minorities as a result of objections raised by the Orthodox Church.[18] Concerns that the close relationship between the Orthodox Church and the state entrenches homophobia in Moldova have been widely raised.[19] It can be considered here whether the state is using the religious non-state actor as a proxy to promote its political agenda or is rather being manipulated by it, in service of the Church's religious agenda. Either way, it is clear that some religious entities enjoy a unique position in society that can be used for rights-contrary ends.

Examples of Judaism impacting on rights with state complicity can also be pointed to. The relationship between the state of Israel and religion has been described as "labyrinthine" owing to the complexity of its hybrid system of being both a majority Jewish state and a democratic state with no established religion, with complex linkages between state and religious institutions.[20] The government continues to enforce Orthodox interpretations of religious law and does not

16 Mythili Sampathkumar, 'Donald Trump defunding of UN's women's health service will cause "millions to suffer"' *Independent*, 4 April 2017, accessed 27 April 2017, http://www.independent.co.uk/news/world/americas/us-politics/donald-trump-abortion-defunding-global-mexico-city-rule-un-population-fund-a7666916.html. Also see: *Hobby Lobby Stores, Inc. v Sebelius*, 723 F.3d 1114 (2013); *Burwell v Hobby Lobby Stores*, Inc. 573 US__ (2014); *Burwell v Hobby Lobby Stores, Inc.* 134 S Ct 2751 (2014).

17 *Report of the Special Rapporteur on freedom of religion or belief, Heiner Bielefeldt*, UN Doc A/HRC/19/60/Add.2 (27 January 2012), 10 [31–33].

18 Ibid 10 [35–38, 46].

19 See for instance, 'Moldova fails to adequately protect lesbian, gay, bisexual, transgender and intersex (LGBTI) individuals from discrimination' (Amnesty International Public Statement, 29 March 2011), accessed 22 March 2017, http://www.amnesty.org/en/library/info/EUR59/004/2012/en.

20 Consideration of Reports submitted by states parties under article 40 of the Covenant, Initial report of states parties due in 1993, Addendum, Israel, 9 April 1998, UN Doc. CCPR/C/81/Add.13 [532].

recognise marriages unless performed by the Orthodox Rabbinate, that also determines who can be buried in Jewish state cemeteries. The Israeli Defence Force sponsors Orthodox conversion courses for Jewish soldiers who are not recognised as Jewish by Orthodox Rabbinical authorities. Discrimination against women in Judaism is partly supported by the state that continues to prohibit mixed prayer services at Jerusalem's Western Wall where women are also not permitted to access public Torah scrolls or bring their own.[21] The Jewish organisation, 'Women of the Wall', has been campaigning for the right to manifest religion at the women's section of the Wall since the late 1980s when their first such service was disrupted by verbal and physical assaults by ultra-Orthodox Jews.[22] Following a district court decision in April 2013, the Women of the Wall were permitted to pray out loud. They did so in May 2013 with police protecting them from the verbal and physical assaults of some five thousand ultra-Orthodox men and women.[23] They continue to campaign for equal access to the Western Wall and Torah scrolls.[24] The interrelationship of Orthodox Judaism and the institutions of state are such that Israel acknowledged to the HRC that it could not confirm that "freedom from religion" is fully protected, particularly for Jews to whom Orthodox norms apply.[25]

The close connection between religion and the state is also evident in several majority Muslim countries and has resulted in state-sanctioned, rights-contrary practices, such as laws against apostasy and forms of corporal punishment meted out by religious police and religious courts who enforce Sharia law with state authorisation or complicity.[26] The explicit application of Sharia in the legislation of many Islamic states further indicates the strong role played by Islam. The influence of Islamic clerics in issuing *fatwas* is evidence of the power of religious actors; as one example, in 2011 the grand mufti of Saudi Arabia issued a *fatwa* asserting that street protests were incompatible with Islam, thereby quelling Arab Spring type uprisings in Saudi Arabia and demonstrating the role that religious actors can play in bolstering state legitimacy.[27] Indeed, the very fact of the Organisation of Islamic Cooperation (OIC) being a political group forged on ties of a

21 *International Religious Freedom Report for 2015*, US Department of State, 2015, accessed 22 March 2017, http://www.state.gov/j/drl/rls/irf/religiousfreedom/index.htm#wrapper.

22 See for instance, http://womenofthewall.org.il/about/history/ accessed 20 June 2013.

23 See for instance, http://womenofthewall.org.il/about/legal-status/, accessed 20 June 2013.

24 See for instance, http://www.womenofthewall.org.il/legal-struggle/, accessed 16 December 2016. For the High Court judgment that at first rejected their petition, see H.C.J. 257/89, 2410/90, *Hoffman v Custodian of the Western Wall*, 48(2) P.D. 265.

25 Consideration of Reports submitted by states parties under article 40 of the Covenant, Initial report of states parties due in 1993, Addendum, Israel, UN Doc. CCPR/C/81/Add.13 (9 April 1998) [532].

26 On apostasy, see Chapter 1, section 2.1.

27 Ann Elizabeth Mayer, *Islam and Human Rights* (Westview Press, 2013) 2.

common faith, points to the interconnectedness of political and religious ideology and interests; with 57 member states, the OIC is the second largest inter-governmental organisation after the United Nations and claims to be the "collective voice of the Muslim world".[28]

The special treatment of religion is evident not only in countries where there are strong ties between Church and state. Even in secular Australia, non-discrimination legislation effectively exempts religious actors from prohibitions on discrimination. The *Sex Discrimination Act* was amended in 2013 to prohibit discrimination on grounds of sexual orientation, gender identity and intersex status. However, exemptions are provided for certain religious actors who raised doctrinal concerns about sexual orientation and gender identity, and therefore remain free to discriminate on those grounds.[29] Article 37(d) of that Act explicitly states that non-discrimination requirements do not affect any "act or practice of a body established for religious purposes, being an act or practice that conforms to the doctrines, tenets or beliefs of that religion or is necessary to avoid injury to the religious susceptibilities of adherents of that religion".[30] Article 38 goes on to explain that it is not unlawful for educational institutions established for religious purposes to discriminate on the grounds of a person's sex, marital status or pregnancy so long as that discrimination is "in good faith in order to avoid injury to the religious susceptibilities of adherents of that religion or creed".[31] The message of such legislation is that offence to religious sensibilities trumps discrimination and that discrimination can be in 'good faith' where it manifests religion.[32] No such exemptions are made for manifestation of 'belief'; the privilege is afforded only to religious actors.

The brief examples above demonstrate the very real impact that some religious actors can have on rights and the states obliged to protect them. Of particular concern for present purposes, is the fact that bias evident at domestic state level is mirrored at the international level, most notably in weak regulation of religious non-state actors.[33]

28 See Organisation of Islamic Cooperation, http://www.oic-oci.org/home/?lan=en accessed 22 March 2017.

29 *Sex Discrimination Amendment (Sexual Orientation, Gender Identity and Intersex Status) Bill 2013, Explanatory Memorandum* (The Parliament of the Commonwealth of Australia, House of Representatives, 2013) 8.

30 *Sex Discrimination Act 1984*, Australia, article 37(d).

31 Ibid article 38(1)–(3).

32 Also see David Marr, 'Gillard's bizarre act of faith leaves vulnerable unprotected' *The Age* online, 14 January 2013, accessed 22 March 2017, http://www.theage.com.au/opinion/politics/gillards-bizarre-act-of-faith-leaves-vulnerable-unprotected-20130113-2cnf0.html.

33 Carolyn Evans, *Freedom of Religion under the European Convention on Human Rights* (Oxford, 2001) 71–72. Evans has expressed concern that states have limited minority rights in deference to religious sensibilities of members of majority religions who pressure them to do so. Cismas notes the influence religious actors have on human rights law in Cismas, above n 3, 19.

1.2. Weak regulation of religious non-state actors

At a theoretical, normative level, international human rights discourse intends neutrality in its pluralist position. Although the term 'neutral' is understood as being 'not helping or supporting',[34] there is evidence to suggest that the international rights community actually tends to help and support major religions.[35] Ioana Cismas argues that unlike their non-religious counterparts, religious organisations have benefited from protection of the human right to freedom of religion and belief, notwithstanding that they are not individuals but institutions.[36] Lack of neutrality is also evident in the failure to criticise religious actors for their rights-adverse actions. By way of illustration, the relationship between international rights bodies and the seat of the Catholic Church may be considered. Of the 2.2 billion people in the world who are Christian, approximately half are Catholics.[37] Where Catholic institutions campaign against the use of condoms and condemn those who choose to use them, they put the lives, health and safety of those who believe them at risk.[38] Where such institutions preach abstinence and unprotected sex within the context of a marriage as the sole means of preventing the spread of human immunodeficiency virus (HIV), they disregard the fact that in many countries, married women are one of the groups most vulnerable to contracting the disease, even where their only sexual partner is their husband.[39] This approach also ignores the reality that in some contexts, the use of a female condom may be

34 See Oxford Dictionary online, accessed 22 March 2017, http://oxforddictionaries.com/definition/english/neutral.

35 The same has been said of European jurisprudence, where courts have been noted to uphold moral standards of the majority religion or religions with which the majority strongly sympathise, revealing discrimination against minority or 'unpopular' religions. Nowak and Vospernik, above n 12, 163.

36 Cismas, above n 3, 307. Cismas was referring specifically to article 9 of the European Convention on Human Rights.

37 The Pew Forum on Religion and Public Life, above n 2, 17. It must be noted that the high numbers of Catholics may also be partly attributable to the fact that many become adherents at birth and to subsequently leave must initiate a formal process via a 'declaration of defection' known as *actus formalis defectionis ab Ecclesia catholica*, that is tantamount to an act of apostasy or heresy. Accordingly, among those counted as Catholics may be people who consider themselves to have left the Church but have not formally done so, or who have formally left, but hold fast to their faith. See *Actus Formalis Defectionis ab ecclesia Catholica*, Pontifical Council for Legislative Texts, Vatican City, 13 March 2016, accessed 22 March 2017, http://www.vatican.va/roman_curia/pontifical_councils/intrptxt/documents/rc_pc_intrptxt_doc_20060313_actus-formalis_en.html.

38 Jennifer Gold, 'Catholic condom ban is helping Aids spread in Latin America: UN', *Christian Today*, 23 October 2007.

39 A study in India showed that 90% of women infected with HIV were infected by their husbands. See UNAIDS, *HIV Transmission in Intimate Partner Relationships in India* (2009), accessed 22 March 2017, http://www.aidsdatahub.org/sites/default/files/documents/HIVTransmission_Intimate_Partner_Relationships_India.pdf. UNFPA also notes "Many women are very vulnerable to HIV even though they do not practise high-risk behaviour. In some places, marriage itself is a risk factor." See UNFPA http://www.unfpa.org/hiv/women.htm accessed 11 November 2009. Also see L.

a woman's only defence against the contraction of a STD resulting from a sexual act she has no meaningful choice to abstain from.[40] There is little question that the stubborn denial of scientific evidence that condom use curtails the spread of HIV has a detrimental effect on individuals and communities who trust them.[41] From a rights-based perspective, such expressions are examples of religious expressions potentially threatening the right to health (article 12, ICESCR) and the right to life (article 6, ICCPR). Manfred Nowak suggests that the prohibition of misinformation about health-threatening activities and restrictions on advertising of harmful substances such as tobacco are likely to be justified under the public health limitation provided in article 19(3).[42] There is little evidence to suggest that those same limitations are applied to religious actors; it remains to be tested whether the teaching and dissemination of Catholic messages on sexual morality which compromise life and health could be prohibited by application of article 18(3) of the ICCPR on the grounds of the rights of others (to life and health) and public health.

The Special Rapporteur has also failed to criticise rights-contrary actions of the Catholic Church. In 1999, the then Special Rapporteur, Mr Abdelfattah Amor, undertook a country visit to the Holy See.[43] Mr Amor's report discussed the respect and esteem with which the Vatican regards non-Christian religious traditions including other monotheistic religions of Islam and Judaism, as well as polytheistic religions such as Hinduism. The report also mentioned Buddhism and traditional religions, and non-Catholic Christian religions. However no such statement of respect was afforded to the 'sects' the Vatican disapproves of, or to non-religious or atheist beliefs. But in the context of international human rights law, more relevant than any omission or lack of respect for human rights on the part of the Vatican, is the Special Rapporteur's failure to criticise it. The Rapporteur's report of his in-country visit reads as a compilation of Vatican declarations and encyclicals on topics ranging from relations with other religions, proselytism, procreation, abortion, and the role of women, without any criticism from the Special Rapporteur for stances which contradict international human rights standards, such as its opposition to the use of condoms against HIV/AIDS, its failure to facilitate access to justice for child victims of abuse, and its views on homosexuality. Rather than recommending reforms on the many points on which the Vatican can be said to be espousing views and acting in ways antithetical to human rights, Amor instead provided the Vatican with a mouthpiece to convey its

Mkandawire-Valhmu *et al.* 'Marriage as a risk factor for HIV: Learning from the experiences of HIV-infected women in Malawi' (2013) 8 *Global Public Health* 187.

40 UNAIDS, 'Empowering women to protect themselves: Promoting the Female Condom in Zimbabwe', 1 July 2010, accessed 22 March 2017, http://www.unfpa.org/news/empowering-women-protect-themselves-promoting-female-condom-zimbabwe.

41 See for instance Robertson, above n 4, 413.

42 Manfred Nowak, *CCPR Commentary* (NP Engel Kehl, 2nd edn, 2005) 358.

43 Abdelfattah Amor, *Report submitted in accordance with Commission on Human Rights resolution 1999/39*, UN Doc E/CN.4/2000/65 (15 February 2000).

messages, failed to challenge them, and abstractly concluded that his visit "enhanced protection of freedom of religion and belief".[44] Happily, the UN has since held the Catholic Church to higher account particularly in relation to mishandling of sex crimes perpetrated by its agents against children. In that regard, the self-interest to be served by the contentious nature of its 'dual personality' is evident in its use of state immunity to avoid civil claims on the one hand, while avoiding obligations under international treaties on the other.[45] In this context it is interesting to note that the Holy See's declaration and reservations to the Convention on the Rights of the Child (CRC) did not result in any objections from states parties, notwithstanding their equivalence to reservations of Islamic states that many states criticised as being contrary to the purpose of the Convention.[46] Two reports in 2014 note that "the Holy See has consistently placed the preservation of the reputation of the Church and the protection of the perpetrators above the child's best interests" and recommend that the Holy See reconsider its positions on denying access to contraceptives and sexual and reproductive health information to adolescents.[47] The Committees mandated to monitor the CRC and the Convention against Torture issued these reports; no such report will emerge from the HRC as the Holy See is not a signatory to the ICCPR.

The failure to criticise a major religion can also be seen with respect to Islam. Much of the terrorism perpetrated in recent years has been at the hands of actors who profess Islamic motivations and inspirations. Notwithstanding this, there is a reticence to explore any link between Islam and Islamic terrorism. In the wake of the September 2001 terrorist attacks in the United States (in which self-identified Islamists killed some 3000 people), the subsequent Security Council Resolutions expressed deep concern about terrorism motivated by intolerance and extremism and called upon states to take broad-ranging measures to address linkages between terrorism and transnational crime and other phenomena, but nowhere mentioned religion.[48] In the wake of terrorist attacks in Tunisia, Turkey, Russia, Lebanon and France, the Security Council did however note that terrorism threatening

44 Ibid [179]. The Holy See was subject to more criticism by the Committee against Torture (see *Concluding observations on the initial report of the Holy See*, on 17 June 2014, UN Doc. CAT/C/VAT/CO/1) and the Committee on the Rights of the Child (*Concluding observations on the second periodic report of the Holy See* on 25 February 2014, UN Doc. CRC/C/VAT/CO/2). Both reports were vocal about handling child sexual exploitation and abuse. These observations were delayed given that the Holy See issued its country reports 9 and 14 years late respectively.

45 Cismas, above n 3, 158–159, 185–191, 218–237.

46 Cismas, above n 3, 222. Cismas considers that the nature of the Holy See's reservations justify them being termed "Catholic reservations" as others were called "Islamic reservations".

47 *Concluding observations on the specific periodic report of the Holy See*, Committee on the Rights of the Child, UN Doc. CRC/C/VAT/CO/2, (25 February 2014), [29], [43], [56–57]; *Concluding observations on the initial report of the Holy See*, Committee against Torture, UN Doc. CAT/C/VAT/CO/1 (17 June 2014) [10–14].

48 Security Council Resolution 1373, Adopted by the Security Council at its 4385th Meeting, UN Doc. S/RES/1373 (28 September 2001).

international peace and security includes that "driven on religious or ethnic grounds".[49] Yet regardless of how emphatically Islamic terrorists claim to be committing their crimes in the name of Islam, the international community refuses to believe them.[50] Rather than calling for greater understanding of the possible links between terrorist actions and the religious ideologies and motivations of those who perpetrate them, Security Council resolutions (including one issued two days after the Manchester bombings by Islamic terrorists) continue to reaffirm "that terrorism cannot and should not be associated with any religion, nationality or civilization".[51]

Its failure to consider religious linkages in religion-related terrorism, results in missed opportunities to potentially formulate evidence-based responses to a significant threat to peace and security, and is symptomatic of a wider problem. While the United Nations expresses concern over crimes of intolerance and discrimination practised in the name of religion,[52] and has no hesitancy in labelling its victims Muslim, Christian or Jewish, it will not label perpetrators along religious lines even where they voraciously label themselves thus. Questions are raised as to whether a person can self-identify according to his or her beliefs at the international level. This reticence is understandable in the context of keeping peace between different people around the globe and avoiding persecution of followers of some religions for the actions of others who profess the same faith. Yet the fact that it is controversial to ask whether some religions may inspire terrorism or other acts of violence suggests that some religions are beyond reproach at the level of international human rights law. Islam is the fastest growing religion in the world with 1.6 billion followers;[53] if persons committing acts of terrorism were all

49 Security Council Resolution 2249, Adopted by the Security Council at its 7565th Meeting, UN Doc. S/RES/2249 (20 November 2015).

50 Security Council Resolution 1624, which emerged two months after the 2005 terrorist bombings in London, stressed the importance of religious society, condemned the "indiscriminate targeting of different religions", and spoke of the need to "prevent the subversion of educational, cultural and religious institutions by terrorists and their supporters". However, it did not explicitly condemn terrorist acts committed in the name of religion. See Security Council Resolution 1624, adopted by the Security Council at its 5261st Meeting, UN Doc S/RES/1624 (14 September 2005). Similarly, ten years later, Security Council 2255 of 2015 expressed concern about links "between terrorism and insurgency activities and illicit drugs" but did not mention religion. See Security Council Resolution 2255, Adopted by the Security Council at its 7590th Meeting, UN Doc S/RES/2255 (21 December 2015).

51 Security Council Resolution 2354, Adopted by the Security Council at its 7949th Meeting, UN Doc S/RES/2354 (24 May 2017); Security Council Resolution 2253, Adopted by the Security Council at its 7587th Meeting, UN Doc S/RES/2253 (17 December 2015); Security Council Resolution 2199, Adopted by the Security Council at its 7379th Meeting, UN Doc S/RES/2199 (12 February 2015).

52 Human Rights Council Resolution 6/37, *Elimination of All Forms of intolerance and discrimination based on religion and belief* (14 December 2007) 3.

53 The Pew Research Centre estimates that by 2050, 30% of the world's population – or 2.8 billion people – will be Muslim. The Pew Forum on Religion and Public Life, 'The Future of World Religions: Population Growth Projections, 2010–2050', April 2015, 7.

proclaiming allegiance to unpopular fringe religion, the Security Council may take less trouble to delink their actions from their ideology.

This failure to criticise major religions comes into sharper focus when the relative criticism mounted at minor religions is considered, with the example of Scientology offered below as an example of high persecution met with apparently low protection. The Church of Scientology is often ridiculed for the implausibility of its beliefs and vilified for its role in criminal activity, yet it is rarely defended. There is seemingly more reticence to attribute the acts of Catholic or Islamic actors to Catholicism or Islam in the same way that the sins of Scientologists are attributed to Scientology. Connected to its failure to criticise major religions is the high concern shown for adherents of those religions at the international level. In expressing concern over increased intolerance and violence, the Human Rights Council and the UN General Assembly mention Islamophobia, anti-Semitism and Christianophobia, omitting other victims.[54] The former Special Rapporteur on freedom of religion and belief, Heiner Bielefeldt, makes this same point in noting that several UN resolutions address 'phobias', typically including Islamophobia, Christianophobia and anti-Semitism (or Judeophobia), but make no mention of other phenomena, including 'Bahaiophobia' despite the extreme persecution faced by Baha'is, or indeed non-theistic, atheists and agnostic rights-holders.[55]

Religious actors occupy a unique position in society, capable of both helping and harming individuals within it. Despite this and the impunity with which many of its agents act, human rights discourse has thus far not subjected religious non-state actors to the same scrutiny it has applied to other private actors such as corporations.[56] Arguably, it has not been given the same opportunity to, with few cases brought by those who have suffered at the hands of religious actors. This lack of cases itself represents a failing of the international human rights framework to promote itself as accessible to those whose rights have been violated by religious actors.

2. New, unusual or emerging religions and beliefs

New and emerging religions (or religions falling on the 'fringe' of mainstream belief) have experienced significant persecution around the world, with members not only excluded from public life but even targeted for violent crime.[57] The state

54 See Human Rights Council Resolution 6/37, *Elimination of All Forms of intolerance and discrimination based on religion and belief*, 14 December 2007, and UN General Assembly Resolution 66/168, Elimination of all forms of intolerance based on religion and belief, UN Doc. A/Res/66/168, 11 April 2012, 3. Also see UN General Assembly Resolution 65/224, preambular paragraph 9.

55 Heiner Bielefeldt, 'Freedom of Religion or Belief – a Human Right Under Pressure' (2012) 1 *Oxford Journal of Law and Religion* 1, 15; Heiner Bielefeldt, 'Misconceptions about Freedom of Religion and Belief' (2013) 35 *Human Rights Quarterly* 33, 35–36.

56 For more on non-state actors see Cismas, above n 3.

57 Eileen Barker, 'Why the Cults? New Religious Movements and Freedom of Religion or Belief', in T. Lindholm, W. Cole Durham and B. G. Tahzib-Lie, *Facilitating of Freedom of Religion or Belief: A Deskbook* (Martinus Nijhoff, 2004) 578–579.

may impede their freedom to manifest religion and belief, and they may face threats from public and more established religions that fear losing members to them.[58] Leaders of established religions have also reportedly participated in kidnapping and forcibly 'deprogramming' members of new religious movements.[59] New religions are often seen as having 'wackier' or more 'unusual' beliefs, whereas older religions are accredited with greater legitimacy, not because their precepts have been substantiated but because the persistence of their own 'unusual' convictions has made them more 'usual' over time. This hierarchical approach is evident in the application of limitations by international bodies. In the same way that some belief sets are denied the status of 'religion', so too can limitations be applied to prevent manifestations of religions or beliefs that are considered by the adjudicating authority to be 'bad', and its adherents less worthy of protection.[60] The hesitancy of domestic, regional and international courts to limit what some may consider 'normal' or to accept what others may consider 'strange' entrenches a hierarchy of religion and belief. The result is that high persecution of members of new religious movements has not been met with the same concern as persecution of members of more established ones.

2.1. High persecution of new or 'unusual' religions

At the outset, the terminology used to differentiate established religions from newer movements, including 'sect' and 'cult',[61] has been acknowledged to have pejorative connotations.[62] The measures taken by some governments to investigate and even curtail the activities of 'sects' and 'cults', in the absence of a

58 Peter Cumper, 'The Rights of Religious Minorities: The Legal Regulation of New Religious Movements', in Peter Cumper and Steven Wheatley (eds), *Minority Rights in the 'New Europe'* (Kluwer Law International, 1999) 166.

59 Barker, above n 58, 579–580.

60 See for instance Human Rights Committee, *Communication No. 570/1993*, UN Doc CCPR/C/50/D/570/1993 (1994), *(MAB and ors v Canada, Admissibility)* [4.2] and Human Rights Committee, *Communication No. 117/1981*, UN Doc Supp No. 40 (A/39/40) 190 (1984) (*M.A. v Italy*). This malleability of limitations has revealed the HRC's bias against religions or beliefs founded on extreme right-wing ideologies, as will be noted in Chapter 4 on hate speech. On hate speech see *M.A. v Italy,* UN Doc Supp No 40 (A/39/40), at 190 (1984) (*M.A. v Italy*) and Human Rights Committee, *Communication No. 736/1997,* UN Doc CCPR/C/70/D/736/1997 (18 October 2000) *(Ross v Canada)*.

61 See Human Rights Committee, UN Doc. CCPR/C/94/D/1746/2008 (30 October 2008) (*Goyet v France)* [6.3] in which the author claimed that labelling the Buddhist Soka Gokkai group to which she belonged a 'cult' triggered hostility towards her.

62 Natan Lerner, *Religion, Secularism and Human Rights* (2nd edn, Martinus Nijhoff Publishers, 2012) 85; Natan Lerner, *Religion, Beliefs and International Human Rights* (Orbis Books, 2000) 7, 120; Peter Edge, *Legal Responses to Religious Difference* (Kluwer, 2002) 394; Dorota Anna Gozdecka, *Rights, Religious Pluralism and the Recognition of Difference* (Routledge, 2016) 86. Also see Jeremy T. Gunn, 'The Complexity of Religion and the Definition of "Religion" in International Law' (2003) 189 *Harvard Human Rights Journal* 16, 196, and Abdelfattah Amor, *Implementation of the Declaration on the Elimination of all forms of intolerance and of discrimination based on religion or belief*, UN Doc. E/CN.4/1998/6 (22 January1998) [116] in

definition of either to explain how they are to be differentiated from established religions, raises concern about the potential violation of freedom of religion and belief.[63] What is considered a 'cult' by some is to others (including those who follow it) a 'religion', and distinctions made between them in terms of perceived 'dangers' they pose to their members or others, are often not based on empirical evidence but on the fact of their 'otherness'.[64] To avoid stigmatisation, scholars now tend to use the less connotative term "new religious movements".[65] However, this rebranding has not ended their persecution.

Scientology is offered here as an example of a 'new' and 'unusual' religion to explore how members of new religious movements fare both in terms of their treatment at the state level, and their protection at the international level. Scientology was founded in 1952 by science fiction author L. Ron Hubbard, and professes the goal of spiritual enlightenment and freedom.[66] Through 'Dianetics', Scientology seeks to overcome early painful experiences through 'auditing'. Humans as spiritual 'thetans' are considered to be trillions of years old, meaning that painful experiences may have occurred in previous lifetimes. A Scientologist going through the auditing process can progress through several levels including 'clear' and on to 'Operating Thetan', being a state higher than that of a mortal human. Scientology prescribes an ethical system and includes specific practices for significant occasions such as weddings, christenings and ordination into its ministry.[67] Scientology claims to be compatible with other religious beliefs and offer a bridge between Eastern and Western schools of thought, using science and technology to improve the lives of its practitioners.[68] The Church of Scientology is also known for its enthusiastic recruitment of celebrities and controversies over the secretive means by which it administers and controls its finances and its public image.[69]

Despite being recognised as a religion by several states, Scientology remains an object of ridicule, scepticism and sometimes contempt.[70] Law enforcers have been reluctant to defend Scientologists from efforts of family members to forcibly 'deprogramme' them; one wonders whether attempts by anti-religious families to forcibly deprogramme their loved-one from, for instance, Anglicanism, would be met with the same indifference. Non-national members of the Church of Scientology were

which former Special Rapporteur Abdelfattah Amor notes the term 'sect' has a pejorative connotation despite its intended neutrality at international law.

63 Natan Lerner, *Religion, Beliefs and International Human Rights* (Orbis Books, 2000) 8.

64 Barker, above n 58, 573; Gozdecka, above n 63, 86.

65 Barker, above n 58, 572.

66 Church of Scientology, www.scientology.org, accessed 22 March 2017.

67 Edge, above n 63, 391–393.

68 Church of Scientology, above n 67.

69 See for instance Richard Behar, 'The Thriving Cult of Greed and Power', *Time Magazine* 6 May 1991; Jeremy Vine and John Sweeny, '*Scientology and me*' for BBC Panorama, 14 May 2007.

70 See for instance, Lawrence Wright 'The Apostate: Paul Haggis v the Church of Scientology' *The New Yorker* (online), 14 February 2011, http://www.newyorker.com/reporting/2011/02/14/110214fa_fact_wright, accessed 22 March 2017.

forbidden from entering the United Kingdom until 1980.[71] There have also been allegations of widespread and systemic discrimination against Scientologists in Germany, where followers are targeted and defamed by the media, and banned from political parties.[72] Some sectors of state government introduced requirements that applicants for positions within the civil service divulge any connection they had with the Church of Scientology.[73] The German government responded to growing recruitment of people into Scientology by distributing material in schools warning youth about becoming involved in sects and established a Commission on New Religious Movements which focused on Scientology. The Commission concluded that there was little danger associated with such groups but nonetheless recommended that legislation be enacted to curtail activities of sects.[74] The Hollywood film *Valkyrie* was initially banned from being filmed at military sites in Germany because its lead actor (Tom Cruise) was a Scientologist.[75] The performance of an American Jazz musician in Germany in 2007 was cancelled when the government learned that he was a Scientologist.[76] There have also been reports of 'sect filters' being used to prevent Scientologists from becoming members of many associations and organisations.[77] Further, authorities condoned active discrimination against Scientologists, distributing lists of Scientologists trying to 'infiltrate' business. Trade associations and Chambers of Commerce distributed leaflets instructing how to 'spot' and exclude Scientologists.[78] Defenders of the rights of Scientologists did not pass up the opportunity to highlight that in this particular country, such measures were once upon a time targeted not at Scientologists but at Jews.[79]

71 Peter Cumper, 'Religious Liberty in the United Kingdom' in Johan Van der Vyver and John Witte (eds), *Religious Human Rights in Global Perspective: Legal Perspective* (Martinus Nijhoff Publishers, 1996) 221.

72 Sue Taylor, Church of Scientology, International, 'Scientology' (paper presented at the International Coalition for Religious Freedom Conference on 'Religious Freedom in Latin America and the New Millennium', Sheraton Mofarrej Hotel, Sao Paolo, Brazil, October 10–12, 1998).

73 Cumper, above n 59, 171.

74 James T. Richardson and Valerie A. Lukes, 'Legal Considerations Concerning New Religious Movements in the "New Europe"', in Peter Cumper and Tom Lewis, *Religion, Rights and Secular Society: European Perspectives* (Edward Elgar Publishing, 2012) 295–296.

75 See 'Germany imposes ban on Tom Cruise', *BBC* (online), 26 June 2007, http://news.bbc.co.uk/2/hi/6240312.stm?lsm accessed 22 March 2017.

76 See for instance, Emine Saner, 'Germany 1, Scientology 0', *Guardian* (online), 27 June 2007, http://www.guardian.co.uk/world/2007/jun/27/germany.features11 accessed 22 March 2017.

77 See *Human Rights Report: Germany,* US Department of State 2008 (25 February 2009), http://www.state.gov/g/drl/rls/hrrpt/2008/eur/119081.htm accessed 22 March 2017.

78 Kevin Boyle and Juliet Sheen, *Freedom of Religion and Belief: A World Report* (Routledge, 1997), 312–313.

79 See for instance, Frank Rich, 'Show me the money', *New York Times* (online), 25 January 1997, http://www.nytimes.com/1997/01/25/opinion/show-me-the-money.html?ref=scientology accessed 22 March 2017.

2.2. Low protection of new or 'unusual' religions

The treatment of Scientologists at the domestic level does not imply that it is condoned at the level of international human rights law. However, there is some evidence to suggest that it is. The three authors in the HRC case of *Arenz v Germany* had their membership in the Christian Democratic Union (CDU) revoked when it became known to that political party that they were Scientologists.[80] Among the state party's challenges to the admissibility of the authors' subsequent complaint to the HRC, was that their claim under article 18 of the ICCPR was inadmissible because the 'Scientology Organisation' could not be considered a religious or a philosophical community, but rather an organisation aimed at economic gains and acquisition of power.[81] The authors responded that article 18 of the ICCPR applied to newly established and minority religions.[82] The HRC found the case inadmissible as the authors failed to substantiate how the conduct of the domestic courts amounted to arbitrariness or denial of justice, effectively upholding the right of political parties to expel members on the basis of their religion (freedom *not* to associate), over the human rights of the three authors including their freedom to manifest their religion and belief. It is asserted that the same decision would not have been made had the authors been expelled from the CDU for being Jewish or Islamic, especially when one bears in mind the political power of the CDU which is not a fringe political party, but is part of Germany's coalition government headed by Angela Merkel.

The Universal Periodic Review (UPR) is a Human Rights Council mechanism tracking the human rights situation of the 193 Member States of the United Nations, through a review that takes place every five years. The database of recommendations and voluntary pledges contains no mentions of Scientology.[83] This lack of scrutiny speaks to the low protection accorded to them. On the human rights website www.bayefsky.com,[84] a search of the word 'Christianity' yields 150 documents. The word 'Islam' appears in 501 documents. 'Judaism' appears in 57 documents, and Scientology in 10.[85] Four of those are documents that mention the case of *Arenz v Germany* described above. Of the other six, the first is a state party report that mentions Scientology in the context of the religious affiliation of Canadian children (CRC/C/11/Add.3 (1994)). The second is a summary of a meeting in which Australia's recognition of Scientology as a religion for tax purposes was noted (CCPR/C/SR.1858 (2000)). The third is a record of a summary meeting praising the Strasbourg Administrative Court ruling, according to which authorities can no longer refuse to register a religious association on

80 *Arenz v Germany*, Human Rights Committee, *Communication No 1138/2002*, UN Doc CCPR/C/80/D/1138/2002 (2004).

81 Ibid [5.4].

82 Ibid [6.8].

83 http://www.upr-info.org/database/, search conducted on 16 December 2016.

84 The website www.bayefsky.com, founded by Professor A. F. Bayefsky of York University, Toronto, Canada, provides data on the UN human rights treaty system by its monitoring treaty bodies since their inauguration in the 1970s.

85 Search of www.bayefsky.com conducted 16 December 2016.

grounds unconnected with the requirements of public order (CCPR/C/SR.1599 (1997)). In this context, enquiries were made about the practice in relation to new religions such as Scientology. France's interesting answer appears in the fourth document:

> the Church of Scientology was in no way entitled to claim the status of a church or religious congregation by virtue – *inter alia* – of the Act of 9 December 1905 on the separation of church and State, and thus it enjoyed none of the benefits, notably tax benefits, attached to that status. Some of its members in France had been prosecuted and convicted for endangering other persons and for practising medicine illegally. More generally, sects as propagators of beliefs were not subject to prosecution by the authorities, but the latter could make use of all the legal means at their disposal in cases where a sect, or any of its members, was guilty of practices that were illegal or contrary to public order, for instance abduction of minors, unlawful confinement or acts of violence. In any event, it was clear that such procedures applied only to physical persons and not to organisations. In conclusion, he emphasised that the question of sects was a matter of concern both to French public opinion and to the authorities, and that an observation unit had been set up following a parliamentary report.[86]

It is not clear whether Mr Faugere intended this answer to appease the HRC's concerns with respect to France's adherence to human rights, or to demonstrate France's willingness to own up to its areas of deficiency. And nor did the HRC seek clarification; in remaining silent in response to these assertions, it tacitly accepted them and avoided the questions raised by it, including what is a 'sect', what is a 'religion' and who determines which is which?

This question emerges in the fifth document, in which Lord Colville of the HRC expressed concern that 'sects' and their followers were being discriminated against in Bavaria, Germany. He questioned the legitimacy of measures taken by the government in circulating an anti-sect policy among schools, requesting headmasters to report on measures they had taken. Further, Lord Colville expressed concern about the presence of 'sect commissioners' and for the fact that as of 1 November 1996, every applicant for a civil service position in Bavaria had to state whether or not he belonged to the Church of Scientology. While Lord Colville said he would have no objection to Catholic or Lutheran Churches warning their own congregations about other beliefs, he expressed the view that it was dangerous to use government machinery to issue warnings against such groups, for "who knew which group might be targeted later?"[87] The final mention of 'Scientology'

86 Human Rights Committee, *Summary Record of the 1600th meeting: France*, 60th sess., 1600th mtg., UN Doc CCPR/C/SR.1600, (11 November 1997) [29].

87 Human Rights Committee, *Summary record of the first part (public) of the 1553rd meeting: Germany*, 58th sess., 1553rd mtg., UN Doc CCPR/C/SR.1553, 23 January 1997 [3].

concerns Ireland, which is giving financial support to Islamic schools in accordance with its obligation to instruct children in the religion of their parents where parents want such instruction to be given, but has not done so with respect to new religions such as Scientology.[88] These six documents – plus *Arenz v Germany* – amount to the totality of consideration given by international human rights mechanisms to the rights of Scientologists.[89]

Scientology is not the first religion to have endured ridicule and derision in its quest to be taken seriously, and will not be the last. At one point or another, all religions are considered 'new' before their 'unusual' practices become 'usual'.[90] But for the moment, the pluralism that should underpin international human rights to ensure that rights attach to individuals irrespective of their beliefs is called into question. Human rights bodies seem to distinguish between a Catholic individual (or Muslim or Jewish individual) and a Scientologist to the extent that the mistreatment of the latter continues relatively unchecked. The 'Thetan' (the everlasting spirit of Scientology) is treated with more scepticism and ridicule than the Holy Ghost (the divine spirit of Catholicism). The wealth and power of the Church of Scientology is viewed with more suspicion than the far larger fortune acquired by the Catholic Church. And significantly, the evils perpetrated by Scientologists are considered to reflect on Scientology more than the crimes of Catholics are attributed to Catholicism.[91] Indeed, sex crimes perpetrated by agents of the Catholic Church against children around the world have been occurring since long before the Church of Scientology came into existence.[92]

Beyond the low protection of new religious movements, the neglect of older religions that are considered 'unusual' can also be observed, where what is 'usual' is determined by what is dominant. In the present day, persecution, stigmatisation and even prohibition of traditional religious practices evinces bias towards Abrahamic religions as being 'usual' while traditional indigenous practices are deemed

88 Human Rights Committee, *Summary record of the 1847th meeting of the Human Rights Committee: Ireland*, 69th sess, 1847th mtg., UN Doc CCPR/C/SR.1847 (12 November 2001) [46].

89 The rights of Scientologists and their lack of protection have been considered more at the European level. See: *X and Church of Scientology v Sweden*, Application No. 7805/77, 5 May 1979 and *Church of Scientology Moscow v Russia*, Application No. 18147/02, Judgment 5.4.2007.

90 For instance, Mormonism – a religion rooted in Christianity that emerged with Joseph Smith's publication of the Book of Mormon in 1930 – endured a similar history of scepticism before achieving mainstream acceptance. See Orma Linford, 'Mormons, the Law, and the Territory of Utah' (1979) 23 *American Journal of Legal History* 213, 216 and Elijah L. Milne, 'Blaine Amendments and Polygamy Laws: The Constitutionality of Anti-Polygamy Laws Targeting Religion' (2006) 28 *Western New England Law Review* 257, 263–264.

91 Eileen Barker makes a similar point in noting that the suicide of a 'cult leader' is a more evocative media story than the suicide of an Anglican or Lutheran. See Barker, above n 58, 582.

92 For instance, Geoffrey Robertson QC, *The Case of the Pope: Vatican Accountability for Human Rights Abuse* (Penguin, 2010) 14, notes that the first child sex scandal occurred in AD 153. The Church of Scientology was founded in 1954.

'unusual' and ostensibly less worthy of protection.[93] The history of many religions is marked by a parallel history of violence and persecution as its opponents have sought to oppress it, and its followers have killed or died in its defence. In the meantime at the level of international law, the persecution of and discrimination against followers of new or unusual religious movements is met with less concern than is the case for major established religions.

3. Non-religion and atheism at the bottom of the hierarchy

The 'heathens', 'heretics' and 'infidels' of history have long been persecuted by religious and political powers. Atheists have been forced to hide the true nature of their beliefs, and risk discrimination, persecution, punishment or even death for manifesting them.[94] But while atheists and non-believers continue to be persecuted on the basis of their beliefs, their freedom of religion and belief is afforded the least protection.

3.1. High persecution of non-believers and atheists

It was noted more than a decade ago but is perhaps truer today that "the position of non-believers becomes ever more perilous in a world of increasing religious fervour."[95] Irrespective of the legislative protections that may be in place to afford equal protection to the religious and the irreligious, many atheists around the world do not publicly admit their belief for fear of discrimination.[96] In 2007, the then Special Rapporteur on freedom of religion and belief issued an Interim Report to the General Assembly on 'Situations of persons with atheistic or non-theistic beliefs'.[97] That report considers whether religions or beliefs that are theistic, non-theistic and atheistic enjoy protection against discrimination on an equal basis and provides an overview of issues of relevance to atheists and non-theists.[98] The Special Rapporteur expressed concerns over legislation which

93 See for instance, Rosalind I. J. Hackett, 'Traditional, African, Religious, Freedom?' in Elizabeth A. Castelli *et al* (eds) *Politics of Religious Freedom* (University of Chicago Press, 2015) 90–92. The plight of adherents of African religions is touched on in Chapter 3.

94 Currently the death penalty is provided for blasphemy or apostasy in at least 13 countries. See Ahmed Shaheed, Foreword to 2016 edition of *The Freedom of Thought Report* (International Humanist and Ethical Union, 2016) http://freethoughtreport.com/foreword-to-the-2016-edition/ accessed 2 February 2017.

95 Brice Dickson, 'The United Nations and Freedom of Religion' (1995) 44 *International and Comparative Law Quarterly* 327, 356.

96 See UN Secretary General, *Elimination of All forms of religious intolerance,* UN GAOR, 55th sess., UN doc A/55/280/Add.2 (9 August 2000) [7] on Bangladesh.

97 Asma Jahangir, *Elimination of all forms of religion intolerance: interim report of the Special Rapporteur on freedom of religion or belief,* UN Doc A/62/280 (20 August 2007).

98 *Equal* treatment is not intended to imply *uniform* treatment. As Krishnaswami understood in his 1956 report, "since the demands made by various religions upon their members are different and since varying degrees of importance are attached to

exempted certain religious or non-religious groups from equal entitlements, and government consultations which excluded non-religious representatives, thereby risking disproportionate influence of sometimes extreme 'faith leaders' in debate.[99] Seven years later, the then Special Rapporteur noted the discrimination against sceptics, atheists and dissenters forced to conceal their positions in order to avoid harassment by colleagues, customers or employers, while followers of mainstream religions or belief are able to manifest their convictions at work.[100] He also noted "atheists and agnostics suffer in many countries from a climate of intimidation, repression or violence."[101] Atheists have also been disproportionately affected by discriminatory practices of non-state actors in access to employment or services, sometimes with state complicity.[102]

Since 2012, the International Humanist and Ethical Union (IHEU) has released an annual report titled 'Freedom of Thought: A Global Report on Discrimination against Humanists, Atheists and the Non-religious', the most recent version of which was published in 2016.[103] That report surveys the treatment of humanists, atheists and non-religious people in sixty countries, taking into consideration laws on apostasy and religious conversion, blasphemy and religious criticism, compulsory religious registration (usually governed by an exhaustive list of permissible religions), religious tests for citizenship or participation in civil life, religious control of family law, and religious control of public education.[104] The 2016 edition reported that:

> the overwhelming majority of countries fail to respect the rights of humanists, atheists and the non-religious. For example, there are laws that deny atheists' right to identify, revoke their right to citizenship, restrict their right to marry, obstruct their access to or experience of public education, prohibit them from holding public office, prevent them from working for the state, or criminalize the expression of their views on and criticism of religion. In the worst cases, the state or non-state actors may execute the non-religious for leaving the religion of their parents, may deny the rights of atheists to exist, or may seek total control over their beliefs and actions.[105]

different manifestations, uniformity of treatment may in reality lead to discrimination against some religions." See Arcot Krishnaswami, *Study of Discrimination in the Matter of Religious Rights and Practices*, UN Doc. E/CN.4/Sub.2/200/Rev.1 (1960), UN Pub. No 60.XIV.2, 49.

99 Jahangir, above n 98 [73–74].

100 Heiner Bielefeldt, *Interim report of the Special Rapporteur on freedom of religion or belief*, UN Doc. A/69/261 (5 August 2014) [27].

101 *Report of the Special Rapporteur on Freedom of Religion or Belief, Heiner Bielefeldt*, UN Doc. A/HRC/28/66 (29 December 2014) [9].

102 Heiner Bielefeldt, Nazila Ghanea and Michael Weiner, *Freedom of Religion and Belief: An International Law Commentary* (Oxford, 2016) 312.

103 *Freedom of Thought 2012: A Global Report on Discrimination against Humanists, Atheists and the Non-Religious* (International Humanists and Ethical Union, 2012).

104 Ibid.

105 Ibid 9. Also see *Report on the Special Rapporteur of Freedom of Religion and Belief*, UN Doc. A/HRC/31/18 (23 December 2015) [60] noting that blasphemy laws

Negative perceptions of atheists are widespread and often unchecked in countries as diverse as Bangladesh and the United States.[106] Conflation of religious affiliation with political affiliation in some parts of the world has made atheists reticent to openly admit their beliefs for fear that doing so will lead to particular perceptions about their political views.[107] In Indonesia, atheism is seen as synonymous with communism; since the execution of all known communists involved in the attempted coup of 1965, there are few worse labels in that country.[108] After 1965, most people declared themselves to be either Christian or Islamic given that it "became generally accepted that to be a citizen, one needed to be a religious person".[109] In Switzerland, compulsory primary and secondary education on 'religion and culture' connects contemporary atheism with former Communist states.[110]

Atheists are of course not universally disadvantaged. Julia Gillard was Australia's first openly atheist prime minister. In 'coming out' as an atheist, the then Prime Minister said:

> I am not going to pretend a faith I don't feel. I am what I am and people will judge that. For people of faith, I think the greatest compliment I could pay to them is to respect their genuinely held beliefs and not to engage in some pretence about mine.[111]

Gillard's atheism was ultimately not a barrier to her political ascent, which sits in marked contrast to the United States of America, where in 2012 only 54% of people would have been prepared to vote for an atheist.[112] During the 2016 election, that figure was 51%, confirming that while atheism is less of a liability

typically favour certain religions for protection and encroach on the freedoms particularly of atheists, agnostics, dissidents and others.

106 UN Secretary General, *Elimination of All forms of religious intolerance*, UN GAOR, 55th sess., UN doc A/55/280/Add.2 (9 August 2000) [7] on Bangladesh.

107 Boyle and Sheen, above n 79, 248.

108 Boyle and Sheen, above n 79, 204.

109 Ibid.

110 Switzerland Country Report, *Freedom of Thought Report* (International Humanist and Ethical Union, 2016), accessed 2 February 2017, http://freethoughtreport.com/countries/europe-western-europe/switzerland/.

111 Prime Minister Julia Gillard, interview with Jon Faine, ABC Radio, quoted in John Warhurst, 'Reflections on Gillard's atheism', *Eureka Street*, 16 October 2011, accessed 22 March 2017, http://www.eurekastreet.com.au/article.aspx?aeid=28547.

112 Jeffrey M. Jones, 'Atheists, Muslims see most Bias as Presidential Candidates' *Gallup*, 21 June 2012, accessed 22 March 2017, http://www.gallup.com/poll/155285/atheists-muslims-bias-presidential-candidates.aspx. Gillard acknowledges that she would be unlikely to have reached the highest echelon of American politics "being atheist, single and childless". See 'Lally Weymouth interviews Australian Prime Minister Julia Gillard', *Washington Post* (online), 8 March 2013, accessed 22 March 2017, https://www.washingtonpost.com/opinions/lally-weymouth-interviews-australian-prime-minister-julia-gillard/2013/03/08/9d0035c0-8733-11e2-999e-5f8e0410cb9d_story.html?utm_term=.3dc6ee019749.

than it was, it remains the biggest hindrance to a presidential candidate of those traits polled; more so than if the candidate were a Muslim (whom 42% would be less likely to vote for); Jewish (for whom 10% would be less likely to vote for); gay or lesbian (whom 26% would be less likely to vote for); or had had extramarital affairs (whom 37% would be less likely to vote for).[113] Another illustration of the low opinion Americans tend to have of atheists, is evident in the infamous comment of George Bush Senior: "No, I don't know that atheists should be considered as citizens, nor should they be considered as patriots. This is one nation under God."[114] Here, Richard Dawkins proposed the experiment of replacing the word 'atheists' with 'Jews', 'Muslims' or 'Blacks'.[115] Negative perceptions of atheists translate into actual discrimination. IHEU reports:

> Despite strong legal and constitutional protections for the religious and secular alike, the U.S. has long been home to a social and political atmosphere in which the non-religious are sometimes made to feel like lesser Americans or as if atheism is 'un-American'.[116]

The report goes on to cite several examples of discrimination against atheists in the United States, including prohibitions in seven states on atheists holding public office (Arkansas even prohibits atheists from testifying as witnesses at trial), and discrimination against atheists in the military.[117]

State-level discrimination and vilification of atheists of course proves nothing about the rights they enjoy at international law; the material point is that it seems to happen with impunity. While international human rights law is concerned with issues such as the vilification of Islam in an age of terrorism and increasing intolerance against Muslims, comments against atheists are made without any apparent legal, political or social consequences at the domestic and international levels. In his foreword to the 2016 IHEU Freedom of Thought Report, Special Rapporteur on Freedom of Belief, Ahmed Shaheed, stated that report was a reminder that:

> the right to freedom from religion or belief is as fundamental as the right to freedom of religion, and that the same human right protects freedom of non-religious thought and non-religious belief as well; and that for some

113 *Faith and the 2016 campaign* (Pew Research Centre, 2016) 3–5, 24–25. By party affiliation, 41% of Democrats polled would be less likely to vote for an atheist in contrast to 65% of Republicans.
114 George Bush Senior in an interview with Robert I. Sherman initially quoted in *American Atheist* magazine on 27 August 1987 and subsequently reprinted elsewhere.
115 Richard Dawkins, *The God Delusion* (Bantam Press, 2006) 43.
116 United States of America Country Report, *Freedom of Thought Report* (International Humanist and Ethical Union, 2016), accessed 2 February 2017, http://freethoughtreport.com/countries/americas-northern-america/united-states-of-america/#Hobby_Lobby.
117 Ibid.

humanists, atheists, free-thinkers and the unconcerned the protection of this right can mean the difference between life and death.[118]

The question to be asked then, as an urgent matter of life and death, is whether the right of atheists to freedom of religion and belief is protected in international human rights law.

3.2. Low protection of non-believers and atheists

Despite high persecution of atheists, international human rights law often overlooks non-believers. 'Belief' is not a ground of discrimination explicitly recognised by article 26 of the ICCPR which refers only to 'religion'. It can be questioned whether human rights bodies give non-believers and atheists due attention; a search of all recommendations and voluntary pledges in the Universal Periodic Review (UPR) database yields 13 results when the word 'Jewish' is searched, 20 results for the word 'Christian', 166 results for 'Muslim', no results for 'Scientologist' (or Scientology), and only one for the word 'atheist', concerning a recommendation for Greece to decriminalise blasphemy and protect the rights of religious minorities, atheists and agnostics.[119] A search of the word 'atheism' on the Universal Human Rights Index of United Nations Documents also yields one result, being concluding observations of the Committee on the Convention on the Rights of the Child recommending that China let children choose whether to participate in classes on religion or atheism.[120] A search of www.bayefsky.com yields 21 results.[121] Two arise in largely irrelevant asides in the HRC case of *Malcolm Ross v Canada*.[122] Among the documents are eight Summary Records from both the HRC and the CERD Committee from 2001 and earlier. Notable among those is that concerning Algeria, in which a government representative acknowledged that people may have been afraid to publicly proclaim atheism in a contemporaneous crisis (a period of violent clashes between security forces and protestors);[123] and Iran explained its cultural policy of purifying the human

118 See Shaheed, above n 95.

119 The Universal Periodic Review process is a Human Rights Council mechanism of reviewing member states on 5-year cycles. See http://www.upr-info.org/database/, searched on 2 February 2017.

120 Universal Human Rights Index, http://www.universalhumanrightsindex.org/en/index.html, search conducted 2 February 2017, resulted in Committee on the Rights of the Child, *Concluding Observations on China (including Hong Kong and Macau Special Administrative Regions)*, 40th sess., UN Doc CRC/C/CHN/CO/2 (24 November 2005) [44].

121 Search conducted 2 February 2016.

122 *Ross v Canada*, Human Rights Committee, Communication No. 736/1997, UN Doc CCPR/C/70/D/736/1997 (18 October 2000) and Human Rights Committee, *Report of the Human Rights Committee*, UN GAOR, 56th sess., UN Doc A/56/40 (Vol. II, 2000) [5.4].

123 Human Rights Committee, *Summary Record of the 1683rd meeting: Algeria*, UN Doc CCPR/C/SR.1683 (28 July 1998) [46].

environment to eliminate the causes of atheism, corruption, prostitution and despotism.[124] Among the seven concluding observations, Colombia assured the HRC that while Colombia was a Catholic country, it respected the right to atheism.[125] In another, the CERD Committee asked the Islamic Republic of Iran whether atheism would be considered un-Islamic and therefore affect an individual's civil rights.[126] In the following document, the HRC was informed by a representative from Iraq that the choice to believe or not to believe in a religion was a personal matter, but that the law intervened during demonstrations in favour of atheism for the question of faith was "securely anchored in the Arab soul".[127]

The documents concerning Morocco contain the most in-depth discussion of atheism. In one, a Moroccan delegate explained that legislation was in place to make overt acts of atheism criminal offences so as to protect against anarchy and civil war.[128] In the first summary record for Morocco, the CERD Committee acknowledged the delicacy of atheism in a country where Islam was the state religion, but asked whether atheists had freedom of conscience and expression.[129] In response, the Moroccan representative failed to see any issue with criminalising overt acts of atheism given that states were required to criminalise overt acts of racism. He went on to explain that atheism as a belief was not criminalised but attempts to overthrow a regime by force were.[130] In response to Morocco's statements, Committee Member Mr Yutzis expressed his views that while he was not in favour of militant atheism, he was of the belief that fundamentalists rather than atheists threatened stability and that the Moroccan law cast a veil of doubt over the relationship between pluralism and democracy.[131] In the penultimate document, representatives of Morocco explained that it was difficult for some countries to legislate to protect non-believers because of the need to be responsive to public opinion, and that it saw no relationship between 'secularism' and 'atheism'.[132] Committee Member Mr Sherifs raised concern about criminalising acts of atheism, to which Moroccan delegates responded that atheism, as the negation of Islam, was a threat to the foundations of the state and therefore

124 Committee on Economic, Cultural and Social Rights, *Summary Record of the 7th meeting: Iran (Islamic Republic of)*, UN Doc E/C.12/1993/SR.7 (3 June 1993) [13].

125 *Concluding Observations of the Human Rights Committee: Colombia*, UN Doc CCRP/A/35/40 (1980) [268].

126 *Concluding Observations of the Committee on the Elimination of Racial Discrimination: Islamic Republic of Iran*, 26th sess., No.18, UN Doc CERD/A/8418, (1971) [294].

127 *Concluding Observations of the Human Rights Committee: Iraq*, UN Doc CCPR A/35/40 (1980) [382].

128 Committee on the Elimination of Racial Discrimination, *Eleventh Periodic Reports of States Parties due in 1992: Morocco*, UN Doc CERD/C/225/Add.1, (12 May 1993) [70–71].

129 Committee on the Elimination of Racial Discrimination, *Summary Record of the 1020th meeting: Morocco*, UN Doc CERD/C/SR.1020 (29 July 1996) [29].

130 Ibid [53].

131 Ibid [60–61].

132 Committee on the Elimination of Racial Discrimination, *Summary Record of the 1021st meeting: Morocco*. UN Doc CERD/C/SR.1021 (10 March 1994) [6].

naturally considered a criminal offence.[133] In response, Country Rapporteur Mr Garvalov explained the drafting history of the 1981 Declaration intended to include atheistic beliefs.[134] Committee Member Mr de Gouttes asserted that criminalisation of atheism could not be justified by the opinion that it threatened the state and noted that the Committee would wish to further consider Morocco's protection only of Islam, Judaism and Christianity.[135] Mr Yutzis asserted that Morocco's criminalisation of atheism was to invert former claims by other states that religion itself was a destabilising factor with equally negative human rights results. The result, he said, was to put a "straight-jacket of fear" on those who experienced a crisis of faith.[136] In the final document, a Summary Record of the Committee on Economic, Cultural and Social Rights, Morocco again took the opportunity to explain that atheism was not an acceptable moral position in Morocco but a grave violation of public order.[137]

It is heartening to see at least in the context of these summary reports of 1994, that Committee Members expressed concern about the rights of atheists. Such concessions however must be viewed alongside the more frequent and arguably more vigorous defence of rights-holders with religious beliefs. The lack of discourse about atheists – notwithstanding blatant violations of their rights by both States and non-state actors – points to a factor that may compound their struggle to have their freedom of religion and belief meaningfully protected; atheists do not have champions at the international level. Even those states that could be considered 'atheistic' do not champion atheism or the rights of atheists, being generally more concerned with communist political values than they are with atheistic ideological values.

The report issued by then Special Rapporteur Amor following his visit to the Holy See in 1999, underlines the neglect of atheists at the international level. In discussing the Vatican's respect for non-Christian religious traditions, no such statement of respect is offered to non-religious or atheistic beliefs. The Vatican's position on non-theistic beliefs is reflected in its opinion that the inclusion of freedom of belief alongside freedom of religion in the 1981 Declaration and in the ICCPR was the result of a political compromise and that the specificity of religion should be "preserved against the danger of it being reduced to culture and, more generally, against the danger of it being denatured".[138] What is concerning about this report, is not the light it sheds on the Vatican's implication that freedom of religion and belief should be out of reach for atheists, but the failure of the Special Rapporteur to criticise that position. The Special Rapporteur failed to explain to

133 Ibid [15 and 32].
134 Ibid [36–38].
135 Ibid [40].
136 Ibid [43].
137 Committee on Economic, Cultural and Social Rights, *Summary Record of 8th meeting: Morocco*, UN Doc E/C.12/1994/SR.8 (11 May 1994) [20].
138 Abdelfattah Amor, Special Rapporteur, *Report submitted in accordance with Commission on Human Rights resolution 1999/39*, UN Doc E/CN.4/2000/65 (15 February 2000) [127].

the Holy See that making enjoyment of the right conditional would be to 'denature' freedom of religion and belief that attaches to human beings on the basis of their humanity, not on the basis of their religions or beliefs.[139] The Human Rights Council Special Procedures database contains only three joint Special Rapporteur communications concerning the rights of atheists, one relating to the hate speech trial and psychiatric confinement of human rights defender Alexsandr Kharlamov in Kazakhstan in 2013, another concerning the arrest and torture of prominent blogger Asif Mohiuddin in 2013, and the final letter relating to the arrest, detention and torture of Albert Saber Ayyad in Egypt for "defamation of religion" in 2012.[140]

While several cases of the European Court of Human Rights have grappled with questions of freedom *from* religion (albeit with varying results),[141] the same is not true at the international level, where there is a dearth of HRC cases concerning non-religious or atheist rights-holders. One example that can be pointed to is *Leirvåg et al v Norway,* in which the HRC protected the rights of humanist parents to be free from the religion of the state educating their children in accordance with their own convictions.[142] Notably absent are cases brought by sceptical rights-holders who have been prosecuted for apostasy, for instance, or cases brought by freethinkers or atheists whose persecution as 'infidels' has been unchecked, or whose persecution has been at the hands of the state itself. Nowak and Vospernik note that it is surprising that many pressing issues on freedom of religion and belief have not generated more international litigation, given the

139 The Vatican's position may change: newly elected Pope Francis has publicly stated that even atheists be redeemed by Jesus if they do good. See *inter alia* 'Pope Francis: better to be an atheist than a hypocritical Catholic', *Guardian*, 23 February 2017, accessed 22 March 2017 https://www.theguardian.com/world/2017/feb/23/pope-francis-better-to-be-atheist-than-hypocritical-catholic.

140 Reference: Urgent Appeal G/SO 218/2 G/SO 214 (67–17) Health (2002–7) G/SO 214 (107–9) G/SO 214 (3–3 16) G/SO 214 (53–24) G/SO 214 (56–23) KAZ 4/2013 (22 August 2013); Allegation Letter G/SO 214 (67–17) G/SO 214 (56–23) G/SO 214 (107–9) BGD 2/2013 (18 January 2013); Urgent Appeal G/SO 218/2 G/SO 214 (56–23) G/SO 214 (3–3-16) G/SO 214 (53–24) EGY 13/2012 (3 October 2012). In response to the latter, the Egyptian government stated that Ayyad's 'defamation of religion' constituted an offence in the Egyptian Criminal Code, and that such an offence is a justified limitation to freedom of religion and belief. See: https://spcommreports.ohchr.org/Tmsearch/TMDocuments, search conducted 26 May 2017.

141 See *Eweida and Others v The United Kingdom*, European Court of Human Rights, Application Nos 48420/10, 59842/10, 51671/10 and 36516/10 (15 January 2013) and *Lautsi and others v Italy*, European Court of Human Rights, Application No. 30814 /06 (3 November 2009). In the latter, the court's decision (that the proselytising effect of crosses in classrooms was not enough to justify their removal) may have failed to protect children from improper proselytism (the subject of Chapter 3) and right to be free *from* the religion of the state.

142 See *Leirvåg et al v Norway,* Human Rights Committee, Communication No. 931/00, UN Doc CCPR/C/82/D/1155/2003 (3 November 2004) [14.2–14.7]. *Grzelak v Poland,* European Court of Human Rights, Application No 7710/02 (15 June 2010) involved agnostic parents; the Court found a violation of Article 14 taken with Article 9 given the stigmatising absence of a mark in school reports for the religion/ethics subject.

abuses that often occur.[143] Yet this lack of litigation as far as atheists are concerned is not surprising given that the right to be free *from* religion is subordinate to freedom *of* religion.

Beyond the scant jurisprudence that has arisen in defence of the freedom of religion and belief of atheists, efforts at the international level to bridge chasms between cultures and ideologies also betray a pro-theistic bias to the exclusion of atheists. The fact that the United Nations Alliance of Civilizations (UNAOC) itself does not include non-religious representation is a telling illustration of the low position of 'atheists' in the hierarchy of religion and belief.[144] Named in contrast to Samuel Huntington's 'Clash of Civilisations',[145] the omission of non-religious groups from the UNAOC undermines the Special Rapporteur's assertion that "[r]epresentatives of non-religious groups should not be deliberately excluded from official consultations where theistic views are prominently taken into account," and runs the risk of religious bias due to the "numerical strength of religious representatives in comparison to non-hierarchical and non-institutional perspectives from atheists or non-theists".[146] Another example of such exclusion can be seen in the King Abdullah Bin Abdulaziz International Centre for Inter-religious and Intercultural Dialogue (KAICIID). Primarily funded by the Kingdom of Saudi Arabia and co-founded with the Republic of Austria and the Kingdom of Spain, the Centre has high-level representatives of major world religions (Judaism, Christianity, Islam, Hinduism and Buddhism) on its board of Directors. The UN General Assembly welcomed the establishment of the KAICIID centre in a resolution acknowledging "the important role that the Centre is expected to play as a platform for the enhancement of interreligious and inter-cultural dialogue".[147] KAICIID was inaugurated in Vienna on the 26 November 2012 with much fanfare, and also some controversy surrounding the irony of Saudi Arabia's oppression of religious freedom and other human rights at home.[148] In Saudi Arabia it is illegal to identify as an atheist; anti-terrorism legislation introduced in 2014 defines calling for atheistic thought as a form of terrorism.[149] Yet, the UN has given its support to KAICIID. The promotional video

143 Nowak and Vospernik, above n 12, 147–148.

144 United Nations Alliance of Civilizations, www.unaoc.org accessed 22 March 2017.

145 See: Samuel P. Huntington, *The Clash of Civilisations and the Remaking of World Order* (Simon & Schuster, 1996). Huntington asserted that conflict would increasingly be along religious and ideological rather than political and economic lines.

146 Jahangir, above n 98 [79]. The Parliament of the Council of Europe has praised the UN for establishing the UNAOC, but added that "such an initiative should be enlarged to other religions and non-religious groups". Parliamentary Assembly of the Council of Europe, *Resolution 1805 on Blasphemy, religious insults and hate speech against persons on grounds of their religion*, 27th sitting (29 June 2007) [7].

147 General Assembly Resolution, UN Doc. A/Res/66/167 (27 March 2012) 2.

148 See for instance *Abdullah-Zentrum eröffnet*, ORF News, 26 November 2012, accessed 15 February 2013, http://wien.orf.at/news/stories/2560515/.

149 Saudi Arabia Country Report, *Freedom of Thought Report* (International Humanist and Ethical Union, 2016), accessed 2 February 2017, http://freethoughtreport.com/countries/asia-western-asia/saudi-arabia/.

played at the launch event opened with extracts of a 2008 speech given by King Abdullah Bin Abdulaziz, in which he stated:

> Let our dialogue be pro-faith in the face of atheism, virtue in the face of vice, justice in the face of injustice, peace in the face of conflicts and wars, human brotherhood in the face of racism. In God's name we started, and we seek strength from him.[150]

No comment was made about the video for its overt insult to atheists, which perhaps would not have been the case had a religion been mentioned in place of atheism, or even had King Abdullah Bin Abdulaziz overtly asserted pro-monotheism in the face of polytheism. Shortly after that video was played, the then UN Secretary General Ban Ki-moon, speaking at the launch stated, "I fully support your vision of religion as an enabler of respect and reconciliation."[151] The UN's support of KAICIID, a clearly pro-faith, anti no-faith entity reveals its pro-religious bias, or at least its indifference to the lower place of atheists relative to their religious counterparts.

4. Conclusion: Non-religious and atheist rights-holders neglected

> "*Give to Caesar what is Caesar's, and to God what is God's.*"
>
> Matthew, 22:21

Pluralism was asserted in Chapter 1 as an essential principle that should support human rights decision makers to ensure they equally value individuals over their religions or beliefs. However, application of this principle is so far more aspirational than operational. A General Assembly Resolution on combating intolerance reaffirms equality of religions and beliefs at international law, recognising "the valuable contribution of people of *all* religions or beliefs to humanity".[152] It also "[s]tresses that the right of freedom of thought, conscience and religion or belief applies equally to all persons, regardless of their religion or belief and without any discrimination as to their equal protection by the law."[153] But it must be questioned

150 The author attended the opening of the KAICIID Centre. The video was available at the KAICIID homepage, accessed 14 February 2013, http://www.kaiciid.org.

151 See Secretary General SG/SM/14675, Press Release, Secretary General stresses tolerance at the inauguration of the King Abdullah Bin Abdulaziz Centre for Interreligious and Intercultural Dialogue, 26 November 2012, accessed 22 March 2017, http://www.un.org/News/Press/docs/2012/sgsm14675.doc.htm. Support for KAICIID was also expressed in the Vienna Declaration on the Alliance of Civilizations, 27 February 2013, accessed 22 March 2017, http://www.vienna5unaoc.org/fileadmin/user_upload/documents/Vienna_Declaration.pdf.

152 General Assembly Resolution 66/167, UN Doc. A/RES/66/167 (27 March 2012) 2. Emphasis added.

153 General Assembly Resolution 66/168, Elimination of all forms of discrimination and intolerance and of discrimination based on religion or belief, UN Doc A/RES/66/168 (11 April 2012) 2 [2].

whether such equality is truly possible where complex and ephemeral issues arise. In practice, it is unlikely that a domestic court would treat as equal the rights of a Protestant Minister and a Wiccan high priest, or the Jewish rituals of bah mitzvah alongside pagan fire-circles, or the confidentiality of Scientological auditing on a par with the Catholic confessional. The British Navy did stand by its equal opportunity employment policies with the recruitment of its first Satanist in 2004,[154] but at the international level would the HRC be prepared to find in favour of a Satanist, where his religious rights conflicted for instance, with those of a Muslim or Christian or Jew?

In theory the enjoyment of freedom and religion and belief should not expand or contract on the basis of the religion or belief of the rights holder concerned. But in practice, there is evidence that international law is not immune from the tendency to treat some religions and beliefs with respect and others with scepticism or disdain. Jeremy Gunn is of the view that legal systems explicitly or implicitly 'rank' religions, describing some as 'good', others as 'bad', or even some as 'religions' and others 'non-religion'. The result is that monotheistic religions may be considered 'traditional' and polytheistic or non-theistic religions 'primitive' or 'superstitious' while others again (such as the Falun Gong or Scientology) are 'not really religions' but discriminated against as 'sects' or 'cults', at the bottom of the hierarchy.[155]

The international human rights community is falling short of its responsibility to protect members of new and unusual religious movements, despite persecution of their members. All religions have been 'new' at some point in history, and their beliefs and practices will always be considered 'unusual' for people whose own beliefs offer the benchmark of what is 'usual'. Yet there is evident scepticism about their beliefs, despite those beliefs having no more or less veracity than those of mainstream religions. Similarly, the crimes of members of emerging religions are attributed to their religions in a way crimes of followers of established religions are not, notwithstanding that "old religions too have been guilty of murder and child abuse".[156] When heinous crimes are committed in the name of an established religion, the tendency is rather to disassociate the perpetrator from the ideological motivation he or she professes.

Unlike some religious movements, atheism is not 'new'. For as long as religions and beliefs have emerged there have been people who have refused to adhere to them and been persecuted for their dissent. Despite extreme persecution and discrimination of atheists (many of whom remain in the closet today for fear of persecution, prosecution or even death) the human rights community is yet to give their plight proportionate attention. In recent years, discrimination on the basis of race, discrimination against women, anti-Semitism and Islamophobia have been rigorously discussed at the international level, and become recognised phrases in rights parlance. 'Discrimination against atheists' has not received equivalent attention. International

154 'Navy approves first ever Satanist', *BBC News*, 24 October 2004, accessed 15 February 2013, http://news.bbc.co.uk/2/hi/uk/3948329.stm.
155 Gunn, above n 63, 196.
156 Barker, above n 58, 591.

law recognises that atheists and non-believers are entitled to equal enjoyment of freedom of religion and belief as their religious counterparts. But for the moment, in practical terms, non-believers are both particularly vulnerable to abuse by state and non-state actors, and particularly neglected by the mechanisms of international human rights law instituted to protect them. Accordingly, atheists are relegated to the lowest rung on a hierarchy of freedom of religion and belief.

It is their plight and predicament that receive the weight of attention in the case study chapters to follow.

3 Freedom from proselytism

The author Annie Dillard tells an anecdote of an Eskimo who asks a priest whether he would go to hell if he did not know about God and sin. The priest replies that he would not, if he did not know, to which the Eskimo responds, 'then why did you tell me?'[1] Proselytism, understood as "expressive conduct undertaken with the purpose of trying to change the religious beliefs, affiliation, or identity of another,"[2] attracts both reverence and abhorrence of rights-holders with divergent ideological perspectives that the law must attempt to reconcile. At international law, proselytism is *prima facie* a manifestation of religion or belief. There is a relationship between this right and the right to change religion and belief, explained in Chapter 1 to include the right to exchange one religion for another or even to renounce a religion and profess atheism. The negative corollary to the right to change religion is contained in article 18(2) in the form of freedom from coercion, being the right *not* to convert.[3] Questions arise when these two rights conflict. To some, proselytism is reminiscent of religious crusades and colonialism;[4] to others it is an integral manifestation of religious freedom and an obligation deserving of protection.[5] Some scholars assert that "freedom to have or to adopt a religion or belief of his choice" as contained in article 18(2) was intended to protect *against*

1 Annie Dillard, *Pilgrim at Tinker Creek* (1st Perennial Classics edn, 2007) 123.

2 Tad Stahnke, 'Proselytism and the Freedom to Change Religion in International Human Rights Law' (1999) 1 *Brigham Young University Law Review* 251, 252.

3 Heiner Bielefeldt, Nazila Ghanea and Michael Weiner, *Freedom of Religion and Belief: An International Law Commentary* (Oxford, 2016) 65.

4 See *inter alia* Makau Mutua, 'Returning to my roots: African "Religions" and the State' in Abdullahi Ahmed An-Na'im, *Proselytisation and Communal Self-Development in Africa* (Orbis Books, 1999) 170 and Paul Taylor, *Freedom of Religion: UN and European Human Rights Law and Practice* (Cambridge University Press, 2005) 55.

5 Peter G. Danchin, 'Of Prophets and Proselytes: Freedom of Religion and the Conflict of Rights in International Law' (2008) 49 *Harvard International Law Review* 249, 256–257. Danchin raises the examples including the Catholic Church distinguishing 'Christian witness' from improper 'proselytism', the Evangelical Lutheran Church regarding 'evangelistic outreach' as a religious obligation, Jehovah's Witnesses and Mormons evangelising, and proselytism as a religious duty of Muslims to non-believers but prohibited where it is aimed at Muslims.

proselytisers and missionaries.[6] Alternatively it has been argued that not only are proselytisers enjoying their freedom of religion and belief by proselytising, but also that they are aiding in the enjoyment of others' freedoms by exposing them to a wider range of choices of religion or belief. Proselytism, then, can be a protected manifestation of religious freedom, or alternatively, a prohibited form of coercion. For human rights law, the challenge is to balance these competing perspectives in a way that best upholds freedom of religion and belief.

The chapter firstly considers existing understandings of and approaches to proselytism in international human rights law, to show that it is not equally enjoyed as a manifestation of religion and belief by all rights-holders. The hierarchy of religion and belief outlined in the previous chapter becomes evident in permissive approaches to proselytism of major religions and scant defence of non-proselytising rights-holders. Non-religious and atheistic rights-holders are vulnerable to the proselytism directed at them, but do not manifest their own beliefs in the same way, highlighting their disadvantage in the enjoyment of article 18 rights.

Secondly, improper forms of proselytism – including threats or violence, exploitation of circumstances and exposure to religious symbols – are explored, to show that certain forms of proselytism that should be considered improper, are instead permitted and protected as legitimate manifestations of certain religions. The finding here is that rights are not balanced on the basis of the coercive interference of proselytising acts with rights of others, but rather on the basis of the religion or belief of the source and target of proselytism. Here again, bias towards major religions is revealed, elevating some rights-holders above others on the basis of their religion or belief.

Finally, the chapter analyses circumstances in which proselytism as a manifestation of religion should be limited to equally protect non-believers and atheists alongside religious rights-holders.[7] Relying on the framework offered by Tad Stahnke, it is argued that decisions as to whether proselytism should be limited, should be made on the basis of whether the proselytism undermines choice, rather than on the basis of the religion or belief of the proselytiser or his target. Here the principle of pluralism emerges again to mitigate the risk of bias and level the hierarchy at play in protecting rights.

1. Proselytism as a manifestation of religion

> "*Go and make disciples of all nations, baptising them in the name of the Father and of the Son and of the Holy Spirit, and teaching them to obey everything I have commanded you.*"
>
> Matthew 28:19–20

6 See for instance, K. J. Partsch, 'Freedom of Conscience and Expression, and Political Freedoms in L. Henkin (ed.), *The International Bill of Rights: The Covenant on Civil and Political Rights* (New York/Guildford: Columbia University Press, 1981) 211.

7 For more on the Krishnaswami study as it relates to proselytism, see Natan Lerner, *Religion, Secularism and Human Rights* (2nd edn, Martinus Nijhoff Publishers, 2012) 140–144.

Arriving at a universal understanding of proselytism is challenging. Religious perspectives on proselytism are as diverse as religions themselves, ranging from those religions that require it of their adherents, through to others that prohibit it. In some states, proselytism may only be permitted in one direction, meaning it may be acceptable to proselytise one religion and punishable to proselytise another. These very opposing positions call on human rights adjudicators to balance the freedoms of rights-holders who proselytise as a means of practising their religion on the one hand, with the rights of others whose enjoyment of freedom of religion and belief may be interfered with by being targeted by proselytisers on the other.

1.1. Advantage of proselytism to major religions

At the outset a *de facto* bias is evident in human rights law owing to the reality that some religions proselytise more than others, making the right to do so a powerful tool for some rights-holders and irrelevant for others. It is no coincidence that the two fastest growing religions in the world are the most proselytised. A 2007 *Economist* article considers which of the "the world's two great missionary religions" – Christianity and Islam – is "winning the battle of the books".[8] That article discusses the phenomenal spread of Holy Books throughout the world through vehicles of globalisation, technology and growing wealth. It mentions that the Bible (a copy of which is given away every second) is available in the native language of 95% of the world's population, and that the Kingdom of Saudi Arabia gives away 30 million copies of the Koran every year. The article acknowledges that receiving a book does not necessarily mean receiving a religion; there is no guarantee that the book will be read, understood or accepted, particularly where factors of illiteracy play a role. Nevertheless, a prophetic conclusion made by the author is that "the urge to spread the Word will spark some of the fiercest conflicts of the 21st century" and that both the Bible and the Koran "will continue to exercise a dramatic influence over human events, for both good and ill".[9]

At its most extreme, proselytism has historically manifested in holy wars, religious crusades and forced conversion on pain of death. Echoes of religious warfare are evident today in acts of religiously motivated terrorism with attacks mounted by pious criminals against those who practise a different religion or the same religion differently.[10] Contrasted with these overtly violent acts are more underhand methods used elsewhere, such as the distribution of counterfeit Korans produced by some Christian Evangelicals in a bid to make Muslims (who value literal recitation of the Koran) doubt their faith.[11] Proselytising tactics are also cultivated in the mainstream; a Masters Degree is offered at the Southwestern Baptist Theological Seminary

8 'The Battle of the Books', *The Economist* (online), 19 December 2007, accessed 22 March 2017, http://www.economist.com/world/international/displaystory.cfm?story_id=10311317.

9 Ibid.

10 Consider, for instance, the frequently reported conflicts between Sunni and Shi'ite Muslims, often involving suicide bombings at religious processions.

11 'The Battle of the Books', above n 8.

in Texas, in which "degree candidates will obtain more effective skills for reaching and making Christian disciples of people with an Islamic background."[12] In recognition of growing interreligious tensions, some Christian actors have produced guidelines for "bearing witness" and proselytising among people of different religions or who do not profess any particular religion, drawing on Biblical principles to offer recommendations on exercising the right to proselytise in a way that does not trespass on the rights or religious sensibilities of others.[13] By its very name Islam requires 'submission' to the will of God, yet the principle of 'free choice' is contained in the Koran in that "there is no compulsion in religion".[14] At the same time, the conversion of a Muslim to another religion or to no religion is considered apostasy, for which the Hadith instructs that the converter be killed. It is not surprising then that in some Islamic religious traditions, proselytising by non-Muslims to a Muslim is forbidden, while proselytism *by* Muslims may be regarded as a religious duty.[15] The Cairo Declaration on Human Rights in Islam is unequivocal in its pronouncement that "Islam is the religion of unspoiled nature. It is prohibited to exercise any form of compulsion on man or to exploit his poverty or ignorance in order to convert him to another religion or to atheism."[16]

Ultimately, international human rights law understands proselytism in light of the fact that it is at the core of major religions.[17] In the case of *Sister Immaculate v Sri Lanka*[18] the HRC observed that

> for numerous religions...it is a central tenet to spread knowledge, to propagate their beliefs to others and to provide assistance to others. These aspects are part of an individual's manifestation of religion and free expression, and are thus protected by article 18, paragraph 1, to the extent not appropriately restricted by measures consistent with paragraph 3.[19]

Additional to the protection that proselytism finds in article 18 of the ICCPR, there is also a basis for its protection under article 19 protecting freedom of

12 See Southwestern Baptist Theological Seminary at http://catalog.swbts.edu/school-of-evangelism/master-of-arts-islamic-studies/ accessed 22 March 2017.
13 World Council of Churches, Pontifical Council for Interreligious Dialogue, World Evangelical Alliance, 'Christian Witness in a Multi-Religious World: Recommendations for Conduct' (2011) 35 *International Bulletin of Missionary Research* 194, 194–196.
14 *Koran*, Surah 2:256.
15 Abdullahi A. An-Na'im, 'Islamic Foundations of Religious Human Rights' in Johan van der Vyver and John Witte (eds), *Religious Human Rights in Global Perspective: Religious Perspectives* (Martinus Nijhoff Publishers, 1996) 352.
16 Organisation of Islamic Conference (OIC), *Cairo Declaration on Human Rights in Islam*, 5 August 1990, article 10.
17 See Asher Maoz, 'Proselytism and the Right to Change Religion' in Silvio Ferrari and Rinaldo Cristofori, *Law and Religion in the 21st Century* (Ashgate, 2010) 243–252 for further discussion about proselytism in Christianity, Judaism and Islam.
18 *Sister Immaculate v Sri Lanka*, Human Rights Committee, Communication No. 1249/2004, UN Doc CCPR/C/85/D/1249/2004 (2005) [7.2].
19 Ibid.

expression, interpretations of which suggest that it also protects missionary activities.[20] The recourse that proselytisers have to article 19 of the ICCPR is significant; the logic of free speech is that public discourse should be vigorous. Where it would be nonsensical to suggest that political views can be held but not expressed, the same would be true in respect of religious beliefs that could be held but not manifested, meaning that there is no distinction to be drawn on the basis of the content of the view being expressed. As such, invoking the right to freedom of expression shifts the burden onto the targets of proselytism to show why religious speech should be treated differently to other speech.[21] As John Witte and Christian Green acknowledge; "the religious expression inherent in proselytism is no more suspect than political, economic, artistic, or other forms of expression and should have, at minimum, the same rights."[22] Targets of proselytism, furthermore, have the right to 'receive' information and ideas of all kinds by virtue of article 19 (2) of the ICCPR. The 2009 HRC case of *Mavlonov and Sa'id v Uzbekistan*, reiterated that the right to receive information is a vital component of freedom of expression.[23] That position is taken here too. In the context of proselytism, manifestation of religion and belief should be construed as broadly as possible and be subject to necessary limitations. How these manifestations are limited or not reveals again the pro-religious, anti-irreligious bias in international human rights law.

1.2. Disadvantage of non-proselytising religions and beliefs

Not all religions are proselytised. Indeed, some do not accept let alone seek converts. Arvind Sharma is a key proponent of the view that there is a bias in international law in favour of proselytism by the major proselytising religions, to the significant detriment of non-proselytising religions. In making this argument, he takes issue with the very notion of how religious 'freedom' has been constructed in international human rights law, pointing to two freedoms, being freedom to change from one religion to another, and freedom *from* the need to change, expressed also as freedom *not* to change. Sharma considers that international human rights law is oblivious to this freedom *not* to change, rendering it biased towards missionary religions (Christianity and Islam) and against non-missionary religions, subordinating the right to *retain* religion free of interference to the

20 See for example, Manfred Nowak, *CCPR Commentary* (NP Engel Kehl, 2nd edn, 2005) 450–452.

21 Danchin, above n 5, 269.

22 John Witte Jr and M. Christian Green, 'Religious Freedom, Democracy, and International Human Rights' (2009) 23 *Emory International Law Review* 583, 596.

23 *Mavlonov and Sa'id v Uzbekistan*, Human Rights Committee, Communication No. 1334/2004, UN Doc CCPR/C/95/D/1334/2004 (2009) [8.4]. In that case, concerning the failure of the Uzbek government to re-register an independent Tajik newspaper, the HRC found violations of the editor's right to impart information, and the right of one of its readers to receive it, the latter right being a corollary of the former.

imperative of major religions to *change* them.[24] It is this freedom *from* any need to change, that Sharma considers the key component of the enjoyment of non-proselytising religions, including for Hindu, Jain and Buddhist rights-holders. He ultimately depicts the competing challenge as being between freedom *of* conversion and freedom *from* conversion, arguing that the latter has lost to a skewed perception that does not grasp the right of people to be free *from* proselytism as a fundamental religious freedom.[25] The built-in disadvantage of non-proselytising religions is that while they do not put proselytising religions under the "threat of conversion", they themselves are subject to this threat from them.[26]

Among the reasons Sharma offers for this flawed understanding of international human rights law is the fact it offers no room for the sacred and the secular to interrelate, and does not conceive of a person belonging to more than one religion simultaneously. This, he argues, is an error of reasoning given that in some cultures, a person can have multiple religious affiliations.[27] By way of example, Sharma explains that Hindus are generally opposed to conversion in either direction, whether a Hindu wishes to change from Hinduism or a non-Hindu seeks to become a Hindu. Rather, the Hindu approach is to share the best of Hinduism without requiring conversion, and to adopt the best of other religious without converting to them.[28] Ultimately, Hindu, Buddhist and Jain perspectives of conversion are shown to be less single-minded in their agenda than Islam and Christianity which offer 'competing' claims on a universal truth, requiring that adherents choose an exclusive affiliation to the 'correct' version.[29] Other belief sets construe religion as a quest for human truth, with diverse religions offering different paths and practices in the ongoing pursuit of it. This fundamental distinction, Sharma argues, is not appreciated by international human rights law that instead favours the freedom to proselytise with the goal of conversion, over the freedom to be free from interference by proselytisers in practising one's religion or belief.[30]

Makau Mutua similarly points to the failure of the human rights regime to understand the nature of non-proselytising religions in the context of indigenous African religions. Mutua expresses the view that "the rights regime incorrectly assumes a level playing field by requiring that African religions compete in the marketplace of ideas."[31] Accordingly, non-proselytising religions are unfairly forced to compete, and evangelising religions are protected "in their march towards universalization". The bias of the rights regime to the universalistic goals of Islam and Christianity over indigenous belief sets is thereby exposed for its

24 Arvind Sharma, *Problematizing Religious Freedom* (Springer, 2011) 76–77.
25 Ibid 79.
26 Ibid 256.
27 Ibid 79, 255.
28 Ibid 129–132.
29 Ibid 129–136.
30 Ibid 166–167.
31 Makau Mutua, *Human Rights: A Political and Cultural Critique* (University of Pennsylvania Press, 2008) 95.

failure to acknowledge their non-proselytising nature and its failure to protect those rights-holders *from* the 'invasion' of ideas proselytised to them by practitioners of major religions.[32] The point noted above by Sharma, that multiple religions may be practised simultaneously, also resonates in the African context. Many people who incorporate traditional religious practices into their lives (such as ancestral veneration, and visits to healers) may nonetheless identify as Christian or Muslim.[33] The same is true in other continents where colonisers imposed religion onto communities who fused the newly adopted set of beliefs with their traditional religions and practices.

Both Mutua and Sharman are silent on the plight of non-believers to also be free *from* proselytism, but the concerns they raise in respect of non-proselytising religions are applicable to them, both in the lack of proselytism that is exercised as a manifestation of their belief, and their susceptibility to proselytism by others, signifying their need to be free *from* it in fully enjoying their freedom of religion and belief.

1.3. Non-applicability of right to proselytise to non-religious rights-holders

The pro-religious bias of proselytism points to the disadvantage of non-religious and atheist rights-holders. Although 'proselytism' is generally discussed in the context of manifesting religion, the term has also been claimed for the expression of non-religious ideas. One commentator noted that "[a]ttempts to convince one's fellow citizens of the merit of a particular idea, such as global warming or the evils of war, is just as much proselytising as is persuasive religious speech [because both] involve an attempt at conversion from one perspective to another."[34] Yet, the fact that non-religious beliefs may be proselytised is not tantamount to the equal protection of that proselytism as a manifesatition of belief. Non-religious rights-holders have a right to express their beliefs and even to attempt to convince others of them, but in practice, manifestation of belief through proselytism is more likely to be supported at the level of international law where it emanates from religious perspectives, than where it seeks to disseminate non-religious or atheistic ideologies. Proselytism is *prima facie* a protected manifestation of religion, and primarily (as discussed above) of major religions for which proselytism is a value.

The term 'proselytism' *per se* is generally not used in reference to promotion of anti-religious or non-religious ideology. The writings of prominent atheists could be argued as seeking to persuade religious people away from their religions, though it is questionable whether criticism of religion is meant to 'convert' religious readers. Atheists have less incentive to convert religious people to atheism

32 Ibid.

33 Rosalind I. J. Hackett, 'Traditional, African, Religious, Freedom?' in Elizabeth A. Castelli *et al* (eds) *Politics of Religious Freedom* (University of Chicago Press, 2015) 95.

34 Kevin H. Theriot, Esq. 'Prince or Pauper? Religious Proselytising and the First Amendment' (2009) 3 *University of St. Thomas Journal of Law & Public Policy* 46, 47.

than religious people have to convert atheists; there is no spiritual incentive for doing so, and propagation of non-belief is not a tenet of non-belief in the way that propagation of belief is a tenet of some religions. Perhaps it is for this reason that door-to-door proselytism more often involves religious parties trying to persuade others of their religion, rather than non-believers or atheists going door-to-door trying to persuade religious people not to be. The latter rather tend to express their views through mediums that can be read – or not – by religious persons. The fact that there are no atheist 'missionary' organisations, is almost certainly owing to the fact that proselytism is not a part of atheism in the way it is part of some religions. There are, of course, organisations that are driven by non-religious beliefs that may even be critical of religious practices. Where an organisation pursues a human rights-based agenda, it may even challenge religious practices that undermine those beliefs. As an example, the International NGO Council on Violence against Women condemns human rights abuses resulting from culture, tradition, religion and superstition including birth superstitions, corporal punishment, cosmetic mutilations, juju curses, female and male circumcision, initiation rites, refusal of life-saving medical treatment, organ removal, ritual killings, sharia law punishments, ritual sexual slavery and witchcraft, among other practices.[35] To the extent that such practices are based on religion and belief, and to the extent that international and non-governmental organisations seek to prevent them, they can be said to be working to undermine religious adherence. Yet challenging a religious practice is not the same as challenging the right to practise that religion, particularly where methods used to mount challenges are non-coercive.

And yet, while atheists and non-religious rights-holders do not manifest their non-theistic beliefs through proselytism *per se*, they are very often targeted by the proselytism of religious rights-holders. The forms that proselytism takes, may involve leveraging strong relationships between religious or state institutions or through exposure to religious symbols at schools, workplaces or courts of law, or daily exposure to religious practices of the majority of the people in society. The discrimination that many face – as infidels, heathens or heretics – may make them susceptible to the dominant religion around them.[36]

2. Forms of improper coercion

As with other protected rights, freedom of religion and belief is subject to exceptional limitations prescribed by law and necessary to protect public safety, order, health or morals or the fundamental rights and freedoms of others. Limitations can be "only for those purposes for which they were prescribed and must be

35 International NGO Council on Violence against Women, *Violating Children's Rights: Harmful practices based on tradition, culture, religion or superstition* (CRIN, 2012) 9–39.

36 The *Freedom of Thought Report* (International Humanist and Ethical Union, 2016) is teeming with examples of atheists and other non-theists feigning adherence to the dominant religion or being murdered for refusing to.

directly related and proportionate to the specific need on which they are predicated".[37] In practice then, certain actions aimed at converting people to a religion or belief should be limited when they cross from being acceptable missionary activities or propagation or dissemination of religion or belief, to become unacceptable. The absence of a neatly demarcated dividing line in law means that significant dispute remains over where the line should be drawn between acceptable, protected proselytism and improper forms of proselytism that must be restricted.

In his 1960 *Study of Discrimination in the Matter of Religious Rights and Practices,* Arcot Krishnaswami foresaw the potential conflicts that could arise between one person's protected right to manifest his or her religion or belief and another person's right to maintain his or hers; a situation which may lead to clashes between various faiths "either because of the contents of the message or the methods used in spreading it".[38] This section illustrates that those clashes are likely to be resolved in a way that biases the rights of certain rights-holders over others, with proselytism less likely to be limited as 'improper' where it emanates from a major religious perspective. Religious rights-holders again are shown to enjoy more freedom to practise article 18 rights than atheists, whose expressions are unlikely to be protected as legitimate manifestations under article 18. At the same time, atheists as non-believers – the infidels, heathens or heretics of a given society – may be particularly vulnerable to coercive forms of proselytism and have no meaningful recourse to assert their right to be free from them.

There is limited international case law shedding light on the distinction between proper and improper proselytism. The European Court of Human Rights cases of *Kokkinakis v Greece* and *Larissis and others v Greece* remain the authoritative jurisprudence on the issue, both of which reveal bias towards proselytisers of major religions over targets from less established ones.[39] In the first case, Kokkinakis, a Jehovah's Witness, called in on the wife of the cantor of the local Orthodox Church in order to engage in discussion about religion and was subsequently charged under Greek national law prohibiting proselytism. Kokkinakis argued to the European Court that the law was incompatible with his religious freedom, and discriminatory in that it would unlikely be used to prosecute a proselytiser of the dominant religion.[40] The majority of the Court found that the limitation was prescribed by law and in pursuit of a legitimate aim, but did not consider measures taken to be proportionate nor "necessary in a democratic society", finding that Kokkinakis had not exceeded the proselytism protected by the ECHR. Accordingly, his rights were deemed violated. However, notwithstanding its decision as far as Kokkinakis was concerned, of relevance in underlying the inherent bias in

37 Human Rights Committee, *General Comment 22*, UN Doc CCPR/C/21/Rev.1/Add.4 (27 September 1993) [4].

38 Arcot Krishnaswami, *Study of Discrimination in the matter of Religious Rights and Practices*, UN. Doc. E/CN.4/Sub.2/200/Rev.1 (1960), UN. Pub. No 60.XIV.2, 39.

39 *Kokkinakis v Greece,* European Court of Human Rights, Application No 14307/88 (5 June 1993) and *Larissis and Others v Greece*, Application Nos. 23372/94, 26377/94 and 26378/94 (24 February 1999).

40 Ibid [29].

the Court's reasoning is the fact that it avoided considering the compatibility of the law itself with the ECHR. The application of that law to Kokkinakis was not exceptional, but usual, and in failing to consider it, the Court revealed its bias towards traditional and established religions over non-traditional or unpopular ones, and its tendency to silence the latter.[41] The extent of bias against minor religions was also apparent in the comments made by dissenting Judge Valticos, describing proselytism as "the rape of the beliefs of others" and Kokkinakis as a "militant Jehovah's Witness, a hardbitten adept of proselytism, a specialist in conversion, a martyr of the criminal courts whose earlier convictions have served only to harden him in his militancy".[42] Furthermore, the European Court's authority as to the distinction between improper and proper proselytism was the World Council of Churches,[43] that considers "bearing Christian Witness" permissible, and everything else as "a corruption or deformation of it".[44] The blatant bias towards the dominant religion in relying on this understanding raises questions about how a non-Christian proselytiser could ever receive protection of his freedom to proselytise.[45] It is to be hoped that this flawed reasoning would not be replicated at the international level.[46]

2.1. Proselytism through threats or violence

General Comment 22 clarifies that article 18(2) of the ICCPR "bars coercion that would impair the right to have or adopt a religion or belief, including the use or threat of physical force".[47] In her 2005 Report to the General Assembly, the then Special Rapporteur on freedom of religion and belief, Asma Jahangir, noted that some proselytising acts cannot be considered manifestations that would be

41 Jeremy Gunn, 'Adjudicating Rights of Conscience under the European Convention on Human Rights', in Johan van der Vyver and John Witte (eds), *Religious Human Rights in Global Perspective: Legal Perspectives* (Martinus Nijhoff Publishers, 1996), 305, 318–325; Danchin, above n 5, 275.

42 *Kokkinakis*, above n 39, dissenting Opinion of Judge Valticos.

43 The World Council of Churches describes itself as "a community of churches on the way to visible unity in one faith and one Eucharistic fellowship, expressed in worship and in common life in Christ. It seeks to advance towards this unity, as Jesus prayed for his followers, 'so that the world may believe' (John 17:21)." See https://www.oikoumene.org/en/about-us, accessed 14 March 2017.

44 *Kokkinakis*, above n 39 [48].

45 In the other key European proselytism case, *Larissis and others v Greece* (above n 39), the targets of proselytism were officers of the Greek air force, and the proselytisers their superior officers. The Court found that the applicants had abused their position of authority and found no reason to depart from *Kokkinakis*. The Court held that no evidence was brought to suggest that the outcome would be different had Orthodoxy been preached, and found no discrimination issue. As in *Kokkinakis*, the Court did not question understandings of "Christian witness".

46 There is evidence to suggest it would not be; during a 1996 country visit to Greece the Special Rapporteur strongly recommended removal of prohibitions on proselytism. See UN Doc A/51/542/Add.1 [12], [134].

47 *General Comment 22*, above n 37.

protected under article 18(1). She opined that a distinction should be made between proselytising acts that invite human rights concerns in respect of article 18(2) and those which are captured in domestic law of a state as criminal acts that should be prosecuted as such.[48] In respect of criminalisation of particular acts, she cautioned that

> it would not be advisable to criminalise non-violent acts performed in the context of manifestation of one's religion, in particular the propagation of religion, including because that might criminalise acts that would, in another context, not raise a concern of the criminal law and may pave the way for persecution of religious minorities. Moreover, since the right to change or maintain a religion is in essence a subjective right, any concern raised with regard to certain conversions or how they might be accomplished should primarily be raised by the alleged victim.[49]

This statement places the onus of challenging proselytism as a legitimate manifestation of religion squarely on the target of it, but notably omits propagation of 'belief' and overlooks the persecution of atheists and non-believers. The Special Rapporteur's suggestion begs the question of whether violent acts performed by way of propagating a religion would also entail mere threats of violence, and by extension, whether such threats of violence should be limited to violence in the immediate earthly realm or can also entail violence that is threatened in the hereafter, given that threats to a person's soul can be just as effective, if not more so, than threats to a person's body.

Below it is argued that spiritual threats should be considered with equal scrutiny as other forms of coercion, balanced against considerations such as the power dynamics at play between the source and the target. The fact such threats are not considered in practice, shows that major, established religions occupy a higher place on the hierarchy of religion and belief. To extrapolate this point further, it is instructive to examine the position of Catholicism – one of the world's most influential religions – on the concept of 'coercion' in proselytism.[50] In 1965, Pope Paul VI promulgated the Vatican's encyclical Declaration on Religious Freedom, titled '*Dignitatis Humanae*', on the right of persons and of communities to social and civil freedom in religious matters. On the point of coercion, the Vatican Council declared:

> the human person has a right to religious freedom. This freedom means that all men are to be immune from coercion on the part of individuals or of social groups and of any human power, in such wise that no one is to be

48 UN Doc A/60/399 (30 September 2005) [65].
49 Ibid.
50 Catholicism has been selected for consideration here because the Vatican Council's encyclical '*Dignitatis Humanae*' offers greater authoritative clarity on its standpoint on coercion than can be gleaned with respect to other major religious traditions.

> forced to act in a manner contrary to his own beliefs, whether privately or publicly, whether alone or in association with others, within due limits.[51]

Prima facie this statement seems compatible with article 18 of the ICCPR, particularly given that the encyclical clearly pronounces against coercion by stating "[i]t is one of the major tenets of Catholic doctrine that man's response to God in faith must be free: no one therefore is to be forced to embrace the Christian faith against his own will."[52] Notwithstanding assertions of Catholicism as "the true religion" and "the one Church of Christ",[53] the right to change religion is well recognised by the encyclical:

> a wrong is done when government imposes upon its people, by force or fear or other means, the profession or repudiation of any religion, or when it hinders men from joining or leaving a religious community. All the more is it a violation of the will of God and of the sacred rights of the person and the family of nations when force is brought to bear in any way in order to destroy or repress religion, either in the whole of mankind or in a particular country or in a definite community.[54]

Despite its apparent support of religious freedom, the Vatican's understanding of the concept of 'coercion' must be more closely examined. First, the encyclical contains a clear defence of proselytism:

> We believe that this one true religion subsists in the Catholic and Apostolic Church, to which the Lord Jesus committed the duty of spreading it abroad among all men. Thus He spoke to the Apostles: 'Go, therefore, and make disciples of all nations, baptising them in the name of the Father and of the Son and of the Holy Spirit, teaching them to observe all things whatsoever I have enjoined upon you' (Matt. 28: 19–20). On their part, all men are bound to seek the truth, especially in what concerns God and His Church, and to embrace the truth they come to know, and to hold fast to it.[55]

Cautiously ensuring that such proselytism does not amount to 'coercion', the encyclical states that:

> in spreading religious faith and in introducing religious practices everyone ought at all times to refrain from any manner of action which might seem to carry a hint of coercion or of a kind of persuasion that would be dishonorable or unworthy, especially when dealing with poor or uneducated people. Such a

51 Second Vatican Ecumenical Council, *Dignitatis Humanae: Declaration on Religious Freedom* (1965) [2].
52 Ibid [10].
53 Ibid [1].
54 Ibid [6].
55 Ibid [1].

> manner of action would have to be considered an abuse of one's right and a violation of the right of others.[56]

Therefore, when considering practical manifestations of Catholic proselytism, one must ask: what constitutes a 'hint of coercion'? Can fiery religious rhetoric amount to coercion? In what circumstances?

On some points in the encyclical, scripture is referred to but not provided in full.[57] In discussing Jesus Christ, paragraph 11 of the Encyclical states that "He did indeed denounce the unbelief of some who listened to Him, but He left vengeance to God in expectation of the day of judgment."[58] Here the encyclical references Mark 16:16 which states simply that "He who believes and is baptised will be saved. He who does not believe will be condemned."[59] The blow of this news to non-believers is softened marginally by noting that Jesus himself instructed that both believers and non-believers should be allowed to exist next to each other, but the relief is short-lived in light of the fact that this is only true until the day of judgment, where the "parable of weeds" contained in Matthew 13:24–29 explains the fate of those who do not submit to Christ. Jesus states that "[t]he kingdom of heaven is like a man who sowed good seed in his field, but while everyone was sleeping his enemy came and sowed weeds among the wheat, and went away…." When the servants ask their master whether he wants the weeds pulled up, the master instructs them not to, "because while you are pulling the weeds, you may root up the wheat with them. Let both grow together until the harvest. At that time I will tell the harvesters: First collect the weeds and tie them in bundles to be burned; then gather the wheat and bring it to my barn."[60] This parable is explained by Jesus thus:

> The one who sowed the good seed is the Son of Man. The field is the world, and the good seed stands for the sons of the kingdom. The weeds are the sons of the evil one, and the enemy who sows them is the devil. The harvest is the end of the age, and the harvesters are angels. As the weeds are pulled up and burned in the fire, so it will be at the end of the age. The Son of Man will send out his angels, and they will weed out of his kingdom everything that causes sin and all who do evil. They will throw them into the fiery furnace, where there will be weeping and gnashing of teeth. Then the righteous will shine like the sun in the kingdom of their Father.[61]

56 Ibid [4].
57 Not providing references in full should be no defence to the message conveyed. Indeed, the US military required the removal of Bible references from equipment provided by weapons manufacturer Trijicon to protect Church–state separation.
58 Second Vatican Ecumenical Council, above n 51 [11].
59 *Bible*, Mark 16:16.
60 *Bible*, Matthew 13:24–29.
61 *Bible*, Matthew 13:37–43.

That the 'evil' ones in this parable are those who do not accept Jesus Christ is clarified by the reference made in the Encyclical to the less convoluted explanation contained in Thessalonians 1:8: "[h]e will punish those who do not know God and do not obey the gospel of our Lord Jesus."[62] In light of the Vatican's view of the fate of unbelievers, one must wonder whether sharing the news contained in Matthew with regard to the fiery furnace, the weeping and the gnashing of teeth, and the punishment contained in Thessalonians, would constitute a "hint of coercion", especially, as the Vatican notes, "when dealing with poor or uneducated people", to say nothing of children.[63]

Christianity is not alone in the severity of its rhetoric. Spiritual threats in Islam akin to those discussed above can be found in the Koran, in which it is explained that: "On the Day when those who disbelieve are brought to the Fire (they will be asked): 'Is this not true?' They will say: 'Yes, most certainly, by our Lord!' He (God) will say: 'Taste the punishment in which you used to believe!'"[64] It is seemingly clear in Islam that Allah will forgive all sins but the sin of disbelief.[65] There is however some disagreement about this point: Kamran Hashemi distinguishes Islam from the "essential mission" of Christianity to proselytise, by explaining that "[t]hough inviting non-believers to Islam is generally encouraged...proselytism for Muslims is not considered as one of the religious obligations or practices."[66] Perhaps the distinction between the different viewpoints of the extent to which Muslims are requested or required to 'invite' non-Muslims to Islam depends on the nature of the invitation offered. Abdullahi Ahmed An-Na'im explains that in the traditional Islamic approach to proselytism, while in theory unbelievers should be offered the choice of adopting Islam, if they reject it they may be killed, enslaved, or ransomed.[67] The result, Tad Stahnke posits, is that "proselytism targeted at Muslims is prohibited, whereas aggressive proselytism by Muslims directed at non-believers is demanded."[68] Indeed, "[a]ll the jurists, perhaps without exception, assert polytheism and Islam cannot exist together; the polytheists, who enjoin other gods with Allah, must choose between war or Islam."[69] Whatever may be the requirements on Muslims to disseminate their religion, it is an undisputed point among Islamic scholars that proselytism by non-Muslims targeting Muslims is not tolerated. However, as with Christianity, the choice for many is between Islam and the pits of hell. Ayaan Hirsi Ali is a former Muslim and now an atheist political activist living in exile following death threats from fanatical Islamists, including one in the form of a note impaled in the chest of her murdered friend, Theo Van Gogh who collaborated with Ali in making a film about

62 *Bible*, Thessalonians 1:8.
63 Second Vatican Ecumenical Council, above n 51 [4].
64 *Koran*, Surah 34, Wind-Shaped Dunes, verse 34.
65 *Koran*, 4:48, 4:116.
66 Kamran Hashemi, *Religious Legal Traditions, International Human Rights Law and Muslim States* (Martinus Nijhoff Publishers, 2008) 31.
67 An-Na'im, above n 15, 352.
68 Stahnke, above n 2, 258.
69 Majid Khadduri, *War and Peace in the Law of Islam* (The Lawbook Exchange, 2006) 75.

violence against women in Islam. Ali describes her childhood, filled with images preachers had tormented her with, of a Koranic Hell full of "sores, boiling water, peeling skin, burning flesh, dissolving bowels. An everlasting fire burns you forever for as your flesh chars and your juices boil, you form a new skin;" a picture she found "genuinely terrifying".[70] It is asserted that the preachers' descriptions of hell to the child Ali would be appropriately defined as coercive proselytism, although there is there is little indication that international law would agree.

Considering the impact of the threat on the target of proselytism would avoid the need to grapple with subjective religious concepts. It would mean that manifestations of religious freedom would be limited where they interfere with another person's enjoyment of his or her freedom of religion or belief, whatever that religion or belief may be. Regardless of whether being presented with the prospect of burning eternally in a fiery furnace constitutes the 'hint of coercion' prohibited by the Vatican's own instruction, it should, in some contexts, be considered a "threat of physical force" prohibited by article 18 of the ICCPR. Where a person is threatened either physically or spiritually, the test should consider the impact of the threat on the threatened person rather than the likelihood of the threat transpiring; the fact that a gun is not loaded is irrelevant to the target who believes it to be.

Such threats of violence may be considered aggravated where there are power imbalances, for instance, when rhetoric is espoused by high religious authorities such as the Vatican Council or by Fatwa. As will be discussed below, the relationship between the source and the target of proselytism must also be considered in determining whether rights of the latter have been trespassed on. Where the proselytiser is a priest or imam describing to a child the degrees of pain awaiting her in the fires of hell, the suggestion that this child is not threatened but is simply freely practising her religion or that of her parents, is the moral equivalent of abandoning a vulnerable person to the coercive proselytism of others, because she is vulnerable. While an educated adult may not be dismayed (or swayed) by threats of eternal damnation, a child may be as much distressed by this prospect explained by a respected adult, as he or she would be by a more immediate physical threat. Threats to freedom of religion and belief and other rights of children will be discussed in Chapter 5, but it is necessary to conclude for present purposes that proselytising religious rhetoric can constitute improper coercion. The key role that particular beliefs play in some religious traditions must be borne in mind if human

70 Ayaan Hirsi Ali, 'How (and Why) I Became an Infidel' in Christopher Hitchens (ed.), *The Portable Atheist*, (Da Capo Press, 2007) 478. In addition to receiving violent threats from Islamic fundamentalists, Ali also faces criticism from Islamic commentators and secular Western liberals who have rejected her views as 'Islamophobic'. See for instance Richard Pérez-Peña and Tanzina Vega, 'Brandeis Cancels Plan to Give Honorary Degree to Ayaan Hirsi Ali, a Critic of Islam', *The New York Times,* 8 April 2014 and Iman Riman, 'Muslim Women protest Australian visit of anti-Islam activist Ayaan Hirsi Ali' 20 March 2017, sbs.com.au, accessed 28 April 2017, http://www.sbs.com.au/yourlanguage/arabic/en/article/2017/03/20/muslim-women-protest-australian-visit-anti-islam-activist-ayaan-hirsi-ali.

rights policies can truly claim to respect freedom of – and from – religion and belief. Regardless of whether burning eternally in hell is a real prospect or not, for many people the threat is real.

In considering whether atheists or humanists 'proselytise' their beliefs through threats of violence, a distinction to be drawn is that they lack doctrine providing them a basis for doing so. This is not to say that they may not threaten violence, but doing so would not be a direct manifestation or expression of their beliefs or its teachings in the same way violence based in religious scripture or doctrine is. Yet on this it is interesting to note that the writings of some atheists have been construed as proselytising. Father Frank Brennan (a Jesuit priest and much-lauded legal academic in Australia) on reviewing a selection of atheist books released in 2007 considered that their authors make "bold claims for the destruction of religion" and propose "a scorched earth policy of killing off all religion".[71] In rights parlance, Brennan could be considered as accusing such authors of 'improper proselytism'. This critical interpretation of the atheistic agenda as being to annihilate religion has led to some atheists being labelled 'militant' in the campaign for religious people to reject their religion and adopt atheism.[72] Yet while the term 'militant atheism' implies violence, it is difficult to see how the atheists branded as 'militant' are using threats or violence to advance their agenda.[73] While a 'militant Christian' could be understood to be a person who bombs an abortion clinic or dons a white sheet to terrorise non-white members of his community, and the label 'militant Muslim' could justifiably be attached to an Islamic terrorist, it is difficult to see how scholars, writers, scientists, philosophers and bloggers who publish works and generate public debate and discourse warrant being labelled 'militant'.

Expressing opposition to religious beliefs, scientifically challenging or even vindictively offending them does not exceed the limits of protected freedoms, and engaging in discussions to convince others to adopt atheism is no more improper than proselytising religious rhetoric is. The label 'militant' would seem more fairly reserved for fundamentalists who use violence in pursuit of their ideological agenda, but is generally imposed on atheists by theists. Philosopher A. C. Grayling notes the logic failure of the term as applied to atheism when he rhetorically asks "how can you be a militant atheist? How can you be a militant non-stamp collector?…You just don't collect stamps. So how can you be a fundamentalist non-stamp collector? It's like sleeping furiously."[74] Grayling notes that

71 Frank Brennan, 'Frank Brennan answers atheist manifestos', *Eureka Street*, 5 June 2007, accessed 22 March 2017, http://www.eurekastreet.com.au/article.aspx?aeid=2955.

72 Phil Fernandes, *The Atheist Delusion: A Christian Response to Christopher Hitchens and Richard Dawkins* (Xulon Press, 2009) 1.

73 Typically included among 'militant' atheists are Sam Harris, Richard Dawkins and the late Christopher Hitchens.

74 Decca Aitkenhead, 'AC Grayling: "How can you be a militant atheist? It's like sleeping furiously"', *Guardian*, 3 April 2011, accessed 22 March 2017 https://www.theguardian.com/books/2011/apr/03/grayling-good-book-atheism-philosophy.

while historically atheists were burnt at the stake by theists, the atheists of today are only exercising their right to speak frankly, much to the chagrin of religious opponents of non-belief who are seemingly concerned that atheists are no longer mute targets of heated religious speech. Indeed, the violence that is most evident in promoting an ideological worldview does not emanate from atheist scientists or humanist bloggers, but theists who use fatal force to silence them.[75]

2.2. Proselytism through exploitation of circumstance

In addition to the threat of physical force to compel believers or non-believers to recant, convert or adhere to a particular religious belief, General Comment 22 notes that "policies or practices having the same intention or effect, such as for example, those restricting access to education, medical care, employment or the rights…of the Covenant, are similarly inconsistent with article 18(2)."[76] Logically, the circumstances in which goods and services are offered or denied in proselytising are those in which the target of proselytism is in particular need of assistance. Examples may include targets who lack access to basic needs or are otherwise vulnerable to incentives. A rights-based perspective must determine the point at which such activities shift from being protected manifestations of religion and belief freedom, into trespassing on the rights of others.

Rudimentary considerations of missionary activities illustrate the complexity here. Social activism is often an encouraged component of practising religion, and indeed the 1981 Declaration explicitly protects freedom "[t]o establish and maintain appropriate charitable or humanitarian institutions".[77] The active role of the Church in education, healthcare and poverty alleviation particularly in Africa is widely recognised; controversy arises when considering whether missionaries have rights to practise their religion in this way, and the competing rights of the people they are engaging with to be free from coercive elements in accessing humanitarian services. Actively providing food and healthcare would seem an uncontroversial manifestation of a religious belief, but where such food and/or healthcare is withheld for religious reasons, the meaningful choice of persons in need is undermined.[78]

Former Special Rapporteur Jahangir draws the line between permissible proselytism and prohibited coercion thus:

> Missionary activity cannot be considered a violation of the freedom of religion and belief of others if all involved parties are adults able to reason on their

75 The murders of humanist and freethinking students, bloggers and publishers in Bangladesh and Pakistan can be noted here alongside the government's inaction to bring perpetrators to justice.

76 *General Comment 22,* above n 37 [5].

77 Article 6(d), *Declaration on the Elimination of All Forms of Intolerance and of Discrimination Based on Religion or Belief,* UN GAOR, UN Doc A/Res/36/55 (25 November 1981).

78 *General Comment 22*, above n 37 [5] noting that restricting access to education, medical care, employment or other rights would be tantamount to coercion.

own and if there is no relation of dependency or hierarchy between the missionaries and the objects of the missionary activities.[79]

Several questions are begged as to how this caution can be heeded in practice. Not all missionaries tie their religious agenda to their humanitarian activities, yet there are compelling examples of some doing so. Mother Teresa, who the Catholic Church beatified in 2013 and canonised in 2016, was widely known for her work with the poor in Calcutta. She was accused by critics including the late Christopher Hitchens of having made "no real effort at medical or social relief, and that her mission is religious and propagandistic and includes surreptitious baptism of unbelievers"[80] and that "her stated motive for the work is that of proselytisation for religious fundamentalism for the most extreme interpretation of Catholic doctrine."[81] The thrust of Hitchens' opposition to the life work of Mother Teresa was that despite a constant stream of monetary resources at her disposal, she failed to deliver meaningful health care or medical treatment, instead glorifying suffering and maintaining the illusion of poverty while channelling funds intended to help the poor towards building Catholic fundamentalist convents in her name.[82]

Despite deploring acts of "unethical conversion" Special Rapporteurs have advised that criminalising them be avoided, recommending instead that they be addressed on a case-by-case basis under domestic legislation[83] so as to avoid prohibitions becoming a pretext circumventing the criteria set out in article 18(3) of the ICCPR.[84] The case of *Sister Immaculate v Sri Lanka* can be looked to in speculating on how the HRC would approach Mother Teresa-type proselytism. In that case, an Order of Catholic nuns filed an application for incorporation in Sri Lankan law, which was rejected on the grounds of unconstitutionality.[85] The Sri Lankan Supreme Court held that the Order's use of charitable activities to "propagate a religion" to "defenceless and vulnerable people" would "result in imposing unnecessary and improper pressures on people, who are distressed and in need, with their free exercise of thought, conscience and religion with the freedom to have or to adopt a religion or belief of his choice as provided in article 10 of the Constitution".[86] On this reasoning, the Sri Lankan Court considered that the Constitution did not recognise a right to propagate a religion, and furthermore, that the propagation of Christianity would impair the existence of Buddhism, contrary to

79 UN Doc A/60/399 [67].
80 Christopher Hitchens, 'Letter to the Editor', *New York Review of Books*, 19 December 1996, accessed 22 March 2017, http://www.nybooks.com/articles/archives/1996/dec/19/mother-teresa/.
81 Matt Cherry, 'An interview with Christopher Hitchens on Mother Teresa', *Free Inquiry Magazine*, Volume 16, Number 4.
82 Christopher Hitchens, *The Missionary Position: Mother Teresa in theory and practice* (Verso, 1995).
83 Asma Jahangir, *Report of the Special Rapporteur on freedom of religion or belief*, UN Doc A/HRC/6/5 (20 July 2007) 7 [8].
84 UN Doc A/67/303 [29].
85 *Sister Immaculate v Sri Lanka*, above n 18.
86 Ibid [2.2].

the article 9 of the Constitution, giving "foremost place" to Buddhism.[87] The HRC held that the Order's right to disseminate its faith was a legitimate exercise of its right to freedom of religion and expression under article 18(1) of the ICCPR, but one that could be limited in accordance with article 18(3).[88] Sri Lanka failed to provide any foundation for its assertions of the threat that such propagation would have on Buddhism, simply concluding that the Order's activities would coercively or otherwise improperly propagate religion.[89] As a result, the HRC found that the limitations imposed on religious freedom were not well founded under article 18(3), meaning article 18(1) had been breached.

Another means of improper proselytising, is demanding that behaviour be modified in accordance with a particular religion or belief. For instance, colonisers gained several Christian converts in parts of Africa by making conversion to Christianity a precondition for receiving health services and education.[90] More recently, non-religious citizens of Ireland have struggled to access education, given that admission criteria for the majority of schools is dictated by the Catholic Church that prioritises inclusion of those who have been baptised into it, coercing many atheists and non-believers to baptise their children.[91] Another poignant example can be seen in policies of the United States government, whereby aid is withheld from organisations that promoted particular forms of family planning or worked with sex workers; a particularly detrimental policy in the fight against HIV/AIDs.[92] In 2003, US President George W. Bush declared that $15 billion would be spent on AIDS relief, but access to such relief came with "moral strings attached", namely, that recipient countries emphasise abstinence over condoms.[93] The policy was criticised for pushing a religious agenda by attaching Christian morality to the AIDS issue. Indeed, the final report of George Bush's 'Faith-based and Community Initiatives' noted that "faith-based organisations form a large portion of [the groups necessary to achieve AIDS relief], providing between 30 and 70 per cent of the health care in the countries of sub-Saharan Africa."[94] The Christian agenda of the Bush administration was not disguised. In his introduction to the final report of the Faith-based and Community Initiative

87 Ibid [2.3].
88 Ibid [7.2].
89 Ibid [7.3].
90 Makau Mutua, 'Human Rights, Religion and Proselytism' in Philip Alston and Ryan Goodman, *International Human Rights* (Oxford University Press, 2013) 622–623.
91 Harriet Sherwood, 'No baptism, no school: Irish parents fight for equal access to education' *The Guardian* (online), 21 October 2015, accessed 2 February 2016 https://www.theguardian.com/world/2015/oct/21/no-baptism-no-school-irish-parents-fight-for-equal-access-to-education.
92 Human Rights Watch, 'Africa: Bush's Trip highlights flaws in US HIV/AIDS policy', 14 February 2008, accessed 22 March 2017, http://www.hrw.org/en/news/2008/02/14/africa-bush-s-trip-highlights-flaws-us-hivaids-policy.
93 'Bush accused of Aids damage to Africa', *Guardian* (online), 30 August 2005, accessed 22 March 2017, http://www.guardian.co.uk/world/2005/aug/30/usa.aids.
94 'Innovations in Compassion, The Faith-Based and Community Initiative: A Final Report to the Armies of Compassion' (The White House, US) December 2008, 6.

(dedicated in typically Bushian parlance, to "the armies of compassion"), outgoing President Bush offered

> sincere gratitude to every individual and organisation that has joined us in this work. As you have loved your neighbor as yourself, you have made a real, measureable impact in lives across America and around the globe. You are part of a great work that is changing the world – one heart, one soul at a time.[95]

More concern has been raised about religious groups proselytising through exploitation of circumstance, than it has about non-religious or atheists. Following the 2004 tsunami in Southeast Asia, concern was raised that different religious groups exploited the situation by offering ideological messages to destitute and vulnerable people, alongside delivering aid.[96] No such concerns were raised about non-theistic organisations attempting to encourage religious people to renounce their faith in favour of none. The fact that there are fewer examples of 'atheist' organisations exploiting such situations to extol atheism than there are examples of religious humanitarian organisations promoting religion, may be a result of there being fewer atheistic or non-religious humanitarian organisations. Rather than leading to the conclusion that non-religious people are less charitable,[97] it is asserted that the contributions they make are less visible because they are not overtly or directly attributed to their atheism or non-religion. While religious organisations define themselves by their religion, secular or non-religious organisations generally do not define themselves by their non-religion, but are 'unreligious' and the extent that the beliefs on which they are based challenge religious practices – or indeed support them – is entirely incidental to their work.

2.3. Proselytism through exposure to religious symbols

There is a dearth of international jurisprudence concerning religious symbols, but questions have arisen at the European Court of Human Rights about the extent to

95 Ibid, introduction.
96 Marianne Kearney, 'Religious groups are exploiting Aceh chaos', *Telegraph*, 14 January 2005, accessed 22 March 2017, http://www.telegraph.co.uk/news/worldnews/1481197/Religious-groups-are-exploiting-Aceh-chaos.html.
97 On the contrary, a University of California, Berkeley study that found that atheists and agnostics are more driven by emotions like compassion than their religious counterparts. See Laura Saslow *et al*, 'My Brother's Keeper? Compassion Predicts Generosity More Among Less Religious Individuals', *Social Psychology and Personality Science*, 26 April 2012, accessed 22 March 2017, http://journals.sagepub.com/doi/abs/10.1177/1948550612444137?journalCode=sppa. A 2015 study of 1170 children showed that religiosity had a negative influence on altruism, finding that non-religious children were more altruistic. See J. Decety *et al*, 'The Negative Association between Religiousness and Children's Altruism Across the World' (November 2015) 25 *Current Biology* (November 2015) 2951, accessed 22 March 2017 http://www.cell.com/current-biology/pdf/S0960-9822(15)01167-7.pdf.

which mere exposure to religious symbols or messages can have a proselytising effect.[98] Key among them, *Lautsi and others v Italy* involved the displaying of crucifixes in classrooms of state schools.[99] The Court found that states were obliged to refrain from imposing beliefs, even indirectly, where people are dependent on the state for schooling, and emphasised that the 'negative' element of freedom of religion and belief extends beyond the absence of religion to include beliefs such as atheism. While the Lower Chamber of the European Court unanimously found that the presence of crucifixes was contrary to the principles of state neutrality and pluralism,[100] the Grand Chamber of the European Court overturned that decision, concluding that "the decision whether or not to perpetuate a tradition falls in principle within the margin of appreciation of the respondent State."[101] No proselytising effect was found.[102] In leaving the matter within the state's margin of appreciation, the Court was explicitly influenced by the majority status of Christianity in Italy.[103]

No cases have been brought at the international level of atheist symbols being improperly used for proselytism. The non-applicability of proselytism to the non-religious or atheist rights-holder is again evident. While there are ostensibly some atheist symbols used by some atheist movements,[104] they are not widely recognised by non-atheists (or even, indeed, by other atheists), meaning that symbolism is unlikely to be used by them as a means of improperly coercing others into atheism. Even if atheist symbols were to achieve wider recognition, it is hard to imagine a circumstance in which they would be prominently displayed in public places, such as classrooms, as was the case in *Lautsi* with the Christian crucifix. But while symbolism cannot be exercised as a manifestation of non-religious or atheistic beliefs in the same way it is by religious rights-holders, it can nonetheless be improperly used against them. Determining where the point is between proselytism that is a protected manifestation of article 18 and where it constitutes improper proselytism is the subject of the next section.

98 See for instance, *Dahlab v Switzerland*, European Court of Human Rights, Application No. 42393/98 (15 February 2001) and *Leyla Şahin v Turkey*, European Court of Human Rights, Application No. 44774/98 (10 November 2005). In *Dahlab* the wearing of an Islamic headscarf by a teacher in a state school was deemed coercive enough to justify her removal for failing to take it off. In contrast, in *Leyla Şahin* a student was prevented from attending classes for wearing a headscarf in accordance with Islam.

99 *Lautsi v Italy*, European Court of Human Rights, Application No. 30814/06 (3 November 2009).

100 Ibid 15 [31].

101 Ibid 29 [68].

102 Ibid [39–40].

103 Ibid 48–9 [2]. On the margin of appreciation see Myriam Hunter-Henin, 'Law, Religion and the School' in Silvio Ferrari (ed.), *Routledge Handbook of Law and Religion* (Routledge, 2015) 268.

104 The atomic symbol, the 'Darwin fish' and the 'scarlet A' could be offered among other examples.

3. Determining where coercion undermines choice

> "*What religious communities have to come to terms with is that members have a legally guaranteed right to leave.*"[105]

It is submitted that proselytism constitutes improper coercion where it interferes with freedom of choice. Put simply: one is coerced if one cannot meaningfully choose. Proselytism, assessed from the perspective of its target, can reduce a person's choices or present him with more choices; coercion should therefore be measured by the extent to which a target's capacity to choose is negatively interfered with. Such a test would prohibit situations where food or health services are dangled before a hungry person, or where a person's prospects for happiness are threatened if he or she does not 'choose' whatever brand of belief is on offer.[106]

Tad Stahnke offers a framework as a starting point to determine what may constitute 'improper proselytism', albeit an incomplete one by his own admission. His framework considers four interrelated variables: 1) the attributes of the source, 2) the attributes of the target, 3) the location where the action alleged to be improper proselytism takes place, and 4) the nature of the action.[107] The touchstone of this proposed framework, according to Stahnke, is the notion of coercion, namely that the more proselytism interferes with a person's ability to make free choices in matters of religion and belief, the more he or she is likely to have been coerced. The particular coercive authority that a source exerts would be relevant here, alongside the susceptibility of the target. The location of the alleged coercion may be relevant for instance, where the target is unable to freely move in or out of that location, and the nature of the exchange between the source and target may reflect more or less coercion.[108] To these points, Peter Danchin adds 'context' as a necessary consideration. Each of these attributes is considered in turn below.

3.1. Attributes of the source and target of proselytism

The attributes and authority of the source relative to the target is the first factor Stahnke offers in determining whether proselytism is improper. Where the source of proselytism has more power than the target, alarm should be raised that the latter may be vulnerable to coercion. Power imbalance would be present in instances where the source of proselytism is the state or an agent of it, is the employer or professional superior of the target, or is economically advantaged vis-à-vis the target.[109] In these situations the target may have a strong incentive to

105 Bielefeldt, Ghanea and Weiner, above n 3, 73.

106 Choice is understood here in the legal sense, to define the scope of legal protection accorded to an individual, not to describe or diminish the spiritual dimensions of their belief or depth of their conviction. See Bielefeldt, Ghanea and Weiner, above n 3, 71.

107 Stahnke, above n 2, 326. Also see Tad Stahnke, 'Proselytism' in Silvio Ferrari (ed.), *Routledge Handbook of Law and Religion* (Routledge, 2015) 404–411.

108 Ibid 327.

109 Such as *Larissis and others v Greece* (above n 39) in which subordinate airmen were found to be coerced as proselytisers were officers of superior rank.

maintain a good relationship with the source, influencing his decision to reject or adopt whatever religious belief or affiliation is being proselytised.[110] The susceptibility of a target of proselytism to a particular message should also be capable of confirming such an assumption, allowing, for instance, for a child's fear of hell or an uneducated adult's fear of juju to be relevant in proving coercion. Accordingly, the relationship between the source and the target of proselytism, must be balanced alongside inquiry into the latter's capacity to rebut or incapacity to deflect it.

Stahnke further explains that the greater the perceived vulnerability of the target, the more likely that the proselytism directed at her will be coercive.[111] To this consideration is added an inquiry into the knowledge the source has of the target's vulnerability; culpability may be less where he or she is oblivious, or conversely may be higher where deliberate exploitation of that vulnerability is found. The *mens rea* of the source shows again the interconnectivity of the factors to be considered in determining whether proselytism is improper. Separate from the nature of the vulnerable relationship that the target may have with the source, the attributes at issue here relate to the nature of the specific target. Stahnke notes that "[c]ertain people may be susceptible to a change in religious beliefs, as they might be susceptible to persuasion in any matter" and includes children[112] as well as people who are vaguely described as "uneducated, naïve or generally weak or unsure of themselves".[113]

Particularly subjective considerations are involved in determining a target's vulnerability. For instance, the posthumous threats discussed above may come into play. Stahnke mentions an Orissa High Court case involving legislation referring to the "threat of divine displeasure" within the definition of prohibited conversion by force.[114] The Indian court supported the provision on the basis that it was needed to protect those with "undeveloped minds", potentially to imply that a person with a "developed mind" would be less susceptible to threats, in turn implying that there is something baseless in the threat: an implication that exceeds what a court of law can speculate about. Indeed, the implication that a person holds a particular belief because her mind is "undeveloped" would offend many believers. The susceptibility of young children whose ideologies have not yet been formed has also been noted as crucial in determining the effect of proselytism on them.[115] The same concerns are true in respect of Stahnke's suggested criteria of "uneducated" amounting to "vulnerable", which proselytisers could argue amounts

110 Stahnke, above n 2, 328–329 and Stahnke, above n 107, 406–407.
111 Stahnke, above n 2, 332 and Stahnke, above n 107, 407–408.
112 The rights of children are the subject of Chapter 5.
113 Stahnke, above n 2, 332.
114 *Mrs. Yulitha Hyde And Ors v State Of Orissa And Ors*, 1973 A.I.R. 116 (Ori) 121 (24 October 1972). Also see Bielefeldt, Ghanea and Weiner, above n 3, 197.
115 In the case of *Dahlab* (above n 98), the Court emphasised the susceptibility of young children whose ideologies are still being formed, in determining whether there may be any proselytising effect from exposure to religious symbols. The Court failed to apply this same reasoning in the later case of *Lautsi*, above n 99.

to an assertion that education is somehow antithetical to whatever religion or belief is being offered. Determining who is and who is not a vulnerable target becomes confused again when specific individuals are considered. Clearly someone suffering from learning disabilities or mental disorders would be deemed more vulnerable than those who are not. However, a person suffering hardship and lacking a support network may be more susceptible to proselytism at that particular time of his life than he would at another. What appears from one perspective to be vulnerability, to another may simply be openness to receiving and accepting a particular message. In short, these issues are obscured by the ethereal nature of religion and the agendas of proselytisers, making it difficult to distinguish vulnerability to coercion from susceptibility of a person to religion or belief.[116]

Situations where an economic imbalance between source and target would come into play include a wealthy and potentially foreign source of proselytism visiting a less developed country to deliver humanitarian aid and to proselytise. Here the target's need for the aid could comprise an incentive to also accept (or at least feign acceptance of) the religion or belief being proselytised. This consideration overlaps with others already discussed, notably, that the susceptibility of the target to the message would increase where she lacks understanding of wider contexts, meaning that she may be unable to separate the message (for instance, Jesus loves you) from the goods she receives (so that, Jesus feeds you).

3.2. Location and nature of proselytism

Stahnke asserts that the location where the proselytism takes place can reflect on how welcome it is. Where proselytism is invited it is less likely to be coercive; for instance, proselytising in the place of worship of the source where the target is willingly present, would not raise as much concern as would proselytising in the place of worship or classroom of the target.[117] In a place of worship, the listener is likely to be a willing audience, whereas the audience in a park or other public place can include those who have not chosen to listen.[118] Where proselytism takes place in the home of the target, this location could either show that the target's privacy had been trespassed upon, or conversely prove that the target is a willing listener who invited the source to share his views. Deciding in this case would require balancing other considerations, such as the vulnerability of the target.

The key role that location can play in increasing the likelihood of coercion, paired with increased vulnerability of the target, concerns situations where the audience is captive, such as in prison settings.[119] In the case of school environments,

116 Here see *Kokkinakis* (above n 39) [9–10], where the Court's reasoning implied that "skilful explanation" could constitute improper proselytism, and a lack of "grounding in doctrine" an attribute of heightened vulnerability to it.
117 Stahnke, above n 2, 334 and Stahnke, above n 107, 408–409.
118 Ibid 334.
119 The US InnerChange Freedom Initiative can be offered as an example. Funded by the Bush administration, the initiative offered participating inmates benefits including the possibility of being transferred to a safer, better equipped and more centrally located

where students may be exposed to religious symbols,[120] the environment is one in which students are required to submit to the authority of their teachers, imbibe information they receive in that environment, and respect the institution that teaches them. Particular vigilance is required to maintain the neutrality of such environments where the audience of messages is not comprised of captive adults, but of impressionable children.

Stahnke's final consideration concerns the nature of the proselytism, which he says can range from simple communication of one's beliefs, through to threats or use of violence.[121] Between these extremes are more grey approaches, such as offering benefits in exchange for changing religion or belief affiliation, or conversely denying rights or privileges in the earthly world or the hereafter. The result of exploring this grey area requires not only taking into account the nature of proselytising acts, but also in considering what is being offered to the target in exchange for his or her change of religion or belief. Stahnke asserts that there must be a division here between tangible and intangible benefits. The latter, which may include eternal life, would be intangible spiritual benefits in Stahnke's view, which "are, of course, one of the primary reasons for holding religious beliefs, and it is difficult to imagine making a principled division between proper and improper in this area".[122]

This dismissal of the 'intangible' is not entirely convincing. As discussed above in relation to spiritual coercion, while religion and belief are essentially intangible, the experience of it may be more significant and add more value to a person's life than the more tangible aspects of their existence do. Respecting the spiritual benefits that can result from intangible beliefs requires that consideration also be given to coercion that can result from intangible threats. The very real impact on targets of 'intangible' threats or benefits can be evidenced in the example (albeit an extreme one) of child sexual abuse within the Catholic priesthood. One mechanism for securing a child's silence is to threaten him with spiritual punishment if he reveals the abuse, and in some instances, giving spiritual rewards or absolution in exchange for sexual acts.[123] Another example which demonstrates the real impact that a possibly unreal incentive can have on a believer can be found in the motivations of a suicide bomber – sometimes a child – prepared to end his life and the lives of others in exchange for rewards he believes await him in paradise.[124] To disqualify such 'intangible' threats or incentives from scrutiny is to undermine the very tangible impact that they can have on their targets.

facility in exchange for receiving Christian counselling. See Alex J. Luchenitser, '"InnerChange": Conversion as the Price of Freedom and Comfort – A Cautionary Tale about the Pitfalls of Faith-based Prison Units' (2007) 6 *Ave Maria Law Review* 445, 451 and 459.

120 See *Lautsi,* above n 99 and *Dahlab,* above n 98.

121 Stahnke, above n 2, 335 and Stahnke, above n 107, 409–410.

122 Stahnke, above n 2, 337.

123 Geoffrey Robertson QC, *The Case of the Pope: Vatican Accountability for Human Rights Abuse* (Penguin, 2010) 21.

124 See Nasra Hasan, 'An Arsenal of Believers' *The New Yorker*, 19 November 2001, accessed 22 March 2017, http://www.newyorker.com/magazine/2001/11/19/an-arsenal-of-believers in which the author writes: "in order to be accepted for a suicide

At the outset of his framework, Stahnke noted that the four key considerations are interrelated and must, as the case requires, be considered in relation to each other. In considering, then, the intangible benefits presented or threats made in the course of proselytising, due consideration must be given to the vulnerability of the target, his or her relationship to the source and the location where the proselytism takes place. If the statement "You will go to hell if you do not believe in God" was considered to be improper, the net would arguably be cast too wide. However, where this statement is directed at a particularly vulnerable target, such as a child or a mentally impaired person, and comes from a relatively powerful source such as a priest, imam, teacher, caregiver or employer, it could arguably constitute improper proselytism.[125]

3.3. Context of the proselytism

Peter Danchin adds the element of context to those offered by Stahnke. He suggests that the task of balancing competing rights claims is not as simple as determining where the proselytiser's right to religious expression is exercised in a way amounting to prohibited coercion of the target. This, Danchin says, would be a daunting task that would require analysis to "advance some moral conception of harm or coercion in order to mark the precise boundary between proper and improper conduct…between the two equal individual freedoms".[126] Stahnke concurs that the context in which the proselytism takes place is a valid consideration, noting that if people in a given society are continually confronted with attempts to change their views on all fronts (from political opinions to consumer choices), it may be inconsistent to overly restrict information that concerns their religious choices, whereas in societies where information is less available, it may be more problematic to allow religious information to flow more freely.[127]

Paul Taylor agrees with this approach when he says "[f]or some countries, distaste of proselytism is rooted in issues of culture or national identity quite separate from matters of doctrine."[128] The examples that Taylor offers in this context include Armenia, Bulgaria and Greece where the dominant religion is commensurate with national identity and is seen as being potentially threatened by proselytising from competing religions.[129] A caution must be issued here. It is surely in those countries where religion is bound to national identity, that the religious freedoms of individuals who diverge from the dominant religion are most threatened. This is particularly the case for atheists who have explicitly rejected religion. The preservation of national identity is not a protected human right. The rights

mission the volunteers had to be convinced of the religious legitimacy of the acts they were contemplating, as sanctioned by the divinely revealed religion of Islam."

125 Complex questions arise under article 18(4) when parents are the source of such a statement. See Chapter 5.

126 Danchin, above n 5, 284.

127 Stahnke, above n 2, 286.

128 Taylor, above n 4, 65.

129 Ibid.

and freedoms of others comprise a justifiable ground for limiting a person's protected right to manifest religion through proselytism, but should be relied on without allowing notions of cultural or contextual relativity to deny protection to individuals in contexts where they may be particularly vulnerable. Indeed, in states where proselytism is feared as something that may be 'perpetrated' by minorities to threaten the dominant religion, the bigger threat to religious freedom emanates from the bias shown to that dominant religion. Such bias could be construed as coercive proselytism not only to individual rights-holders who do not subscribe to the dominant religion, but also to those who already do; their beliefs may be coercively entrenched and they may be denied meaningful choice to leave the religion or question their beliefs. In the HRC case of *Sister Immaculate v Sri Lanka*[130] the Sri Lankan Supreme Court attributed its decision to concern about the impact that an Order of Catholic nuns would have on Buddhism, which is given "foremost place" in the Constitution.[131] Happily, the HRC did not endorse Sri Lanka's decision in this respect. Were it to do so, it would have endorsed the notion that there is a hierarchy among rights-holders determined by their choice of religion or belief. It can be speculated though whether it would have made the same decision had the religion at issue not been Catholicism but a fringe religion.

4. Conclusion: The need to prioritise rights over religions

It is clear that in international law, the non-coercive conversion of a person to a dominant religion or away from it, or even converting him to atheism, is a protected manifestation of religion and belief. However, in practical terms proselytism – as a means of exercising article 18 rights – falls within the privileged purview of theists and is not equally enjoyed by atheists and non-religious rights-holders. While atheists may be the targets of proselytism (and prime ones, at that), they are less likely to be the source of it. Notwithstanding that some atheists have been branded 'militants' who seek to convert religious adherents to atheism, proselytism is not a core tenet of atheism or non-religion, in the way it is of some religions. Furthermore, even where the expressions of atheists could be viewed as being proselytising, it is less likely that their effect would be improperly coercive. The messages of non-religion or atheism are less hostile than religious rhetoric can be; a child may be more threatened by being told by her parents that she will burn forever in hell if she rejects or questions their religion, than she is by being told by atheist parents that there is no such place. But this assertion that expressions of religion are more likely to be improperly coercive than expressions of non-religion and atheism are, is beside the point. The point – as evident from unpacking Stahnke's framework above – is that it is the attributes of the source, target, location and nature of proselytism that matter, not the religions or beliefs – or irreligion – of its source.

Rightly absent from the above criteria for determining what amounts to improper coercion, is the religion or belief being proselytised. What is coercive

130 *Sister Immaculate v Sri Lanka*, above n 18.
131 Ibid [2.3].

must be considered on a case-by-case basis, weighing the attributes of the source, the target and the target's relationship with the source, the location of proselytism, as well as the nature and context in which it occurs. These factors are interrelated in determining whether a given situation constitutes coercive proselytism of the type that should be curtailed, regardless of the religion or belief being proselytised.

Pluralism again emerges as a key guiding principle to ensure that rights-holders are treated even-handedly. The objective in imposing limitations must be furtherance of rights-based interests rather than religious or ideological agendas. The fact that there is a dominant religion in a particular state should not afford its followers special rights or privileges that would be discriminatory to those who do not follow it. In short, the nature of the religion or belief should not be a determinant of whether proselytism is coercive.

In his *Study of Discrimination in the Matter of Religious Rights and Practices,* Krishnaswami acknowledges that the line between what are justifiable and what are not justifiable constraints on proselytism is unclear.[132] The key outcome of his report is the 16 rules he offers towards achieving the religious freedom goals set out in the UDHR, the tenth of which provides guidance on determining the point at which proselytism crosses from being a protected religious manifestation to being a limitable imposition on another's enjoyment of his or her freedom: "[e]veryone should be free to disseminate a religion or belief, in so far as his actions do not impair the right of any other individual to maintain his religion or belief."[133] Limitations to the right to proselytise a religion, then, should not jeopardise the freedom to reject or renounce whatever is being proselytised. In terms of freedom of religion and belief of non-believers and atheists: the mere maintenance of non-belief or rejection of whatever is being proselytised is a right of equal importance to the right to proselytise a religion. If a person is not free to adopt, reject or maintain non-belief or atheism in the face of proselytism, he is improperly coerced.

132 Krishnaswami, above n 38, 41.
133 Ibid.

4 Freedom from hate

Looking to hate speech as a case study shows the relative disadvantage of the non-religious and atheist rights-holders in the hierarchy of religion and belief. This chapter explores the point where an expression manifesting religion and belief constitutes 'hate speech' that should be prohibited as such. In doing so, mandatory prohibitions introduced by article 20(2) of the ICCPR to religious hate speech are explored to assert that hate speech is less likely to be curtailed when it emanates from a religious point of view, and more likely to be curtailed when it expresses a non-religious belief. What is considered at the international level to constitute hate speech that ought to be prohibited as such, and what is a permissible and protectable form of expression, again illustrates the bias inherent in international human rights law, in favour of religious rights-holders, to privilege manifestations that are religious over manifestations that are not.

Though *prima facie*, religious and non- or anti-religious rights-holders are equally entitled to express their views, what emerges from considerations of the workings of article 20(2) is that non-religious expressions are more likely to be limited as hate speech than are equivalent expressions originating from a religious perspective. The implication is that article 20 is biased towards situations where offence is caused *to* religions or the religious rather than *by* religions or the religious. Beyond this, it is argued that article 20(2) of the ICCPR is limited by its inability to address all forms of hate, including religious expressions directed against non-believers and atheists.

On the basis of this analysis the entrenched position of major monotheistic religions in the hierarchy of religions and the relatively weaker position of atheists and non-religious rights-holders is again revealed. Article 20(2) betrays a bias in failing to weigh theistic and atheistic convictions equally in limiting 'hate speech'. The strength of article 20, it is argued, should be measured by its ability to protect all persons from hatred that incites discrimination, hostility or violence, regardless of the particular hated traits.

1. Article 20 and hate speech in the name of religion

> "*The devil can cite Scripture for his purpose.*"
>
> William Shakespeare

Article 20(2) of the ICCPR reads:

> Any advocacy of national, racial or religious hatred that constitutes incitement to discrimination, hostility or violence shall be prohibited by law.

Article 20(2) is an express requirement on states parties to interfere with freedom of expression to prohibit advocacy for national, racial or religious hatred.[1] It is an unusual article, in that it does not provide for a human right as other provisions of the ICCPR do, but rather establishes limitations on other rights.[2] In doing so, it differs from limitations clauses contained in articles 18(3), 19(3), 21 and 22(2) because it is a mandatory limitation to freedom of expression, *requiring* states parties to provide corresponding restrictions, rather than merely permitting them to do so.[3] Article 20 is to be interpreted in conformity with the legitimate limitations contained in other provisions, with article 19(3) concerning freedom of expression being the most commonly linked to it. Though article 20 is a separate article it merely sets forth additional, specific purposes for interference, which could have been included under those in article 19(3). The prohibition of advocacy of hatred may be necessary for the respect of the rights of others and for the protection of public order or *ordre public*.[4]

The fact that free expression is so valued in many countries has meant that article 20 has attracted several reservations particularly from Western democratic states: Australia, Belgium, Denmark, Finland, Iceland, Malta, New Zealand, the United Kingdom and the United States reserve the right not to enact any prohibitions going beyond existing legislation.[5] Belgium and Luxembourg made declarations with respect to article 20, "that article 20 as a whole shall be applied taking into account the rights to freedom of thought and religion".[6]

1 On the interconnection between the prohibition on hate speech and freedom of expression, see *Report of the Special Rapporteur of Freedom of Religion and Belief*, UN Doc A/HRC/31/18 (23 December 2015).

2 *Report of the Special Rapporteur on freedom of religion or belief, Asma Jahangir, and the Special Rapporteur on contemporary forms of racism, racial discrimination, xenophobia and related intolerance, Doudou Diène, further to Human Rights Council decision 1/107 on incitement to racial and religious hatred and the promotion of tolerance*, UN Doc A/HRC/2/3 (20 September 2006) [46]; Jeroen Temperman, *Religious Hatred and International Law: the Prohibition of Incitement to Violence or Discrimination* (Cambridge, 2016) 67, 80.

3 Human Rights Committee, *General Comment 34: Freedom of Opinion and Expression (Art 19)*, UN Doc CCPR/C/GC/34 (29 June 1983) [50–52]; Temperman, above n 2, 67–78.

4 Manfred Nowak, *CCPR Commentary* (NP Engel Kehl, 2nd edn, 2005) 476.

5 UN Treaty Series (Online) *Declarations and Reservations to the International Covenant on Civil and Political Rights*, 1197 UNTS 411, accessed 22 March 2017, https://treaties.un.org/Pages/ViewDetails.aspx?src=IND&mtdsg_no=IV-4&chapter=4&clang=_en#EndDec.

6 Ibid. Both also included freedom of opinion and freedom of assembly and association. The HRC has suggested that a state may not reserve the right to engage in advocacy of hatred; see Human Rights Committee, *General Comment 24: Issues relating to*

Crucially in the context of the rights of atheists, the freedom from hate that article 20 offers is limited only to some forms of hate. The United Nations has observed that the significant violence committed in the name of religion disproportionately targets religious dissidents, members of religious minorities or converts, and that violence is perpetrated in the name of religion against lesbian, gay, bisexual and transgender rights-holders.[7] Notwithstanding that reality, some of this hatred emanating *from* religion is not explicitly contrary to article 20, illustrating again the privileged position of religious rights-holders and the pro-religious bias of international human rights law. Not all hatred is prohibited; article 20 only takes issue with the type of hatred that incites discrimination, violence and hostility, and even then only where national, racial or religious hatred is advocated.[8] The insertion of the word 'discrimination' is inexplicable to Nowak who correctly notes that it "is most difficult to conceive of any advocacy of national, racial or religious hatred that does not simultaneously incite discrimination".[9]

Very few article 20 cases have appeared before the HRC, and those that have reveal a range of approaches, from avoiding opportunities to address questions, to attempting to resolve them.[10] An example of the former is found in the 1981 case before the HRC of *J.R.T and the W.G. Party v Canada* in which the state took action to repress the speech of the Western Guard that had used public telephone services to warn "of the dangers of international finance and international Jewry leading the world into wars, unemployment and inflation and the collapse of world values and principles".[11] The authors alleged violations of their article 19(2) rights, an allegation deemed inadmissible by the HRC, which held that the Party's warnings "clearly constituted the advocacy of racial or religious hatred which Canada has an obligation under article 20(2) of the Covenant to prohibit".[12] In saying this, the Court attributes to Canada an obligation to prohibit advocacy of hatred, though it has no such obligation; its obligation relates to prohibiting *incitement* to discrimination, hostility or violence. The Court did not consider whether the advocacy of hatred at issue constituted incitement. According to Temperman, this questionable finding is tantamount to construing article 20(2) as an admissibility criterion such that any speech that runs counter to the spirit of that article may result in applicants being denied standing. In lacking the standing

reservations made upon ratification or accession to the Covenant or the Optional Protocols thereto, or in relation to declarations under article 41 of the Covenant, UN Doc CCPR/C/21/Rev.1/Add.6 (11 April 1994) [8].

7 *Report of the Special Rapporteur on Freedom of Religion or Belief, Heiner Bielefeldt*, UN Doc A/HRC/28/66 (29 December 2014) [6], [11].

8 On the narrow scope of grounds of incitement, the NGO ARTICLE 19 supports an interpretation of article 20(2) that provides prohibition of incitement on all grounds provided for in international law. *Prohibiting incitement to discrimination, hostility of violence: Policy Brief* (ARTICLE 19, December 2012) 19–21.

9 Nowak, above n 4, 475.

10 Temperman, above n 2, 120.

11 *J.R.T. and the W.G. Party v Canada*, Human Rights Committee, Communication No. 104/1981, UN Doc CCPR/C/OP/2 at 25 (1984) [2.1].

12 Ibid [8(b)].

of other persons, alleged inciters then suffer a form of 'content discrimination'. Temperman is of the view that such an approach suggests that actions that fall within the ambit of article 20(2) do not warrant the protection of article 19 and should be rejected.[13]

In the 1993 case of *Faurisson v France* the author, a former Professor at the Sorbonne University, argued that his freedom of expression had been violated.[14] Faurisson was charged under the Gayssot Act that made it an offence to contest the existence of the category of crimes against humanity as defined in the London Charter of 8 August 1945, on the basis of which Nazi leaders were tried and convicted by the International Military Tribunal at Nuremberg in 1945–1946. In a magazine interview, Faurisson stated that "No one will have me admit that two plus two make five, that the earth is flat, or that the Nuremberg Tribunal was infallible." Faurisson's complaint to the HRC related to his belief that his freedom to doubt and conduct academic research and freely express himself were curtailed by the Gayssot Act, which he believed to be targeting him personally. The HRC abandoned the earlier approach taken in *J.R.T and the W.G. Party v Canada*, finding the case admissible and deciding the case on the merits. In doing so, it found that there was no breach of Faurisson's article 19 rights, given that the state's actions were justified by virtue of article 19(3), but it did not consider the relevance of article 20(2).[15] On the facts of the case, some members argued the implicit application of article 20. Rajsoomer Lallah for instance asserted that article 20 of the ICCPR should have been evoked in the HRC's reasoning to exonerate the state.[16]

In the 1997 case of *Malcolm Ross v Canada*,[17] the applicant stated that his distribution of material asserting that the Jewish faith was a threat to Christianity was religious expression, and that his consequent removal from his teaching position for activities outside the work place was a breach of his rights under article 18 and 19 of the ICCPR. The state party responded that Ross's activities were designed to incite hatred against Jews and that in acting in the way it did, it was simply upholding article 20(2) of the ICCPR. The HRC found that the permissibility of such restrictions was an issue for consideration on the merits.[18] In so doing, the HRC found that the author's comments called upon Christians not only to question Jewish beliefs and teachings but to hold Jews in contempt as undermining freedom, democracy and Christian beliefs and values. The HRC concluded that the restrictions imposed on Ross were warranted to protect the "rights or reputations" of persons of Jewish faith or ancestry, including the right to

13 Temperman, above n 2, 90–91.
14 *Faurisson v France*, Human Rights Committee, Communication No. 550/1993, UN Doc CCPR/C/58/D/550/1993 (1996).
15 The court found that the limitations of Faurisson's rights were justified under article 19(3) grounds of protecting the rights and reputations of others.
16 See the opinion of Rajsoomer Lallah in *Faurisson*, above n 14 [11].
17 *Ross v Canada*, Human Rights Committee, Communication No. 736/1997, UN Doc CCPR/C/70/D/736/1997 (18 October 2000).
18 Ibid [10.6].

have an education in the public school system free from bias, prejudice and intolerance. The restrictions imposed on Ross were also noted by the HRC to derive from the principles reflected in article 20(2) of the ICCPR, reinforcing the relationship of this article with the limitations provided for in article 19(3).[19]

Thus far, the HRC has not been called upon to consider religious hatred complaints made under article 20.[20] Salient cases, discussed above, have been more relevant to racial hatred than religious hatred (though this depends on whether Jews are hated for their race or their religion or a combination of both).[21] Some of the HRC's Concluding Observations shed light on its approach to article 20. On Poland, the HRC emphasised that the state party should intensify its efforts to combat and punish incidents of desecration of Catholic and Jewish cemeteries and acts of anti-Semitism that violate articles 18, 20 and 27.[22] The HRC also implied that the local advertising campaign in Switzerland against minarets may have breached article 20, in calling on the state to respect freedom of religion and combat incitement to discrimination, hostility and violence.[23]

Relevant to the end of equally protecting religious and non-religious belief, it is interesting to consider the point at which the HRC would determine that a *religious* expression advocating hatred on the grounds of religion or belief (or lack of either) would become advocacy of violence. Only "religious hatred" is specified in Article 20; 'belief' hatred is not. It must therefore be considered whether, if called upon to consider such a case, the HRC would find article 20 adequate to address all forms of hate speech that commonly arise in religion, such as vilification of non-believers. For instance, where a Christian expresses hatred for 'non-believers' would article 20 intervene to protect all non-believers of Christianity (including Sikhs, atheists, Hindus, Buddhists, Muslims, Jews, agnostics and others)? Or would article 20 be construed as addressing only hate speech that targets a *particular* religion or belief?

Finally, the pro-religious bias of international human rights infrastructure must be pointed to by noting that the UN Human Rights Council, and its predecessor

19 Ibid [11.5].

20 Article 20 cases that were found inadmissible include Human Rights Committee cases of *Andersen v Denmark*, Communication No. 1868/09, UN Doc CCPR/C/99/D/1868/2009 (7 September 2010); *Ernst Zündel v Canada*, Communication No. 953/2000, UN Doc CCPR/C/78/D/953/2000 (27 July 2003) and *Kasem Said Ahmad and Asmaa Adol-Hamid v Denmark*, Communication No. 1487/2006, UN Doc CCPR/C/92/D/1487/2006 (18 April 2008).

21 Some cases of racial hated have been brought under article 4 of the International Convention on the Elimination of Racial Discrimination. See for instance *Ahmad v Denmark* (CERD 16/99), *Jama v Denmark* (CERD 41/2008) and the *Jewish Community of Oslo et al v Norway* (CERD 30/2003).

22 Human Rights Committee, *Consideration of Reports Submitted by States Parties under Article 40 of the Covenant*, UN Doc CCPR/CO/82/POL, 82nd Sess. (2 December 2004) [19].

23 Human Rights Committee, *Consideration of Reports Submitted by States Parties under Article 40 of the Covenant*, UN Doc CCPR/C/CHE/CO/3, 97th Sess. (3 November 2009) [8].

the Human Rights Commission, have passed several resolutions condemning "defamation of religions".[24] These resolutions were controversial for the significant threat they pose to freedom of expression.[25] The language of these resolutions seems to reach far beyond religious vilification to protection of the religions themselves, not only from hate but also from lesser forms of denigration and offence. Indeed, Special Rapporteurs on both race and religion stated that "international human rights law protects primarily individuals in the exercise of their freedom of religion and not religions per se," noting that "the right to freedom of religion or belief, as enshrined in relevant international legal standards, does not include the right to have a religion or belief that is free from criticism or ridicule."[26] Indeed, there is no right to not be 'offended'.[27] As Dennis De Jong notes "hurt feelings as such do not matter...[h]owever, speeches aimed at mobilising parts of the population against adherents of a particular religion or belief do come under the realm of article 20 and are therefore prohibited."[28] The issue of defamation was finally set aside in the Council in 2011 when it became clear that majority support no longer existed for the notion.[29] Nevertheless, these resolutions display the clear interest many states have in protecting adherents of religions from defamation of their religion, being 'all religions' generally, and Islam in particular.[30] Certainly, defamation of non-religious beliefs including atheism has not received any such consideration or concern.

24 See for instance, Commission on Human Rights resolutions 1999/82 of 30 April 1999, 2000/84 of 26 April 2000, 2001/4 of 18 April 2001, 2002/9 of 15 April 2002, 2003/4 of 14 April 2003, 2004/6 of 13 April 2004, and 2005/3 of 12 April 2005. Also see Human Rights Council resolutions 4/9 of 30 March 2007, 7/19 of 27 March 2008 and 10/22 of 26 March 2009.

25 *Report of Special Rapporteurs*, above n 2 [8 and 17], in which the Special Rapporteurs note the close links between defamation of religion and freedom of expression.

26 Ibid [27 and 36].

27 *Report of the Human Rights Council*, HRC Res 16/18, UN Doc A/66/53 (24 March 2011). See, however, *Wingrove v the United Kingdom*, Application No. 17419/90 (26 November 1996). In that case the European Court of Human Rights invoked the notion of protecting "religious feelings" to support a total ban on a video containing content depicting sexual conduct between individuals revered in Christianity, which was deemed blasphemous under British law. The Court reasoned that the video would "outrage the feelings of Christians".

28 Dennis De Jong, 'Freedom of Religion in Light of Recent Challenges', in Nazila Ghanea, Alan Stephens and Raphael Walden (eds), *Does God Believe in Human Rights?* (Martinus Nijhoff Publishers, 2007) 182, 193.

29 Given that impetus to combat defamation of religion has risen at times when some consider their religion to be particularly defamed, it is possible that the issue could emerge again. Indeed, there was a push to reintroduce the notion to the Human Rights Council following the release of 'The Innocence of Muslims' on YouTube in late 2013, which insulted Mohammed and sparked violence throughout the world resulting in many deaths. See Brett G. Scharffs, 'International Law and the Defamation of Religion Conundrum' (2013) 11 *The Review of Faith and International Affairs* 66, 66–67.

30 *Combating Defamation of Religions*, G.A. Res. 65/224, § III.A, UN Doc A/RES/65/224 (11 April 2011). The emphasis on Islam stands to reason in light of the role

The *Rabat Plan of Action on the prohibition of advocacy of national, racial or religious hatred that constitutes incitement to discrimination, hostility or violence* was launched by the United Nations High Commissioner for Human Rights in February of 2013. That plan – which Jeroen Temperman considers a sensible path towards shifting attention away from blasphemy laws towards taking incitement seriously – offers six test questions to determine whether conduct amounts to 'incitement' warranting prohibition.[31] Those questions relate to the severity of the speech, the intent of the speaker, the content of the speech, the extent of the speech, and the context of the speech, as well as the likelihood that the speech will cause harm. Quite rightly, the questions do not touch on the traits of the hated person.[32] But in practice, a pro-religious approach is taken to article 20 to show more concern about hatred of some people over others.

2. Pro-religious bias of article 20

> "*Nobody has ever really believed in freedom of religion. Where religion is concerned, the hardest virtue is tolerance, and to find out what a person's religion is one has only to discover what he becomes violent about.*"[33]

In 2010, the General Assembly, noted

> with deep concern the serious instances of intolerance, discrimination and acts of violence based on religion or belief, intimidation and coercion motivated by extremism, religious or otherwise, occurring in many parts of the world, including cases motivated by Islamophobia, Judeophobia and Christianophobia...[34]

of the Organisation of Islamic Conference in promoting resolutions on defamation of religion and its professed aim to "protect and defend the true image of Islam, to combat defamation of Islam and encourage dialogue among civilizations and religions." See http://www.oicun.org/2/23/ accessed 22 March 2017. In 2011, the Special Rapporteurs on religion and belief, and racism, racial discrimination, xenophobia and related intolerance sent a joint letter to the United States of America concerning the alleged burning of the Koran by Church members of the Dove World Outreach Center. It was unclear from that letter how this act constituted a violation of the article 18 rights of members of the Islamic community. Reference: Allegation Letter G/SO 214 (78–15) G/SO 214 (56–23) USA 4/2011 (24 March 2011).

31 Jeroen Temperman, 'Blasphemy, Defamation of Religion, Religious Hate Speech' in Silvio Ferrari (ed.), *Routledge Handbook of Law and Religion* (Routledge, 2015) 390.

32 *The Rabat Plan of Action on the prohibition of advocacy of national, racial or religious hatred that constitutes incitement to discrimination, hostility or violence*, UN Doc A/HRC/22/17/Add.4, annex, appendix (11 January 2013) [29]. Also see *Report of the Special Rapporteur on freedom of religion or belief, Heiner Bielefeldt*, UN Doc A/HRC/25/58 (26 December 2013).

33 W. H. Auden, 'Port and nuts with the Eliots' (on 'Notes towards the definition of culture' by T. S. Eliot) *New Yorker*, 17 July 1948.

34 *Combating Defamation of Religions*, G.A. Res. 65/224, § III.A, UN Doc A/RES/65/224 (11 April 2011). Also see Commission on Human Rights, *Resolution 2005/40*

But what of the intolerance and violence motivated by phobia of people who are not Muslims, Jews or Christians? Even former Special Rapporteur Heiner Bielefeldt notes that none of the many resolutions echoing such concern since have mentioned Bahaiophobia in response to the persecution Baha'is endure, or others including Jehovah's Witnesses, as well as non-theistic, atheistic and agnotistic adherents.[35] In that context, Bielefeldt notes that this "limited tolerance" mirrors Islamic tolerance of "religions of a book", being the three monotheistic religions of Judaism, Christianity and Islam, exempting polytheists, atheists and converts from Islam. This narrow focus, he contends, is reflected today in the votes of Islamic countries (and other countries that recognise only a narrow list of religions) at UN forums where religious questions arise, and is contrary to the universalism of international human rights law which attaches to human beings on the basis of their human dignity, not on the basis of their religion or belief.[36] The question must be asked, then, whether article 20 confronts the hate speech issued by those who belong to those religions in defence of those who do not?

At the outset it must be acceded that hatred itself may be sometimes justified. While hatred on the basis of race is always illogical in light of the arbitrariness of birth and the irrelevance of the components of DNA that comprise skin colour, hatred on the basis of religion may be based on more substantial considerations pertaining to a person's actions, character, choices and treatment of others. Peter Cumper concurs that "a blanket repudiation of 'hatred' is open to question".[37] While racial hatred is inevitably irrational and should never be condoned, "there may be occasions where toleration of *religious* hatred is permissible."[38] He raises examples of beliefs of sects that permit young children to be severely beaten to have evil spirits exorcised from their bodies, to which hatred, he argues, is an appropriate reaction, and religious groups that engage in child sacrifice or teach that murder is a sacred duty.[39] It could be argued that not only is hatred an "appropriate response" to such beliefs and practices, but also that it is perhaps necessary; tolerance is *prima facie* a virtue, but it is unacceptable to tolerate intolerable practices. On this point, Abrahamic religions and human rights agree. But while rights advocates may hate those people that violate rights, religious advocates may hate people on far broader grounds; followers of many faiths are exhorted to hate 'sin' and perpetrators of evil, or people who reject God.[40] Indeed, Dennis de Jong believes most religions or beliefs can be interpreted as

on Elimination of All Forms of Intolerance and of Discrimination Based on Religion or Belief, UN Doc E/CN.4/RES/2005/40 (19 April 2005) [6].

35 Heiner Bielefeldt, 'Misconceptions about Freedom of Religion or Belief' (2013) 35 *Human Rights Quarterly* 33, 35–36.

36 Ibid 36–37.

37 Peter Cumper, 'Inciting Religious Hatred: Balancing Free Speech and Religious Sensibilities in a Multi-Faith Society', in Nazila Ghanea, Alan Stephens and Raphael Walden (eds), *Does God Believe in Human Rights?* (Martinus Nijhoff Publishers, 2007) 249.

38 Ibid.

39 Ibid.

40 Ibid 248.

permitting violence to follow hatred, pointing to the Crusades and colonialism of Christianity, the *jihad* of Islam, and the Hindutva or radical Buddhism, noting that "such religiously inspired violence is in direct conflict with international human rights and humanitarian law."[41]

Aside from the fact that hatred (whether of or by the religious) is in some circumstances warranted, hatred cannot of itself be practically prohibited; hatred itself as an internal feeling is not and cannot be prohibited, but 'incitement' to discrimination, hostility or violence must be. The challenge is that the circumstances in which hatred is warranted differ in religious and rights perspectives, as does the tipping point at which such hatred can be considered incitement. Some religious teachings may promote hatred of certain people (homosexuals for instance, perhaps Jews, or maybe infidels or non-white races).[42] Here the conflict between manifestation of religion and other human rights becomes immediately apparent; while such hatred could be prohibited on the basis that it incites discrimination or violence against the object of hatred, from a religious point of view such hatred may constitute a fundamental part of the belief in question and therefore be protected as a religious manifestation. Consider, for instance, the rights of a woman leaving an abortion clinic who is subject to hateful taunts from Christian fundamentalist pro-life advocates who accuse her of a being a murderer destined for hell. Is human rights law, particularly article 20 of the ICCPR, adequately equipped and applied to address this conflict?

Jurisprudence and academic literature on religious hatred primarily concern hatred *of* the religious rather than hatred *by* the religious. In 2006, Asma Jahangir, then the Special Rapporteur for Freedom of Religion and Belief, expressed the concern that "[i]ntolerance of any form or expression of religion is becoming a very negative outcome of certain forms of radical secularism."[43] This said, in the same year Special Rapporteurs of both freedom of expression and freedom of religion and belief jointly issued a report touching on this issue of hate speech originating in religious expression.[44] Its authors note that expressions directed against religious and belief communities "are not necessarily secularists, but also members of religious communities. Religious groups and communities are therefore not only the target of critical forms of expression but also in many cases the origin."[45] This acknowledgement that religious individuals or communities may be the source of hateful expressions is a welcome development. However, the statement would have been more appropriate had it been issued without the suggestive comment that the authors of such expressions are "not necessarily

41 De Jong, above n 28, 190.

42 Multiple grounds of hatred may be evoked at once; sexual minorities in Bangladesh are often viewed as 'atheists' as their conduct is seen to contravene religious mores, notwithstanding that they may be religious. Heiner Bielefeldt, Nazila Ghanea and Michael Weiner, *Freedom of Religion and Belief: An International Law Commentary* (Oxford, 2016) 386.

43 *Report of Special Rapporteurs*, above n 2, 6.

44 Ibid.

45 Ibid 8 [25].

secularists" for the same reason it would have been inappropriate and borderline discriminatory to say 'Muslims are not necessarily radicals'.

Three years later, in her last general report to the Human Rights Council, Asma Jahangir took her final opportunity as Special Rapporteur to express strong concerns about hate speech. In doing so she noted that preaching of hatred by religious leaders is an indicator of incitement to discrimination, hostility or violence, and expressed her increasing concern about discrimination and violence incited and perpetrated on the grounds or in the name of religion, often against those who are dispassionate about religion.[46] In 2016, outgoing Special Rapporteur Heiner Bielefeldt noted in even stronger terms in his final interim report, that governments often fail to protect religious minorities from hate crimes, and may even themselves act as guardians of religious doctrines against so-called 'unbelievers', 'heretics' and people demonstrating religiously 'deviant' behaviour contrary to the universality of freedom of religion and belief.[47]

But this increased concern has not been met with increased jurisprudence. The lack of cases brought by victims of hate speech *from* a religious basis represents a failing of the international human rights framework to present and promote itself as accessible not only to people whose religious beliefs have been attacked but also to those who have been attacked by religious beliefs. It may also speak to the grave danger such potential authors would face in attempts to exhaust domestic channels before having recourse to international mechanisms. Similarly, while concern is expressed over anti-Semitic, anti-Islamic acts and hatred of other religious groups, there is a lack of Concluding Observations on religious hatred by religious groups of the irreligious or atheists for their lack of belief or rejection of religion.[48]

2.1. Hatred in the name of religion

That religious beliefs may be sources of hate speech is borne out in the fact that there is sometimes a positive link between religiosity and prejudice.[49] Social scientists define fundamentalists as those who believe "that one religion uniquely represents the fundamental truth, that this truth is opposed by evil, and that only followers of this religion have the desired relationship with God".[50] Defined thus, it can be said that "[a]ll religions are to a greater or lesser extent 'fundamentalist'

46 *Report of the Special Rapporteur on freedom of religion or belief, Asma Jahangir*, UN Doc A/HRC/13/40 (29 December 2009) [28].

47 *Interim report of the Special Rapporteur on freedom of religion or belief, Heiner Bielefeldt*, UN Doc A/71/269 (2 August 2016) [27].

48 See for instance, Egypt, ICCPR, A/58/40 vol. I (2002) 31 at 77(18); Israel, ICCPR, A/58/40 vol. I (2003) 64 at para. 85(20).

49 Deborah Jones Merritt & Daniel C Merritt, 'The Future of Religious Pluralism: Justice O'Connor and the Establishment Clause' (2007) 39 *Arizona State Law Journal* 895, 926.

50 Lynne M Jackson & Bruce Hunsberger, 'An Intergroup Perspective on Religion and Prejudice' (1999) 38 *Journal for Scientific Study Religion* 509, 512.

in character in that they recognise that theirs is the just rule, the correct avenue to truth."[51] Beyond this unavoidable element of fundamentalism in worldviews, researchers have found a correlation between religiosity and prejudice based on religion or belief, race, ethnicity, sexual orientation, gender and several other characteristics.[52] Research has also revealed a negative relationship between religiosity and 'universalism', defined as "[u]nderstanding, appreciation, tolerance and protection for the welfare of all people and for nature".[53] It logically follows that the more 'fundamental' a person is in his or her beliefs, the less likely he is to be tolerant and subscribe to values of pluralism.

While it can be acceded that the relationship between religion and violence is not 'immediate' but is brought about by actors who invoke religion or religious tenets to incite violence,[54] it is worth considering the fuel they use to fan such flames. Because certain passages of the Bible and the Koran can be used as tools of incitement to hatred, hate speech legislation in many countries provides for exceptions when the speech concerned is quoted from a religious text to the detriment of its targets.[55] For instance, in 2012 a UK preacher, Michael Overd, was acquitted of charges of homophobic hate crime after he approached a gay couple in the street and told them they were sinners who would burn in hell. He asserted that he was only quoting passages from the Bible in accordance with his free expression.[56] Amos N. Guiora points to a more blatant example of incitement, being the religious hate speech of prominent rabbis directed at former Israeli Prime Minister Yitzak Rabin in the lead up to his assassination in 1995. Religious justifications for Rabin's murder had been discussed at conferences, appropriate methods to kill him were published, and rabbis chanted outside his house that he be put to death, yet none was prosecuted following his murder. Guiora considers

51 Patrick Thornberry, *International Law and the Rights of Minorities* (Clarendon Press, 1991) 324.

52 See for instance, Bruce Hunsberger and Lynne M. Jackson, 'Religion, Meaning and Prejudice' (2005) 61 *Journal of Social Issues* 807, 811.

53 Shalom H. Schwartz and Sipke Huismans, 'Value Priorities and Religiosity in Four Western Religions' (1995) 58 *Social Psychology Quarterly* 88, 90. The authors found a negative relationship across four religious faiths (Protestantism, Judaism, Roman Catholicism and Greek Orthodoxy).

54 *Report of the Special Rapporteur on Freedom of Religion or Belief, Heiner Bielefeldt*, UN Doc A/HRC/28/66 (29 December 2014) [15].

55 For instance, section 8 of the Australian *Racial and Religious Tolerance Act 2011* prohibits inciting hatred on the ground of another religious belief or activity of another person. Section 11 provides an exception where the conduct was in good faith for a religious purpose, including conveying or teaching a religion or proselytising. Temperman also notes that Georgia, FYR Macedonia, Malta and Slovakia prohibit advocacy of only racial or ethnic hatred, but not religious hatred. Temperman, above n 2, 77.

56 See 'Gay men told they would burn in hell by preacher', *BBC News*, 9 February 2012, http://www.bbc.co.uk/news/uk-england-somerset-16967037 and 'Michael Overd cleared of verbally abusing gay men in Taunton', *BBC News*, 10 February 2012, http://www.bbc.co.uk/news/uk-england-somerset-16984133 both accessed 22 March 2017.

this failing symptomatic of too permissive a view of free expression that should have been limited for inciting violence.[57]

Peter Cumper agrees that there are several passages of religious texts which, where taken literally, are "capable of inciting hatred on the grounds of religion".[58] Examples of such passages include the following:

> Those who (knowingly) conceal and reject Our Revelations, We Will land them in a Fire to roast there. Every time their skins are burnt off, We will replace them with other skins, that they may taste the punishment. Surely God is All Glorious with irresistible might, All Wise.[59]
>
> If your very own brother, or your son or daughter, or the wife you love, or your closest friend secretly entices you, saying, 'Let us go and worship other gods'...do not yield to him or listen to him. Show him no pity. Do not spare him or shield him. You must certainly put him to death. Your hand must be the first in putting him to death, and then the hands of all people. Stone him to death, because he tried to turn you away from the Lord your God...[60]

Notwithstanding the substantive basis for hate speech that religious texts provide, it is neither possible nor desirable to criminalise quoting from them; doing so would breach freedom of religion and expression of countless individuals and deprive humanity of the goods of its cultural heritage. Rather, consideration must be given not only to the content of the scripture in question but to the inciting effect of expressing it in a particular context. The fact that religious expressions can amount to hate speech was acknowledged at the domestic level in 2002 when a UK court found a man guilty of inciting racial hatred for having distributed leaflets containing quotations from the 'Hadith' calling upon on Muslims to fight and kill Jews.[61] The defendant's submission that he had merely been quoting from a religious text, was rejected by Justice McCullen on the basis that "words created 1400 years ago are equally capable of containing race hate as words created today."[62] Indeed, the very suggestion that the power of the words in the Koran has diluted over time would itself be an affront to the religious beliefs of many.

Ultimately, what matters is whether a statement in context is capable of inciting hatred; the fact that a source of a statement is religious should not change its characterisation as inciting discrimination, hostility or violence. A telling example is found in the 2006 Australian case of *Catch the Fire Ministries Inc and Ors v Islamic Council of Victoria Inc and Attorney-General for the State of Victoria* at

57 Amos N. Guiora, *Freedom from Religion* (Oxford University Press, 2009) 32–38.
58 Cumper, above n 37, 247.
59 *Koran*, Surah 4, Women, Verse 56.
60 *Bible*, Deuteronomy 13:6–10.
61 While domestic courts do not make international law decisions, their decisions have significant bearing on the interpretation and enforcement of international law, including human rights law.
62 'Muslim guilty of inciting racial hatred', *BBC News*, 3 May 2002, accessed 22 March 2017, http://news.bbc.co.uk/2/hi/uk_news/england/1966839.stm.

the Victorian Supreme Court of Appeal (hereafter the Catch the Fire Case).[63] The appeal case followed from proceedings at the lower Victorian Civil & Administrative Tribunal (VCAT) instituted by the Islamic Council of Victoria. The Islamic Council alleged that the Catch the Fire Ministries had contravened section 8(1) of the *Racial and Religious Tolerance Act 2001*, which states that:

> A person must not, on the ground of the religious belief or activity of another person or class of persons, engage in conduct that incites hatred against, serious contempt for, or revulsion or severe ridicule of, that other person or class of persons.

The Islamic Council argued that statements of a Catch the Fire pastor at a gospel assembly, a newsletter written by another, and an article on its website incited hatred against, serious contempt for, or revulsion or severe ridicule of the Islamic faith. The tribunal agreed. Catch the Fire Ministries appealed to the Supreme Court on a number of grounds, including that the tribunal erred in its construction of section 8 and that a number of the tribunal's findings were not substantiated by evidence. The Supreme Court found that the lower court erred in pointing to evidence that offence had been caused as proof that hatred had been incited. Similarly, the tribunal's characterisation of the Catch the Fire Ministries' comments as being false and unbalanced were beside the point. In this context Justice Nettle noted that:

> Statements about the religious beliefs of a group of persons could be completely false and utterly unbalanced and yet do nothing to incite hatred of those who adhere to those beliefs. At the same time, statements about the religious beliefs of a group of persons could be wholly true and completely balanced and yet be almost certain to incite hatred of the group because of those beliefs. In any event, who is to say what is accurate or balanced about religious beliefs?…In my view it was calculated to lead to error for a secular tribunal to attempt to assess the theological propriety of what was asserted at the Seminar.[64]

The Supreme Court also noted that the tribunal failed to distinguish between hate speech directed at religious beliefs, and that directed at holders of those beliefs.[65] To establish incitement of hatred contrary to section 8, the former was wholly irrelevant. The expressions at issue had to attack Muslims themselves to incite hatred of them; the expressions here were found to have attacked Islamic beliefs with the aim of encouraging Christians to share the Christian faith with them.[66]

63 *Catch the Fire Ministries Inc & Ors v Islamic Council of Victoria Inc* [2006] VSCA 284 (14 December 2006).
64 Ibid [36].
65 Ibid [76].
66 Ibid [90].

The Supreme Court ordered that another tribunal member hear the case again without further evidence. The Supreme Court's reasoning is commendable for acknowledging that while viewpoints emanating from a religious position may not be balanced or fair, they do not necessarily amount to hate speech. In lay terms, the decision upholds the valuable notion that the entitlement to criticise another person's religious belief is an essential ingredient in freedom of expression and freedom of religion and belief. Justice Nettle explained that section 8 does not prohibit statements about religious beliefs as such, even where they may offend or insult. Rather, section 8 is to be applied against *incitement*.[67]

In keeping with the focus of this monograph on the extent to which atheists and non-believers enjoy freedom of religion and belief relative to their religious counterparts, Justice Nettle's statement confirms that expressions criticising religion must not be repressed. However, section 8 of the *Racial and Religious Tolerance Act 2001* prohibits vilification of a person or class of persons on the ground of "religious belief". Irrespective of the fact that the Islamic Council was ultimately unsuccessful in its claim, it had standing to bring the issue before VCAT. If Catch the Fire Ministries had targeted atheists on the basis of their beliefs, they may have had no such recourse to the *Racial and Religious Tolerance Act*. At the international level, article 20 of the ICCPR suffers from the same failing.

2.2. Homophobia: Prohibited discrimination or a religious right?

The failings of article 20 to address all forms of hate are particularly evident when considered in the light of hatred of gays and lesbians, or homophobia. Their plight showcases the particular advantage that religious actors have in international human rights law. Incitement to violence in the name of religion against people on the basis of sexual orientation has emanated from religious leaders and authorities, manifesting in organised violence, family violence and even curative 'gang rapes'.[68] While rights-based understanding of non-discrimination in international law has broadened to capture grounds of gender and sexuality,[69] hatred directed at them on the basis of their sexuality remains uncaptured by article 20, as sexual orientation is not entailed by nationality, race or religion.

Clashes between religious precepts and human rights principles are evident with respect to religious views about gays and lesbians, or perhaps more specifically, about gay and lesbian sexual activities. Several passages of the Bible explicitly state or imply that homosexuality is sinful. Indeed, a lay reader of certain passages could construe Bible morality as teaching that gang rape of a woman is far less sinful than men having consensual sex with one another. When Lot was hosting male visitors (actually incognito angels sent by God), men from all over the city of

67 Ibid [15].

68 *Report of the Special Rapporteur on Freedom of Religion or Belief, Heiner Bielefeldt*, UN Doc A/HRC/28/66 (29 December 2014) [11]

69 *Discriminatory Laws and Practices and Acts of Violence against Individuals Based on Their Sexual Orientation and Gender Identity: Report of the United Nations High Commissioner for Human Rights*, UN Doc A/HRC/19/41 (17 November 2011).

Sodom surrounded the house, and called to Lot: "Where are the men who came to you tonight? Bring them out to us so that we can have sex with them."[70] Lot bravely confronted the men, and said, "No, my friends. Don't do this wicked thing. Look, I have two daughters who have never slept with a man. Let me bring them out to you, and you do can what you like with them. But don't do anything to these men, for they have come under the protection of my roof." In the end, the daughters were spared from being gang-raped; the angels told Lot to flee with his family and God destroyed every living thing (including the vegetation) in the city.[71]

The girls in the book of Judges did not fare so well. In a similar story therein, men of the city also demanded that male visitors be presented for sex. The host of the visiting men went outside and said, "No, my friends, don't be so vile. Since this man is my guest, don't do this disgraceful thing. Look, here is my virgin daughter and his [the guest's] concubine. I will bring them out to you now, and you can use them and do whatever you wish. But to this man, don't do such a disgraceful thing."[72] The man who was under threat sent his concubine outside in place of himself, "and they raped her and abused her throughout the night and at dawn they let her go".[73] The woman's 'master' who had given her over to be gang-raped found her in the morning collapsed at the door. He said to her, "Get up; let's go."[74] Discovering that she was dead, he loaded her body on his donkey and upon arriving at home, cut it into twelve parts that he sent to different areas of Israel.[75]

The 'correct' interpretation of such passages is difficult to ascertain. Is the message that rape of a man is a worse crime than rape of a woman? That a male visitor is to be afforded more protection than one's own daughter? That the dead body of a rape victim should be dismembered and dispersed?[76] Readings of such passages have been attempted in a way that does not condemn homosexuals or homosexual acts. Notably, in 1980 John Boswell sought to enhance interpretation of the Scriptures with wider Christian scholarship. In his view, the sins of the Sodomites had naught to do with homosexuality. As condemnation of homosexuality is relatively recent with early Christian literature essentially silent on the issue, Boswell instead argues that the moral of the story of Sodom does not concern sins of the flesh, but rather concerns general wickedness, chief among

70 *Bible*, Genesis 19:5.

71 *Bible*, Genesis 19:23–26. Lot's family was spared, other than his wife who defied instructions not to look back when she was fleeing and was turned into a pillar of salt for doing so. Curiously, Lot ended up hiding in a cave with his daughters who got him drunk and took turns having sex with him so the family line could continue (*Bible*, Genesis 19:30–38).

72 *Bible*, Judges 19:23–24.

73 *Bible*, Judges 19:25.

74 *Bible*, Judges 19:28.

75 *Bible*, Judges 19:28–29.

76 See Rehman and Polymenopoulou's interpretation that these passages and their equivalent in Koranic Surah XI are a condemnation not of homosexuality but of lust. Javaid Rehman and Eleni Polymenopoulou, 'Is Green a Part of the Rainbow? *Sharia*, Homosexuality, and LGBT Rights in the Muslim World' 27 *Fordham International Law Journal* (2013–2014) 1, 14–18.

them being inhospitality.[77] According to Boswell, in the few places where homosexual acts are explicitly mentioned (including Leviticus 18:22 and 20:13) it is considered ritually unclean (like eating pork, or sex during menstruation) but not intrinsically evil (such as rape or theft).[78] Indeed, Leviticus 20:13 reads:

> If a man lies with a man as one lies with a woman, both of them have done what is detestable. They must be put to death; their blood will be on their own heads.[79]

And Corinthians 6:9–10 states that:

> Neither the sexually immoral nor idolaters nor adulterers nor male prostitutes nor homosexual offenders nor thieves nor the greedy nor drunkards nor slanderers nor swindlers will inherit the kingdom of God.[80]

Regardless of whatever precise 'meaning' is to be inferred from these passages, several interpretations conclude that the Bible is at least antithetical to homosexuality.[81]

The Koran has also offered its readers fodder for disapproving of homosexuals and their sexuality:

> What! will you continue to come with lust to men in place of women? You are indeed an ignorant people with no sense (of decency and right and wrong).[82]

In relation to gay sex, the Hadith also instructs:

> Kill the one that is doing it and also kill the one that it is being done to.

Here again, there is a spectrum of interpretations of such passages, ranging from those concluding that homosexuality is abominable,[83] to others that suggest there are positive references to sexual diversity in the Koran.[84] In June of 2016, the then

77 John Boswell, *Christianity, Social Tolerance, and Homosexuality: Gay People in Western Europe from the Beginning of the Christian Era to the Fourteenth Century* (University of Chicago Press, 1980) 92–99.
78 Ibid 100.
79 *Bible*, Leviticus 20:13.
80 *Bible*, 1 Corinthians 6:9–10.
81 See Dawne Moon, 'Beyond the Dichotomy: Six Religious Views of Homosexuality' 61 *Journal of Homosexuality* 1215, 1216. Moon sets out religious views of homosexuality in Jewish and Christian thought in the United States.
82 *Koran*, Surah 27:55.
83 Rehman and Polymenopoulou, above n 76, 1, 10–12 in which the authors note the unanimity of Islamic schools of thought that homosexuality is forbidden and punishable by death or flogging.
84 For instance, Javaid Rehman, referred to in *Conference Summary: Freedom of Religion and Belief and Sexuality, Organized by the United Nations Special Rapporteur on*

UN Special Rapporteur on Freedom of Religion and Belief, in partnership with 'Muslims for Progressive Values', held a three-day conference on freedom of religion and belief and sexuality, that ambitiously sought to examine conflicts between freedom of religion and the rights of lesbian, gay, bisexual, transgender and intersex (LGBTI) people.[85] That conference discussed the challenges of interpreting the source of Islamic law – the Koran and the Hadith – and of distinguishing between divine inspiration and political interpretations.[86] Also mentioned at that conference was the work of the Justice Project in which Islamic scholars advocate for social justice addressing discrimination on the basis of sexual orientation, gender identity or expression, while challenging the dominance of literalist interpretations of the Koran and Hadith.[87] Such efforts to reinterpret challenging texts in a way that is rights-accordant are to be commended. But it is not the solution for international law. The language of law is not the language of theology. What is relevant to the human rights of gays, lesbians, bisexual, transgender and other rights-holders, is not religious scholarship *per se*, but legal scholarship and the credence it gives to religious interpretations of expressions in making its own interpretations of human rights outcomes.

Domestic law sheds light on how international human rights are unpacked in practice. In 2005 in Sweden, evangelical Christian pastor, Åke Green, was issued with a month-long prison sentence for his comments about homosexuals. The conviction was quashed on appeal with the Appellate court finding that Green's sermon on homosexuality could not be considered incitement against homosexuals, but simply as a sermon faithful to the Bible.[88] In his sermon, Green had referred to homosexual acts (and other "sexual abnormalities") as a "cancerous tumour" on society and implied that homosexuals were more likely than heterosexuals to rape children and animals. The fact that this comment was made in reference to the acts rather than the people performing them was argued by Green as absolving him from having expressed hate speech.[89] The Supreme Court confirmed that the statements made by Green and the context in which he expressed them showed "contempt" for homosexuals, but fell short of hate speech.[90] Indeed, the Supreme Court noted that "the way he expressed himself perhaps cannot be

Freedom of Religion or Belief and Muslims for Progressive Values (Muslims for Progressive Values, 2016) 23. Also see Rehman and Polymenopoulou, above n 76, 1, 25–28 on the appreciation of sexual diversity in the Koran.

85 See *Conference Summary: Freedom of Religion and Belief and Sexuality, Organized by the United Nations Special Rapporteur on Freedom of Religion or Belief and Muslims for Progressive Values* (Muslims for Progressive Values, 2016).

86 Ibid 7–9.

87 Ibid 12. Also see Arash Naraghi, 'The Quran and Human Rights of Sexual Minorities' in *Lesbian, Gay, Bisexual and Transgender Rights in Iran* (International Gay and Lesbian Rights Commission, 2015) 29–55.

88 Cumper, above n 37, 248. Also see http://www.akegreen.org/.

89 The sermon delivered by Pastor Åke Green can be read at http://www.akegreen.org/en-2-left/en-2-9.htm.

90 *Prosecutor General v Green* (Supreme Court, Sweden) Appeal Judgment, Case No B, 1050–05, ILDC 200 (SE 2005) (29 November 2005) 8.

deemed that much more derogatory than the wording of the Bible verses in question."[91] In its reasoning, the Court considered what the European Court of Human Rights would decide if it was asked to do so, and came to the conclusion that it would consider the limitations imposed on Green to be disproportionate. Green's sermon, the Supreme Court reasoned, was based on a theme contained in the Bible, and the legitimacy of that belief was not a question for the court.[92]

It is a shame that neither the European Court of Human Rights nor the HRC was given the opportunity to consider this case. The Supreme Court of Sweden may be correct in its predictions as to what the European Court would hypothetically decide, but it is submitted here that if Green had said in his speech that Islamic practices were a 'cancerous growth' on the body of society, or that Jews will 'force themselves upon animals' or 'corrupt young boys', then the group targeted by Green's assertions would have achieved protection under the Swedish justice system, the ECHR and the ICCPR, owing to its pro-religious bias.

The Supreme Court's decision to acquit Green, whose controversial expressions were biblically based and therefore 'religious' expressions, supports the key submission of this chapter: hatred that is inspired by religion is met with less interference than hatred that is not.[93] Dennis de Jong has commented on the privileged position of religious manifestations in a number of cases in the Netherlands concerning Islamic and Christian teachings or publications condemning homosexuality. Such manifestations, he notes, were generally held to be consistent with international and national law providing that they only concerned religious precepts for the followers of that particular religion.[94] But, he noted, if the sermons or literature advocate persecution of homosexuals who do not belong to the same religion or belief, such manifestations are not protected by freedom of religion and belief, but are to be prohibited by article 20.[95] The implication is that human rights law should not intervene where a gay Christian, Jew or Muslim is persecuted by fellow Christians, Jews or Muslims.

A more recent decision of the Derby Crown Court in the United Kingdom resulted in the prosecution of three men for hate speech against gays, which they expressed from the perspective of their religious beliefs. In advance of an upcoming gay pride parade, a group of five Muslim men distributed flyers to passers-by in the vicinity of their mosque and posted them through doors and letterboxes. The flyer contained passages from the Koran, a picture of a wooden mannequin hanging from a noose, and read 'Death Penalty?'[96] On 20 January 2012, three of

91 Ibid 15–16.
92 Ibid.
93 The above-mentioned acquittal of Michael Overd is one such example.
94 De Jong, above n 28, 194.
95 Ibid.
96 'Convictions show society won't tolerate homophobia', *Derby Telegraph*, 21 January 2012, accessed 22 March 2017, http://www.derbytelegraph.co.uk/convictions-society-won-t-tolerate-homophobia/story-14994895-detail/story.html.

the five men were found guilty of inciting hatred and sentenced to prison.[97] The case was the first in the UK to apply an amendment to the *Public Order Act* of 1986, which by virtue of the *Criminal Justice and Immigration Act* of 2008, criminalised acts intended to "stir up hatred on the grounds of sexual orientation".[98] By prosecuting the defendants in this case, the court confirmed that religious expressions could incite hatred against gays on the basis of their sexual orientation. In this situation, domestic law was available to the court to enable them to make a decision accordingly. At the international level though, hatred directed at gays from religious standpoints is not captured by article 20 because homosexuals are a group defined by their sexual orientation rather than by their nationality, race or religion.

Limiting prohibitions of incitement on the basis of the grounds of hatred disfavours rights-holders who are hated for unlisted traits, and privileges certain groups by protecting them from hatred. Hatred that incites discrimination, hostility or violence that is not based on a person's nationality, race or religion, then, is not prohibited. In short, setting the limits of article 20 in terms of hated traits rather than the nature and extent of the hatred and its inciting effect serves to condone hate speech directed at some people for some reasons.

However, there is some sign that lesbian, gay, bisexual, transgender and intersex (LGBTI) people are increasingly being given attention by the international human rights community. In 2006, the HRC expressed concern over violent crimes against sexual minorities in the US and requested that such crimes be included in federal hate crime legislation, though it cited articles 2 and 26 in doing so, rather than article 20.[99] In Concluding Observations on Sweden in 2009, the HRC spoke of homophobic and racial hate crimes, citing articles 20 and 26 in relation to the latter.[100] A year later in 2010, the HRC noted the rise in hate speech directed at LGBT people in Poland and recommended that the state amend its penal code to include hate speech based on sexual orientation.[101] In the year before, the HRC named "religious leaders" among those manifesting hate speech against LGBT people in the Russian Federation, alongside public officials and the media, although it made this comment in relation to article 26 (protection from discrimination), not article 20 protection from hate speech.[102] In more recent

97 'Derby men guilty over gay hate leaflets', *BBC News*, 20 January 2012, accessed 22 March 2017 http://www.bbc.co.uk/news/uk-england-derbyshire-16656679.

98 *Criminal Justice and Immigration Act 2008* (UK), section 74.

99 Human Rights Committee, *Consideration of reports submitted by States Parties under article 40 of the Covenant*, UN Doc CCPR/C/USA/CO/3, 87th Sess. (10–28 July 2006) [25].

100 Human Rights Committee, *Consideration of reports submitted by States Parties under article 40 of the Covenant*, UN Doc CCPR/C/SWE/CO/6, 95th Sess. (7 May 2009) [19].

101 Human Rights Committee, *Consideration of reports submitted by States parties under article 4 of the Covenant, Concluding Observations of the Human Rights Committee*, UN Doc CCPR/C/POL/CO/6, 100th Sess. (15 November 2010) [8].

102 Human Rights Committee, *Consideration of reports submitted by States parties under article 40 of the Covenant*, UN Doc CCRP/C/RUS/C/6, 97th Sess. (24 November 2009) [27].

years, Human Rights Council Resolutions have directly concerned sexual orientation and gender identity, including in landmark Resolution 17/19 of 2011 on 'Human Rights, Sexual Orientation and Gender Identity', as well as Resolution 27/32 of 2014 and Resolution 32/2 of 2016.[103] Unfortunately none of these resolutions explicitly mentions hate speech. Ultimately, LGBTI rights-holders do not receive full protection of article 20. Instead, hate speech against them is sometimes permitted – or simply not opposed – on the grounds that it is permissible religious expression.

3. Weak protection of non-believers and atheists from hate speech

> "*Do not I hate them, O Lord, that hate thee? And am not I grieved with those that rise up against thee? I hate them with perfect hatred: I count them mine enemies.*"
>
> Psalms 139:21–22

In light of the pro-religious bias established above, it is necessary to consider whether or not vilification of non-believers or atheists can constitute religious hatred. If this form of hatred were to fall between the gaps of article 20, a severe failing of the ICCPR would be evident in its inability to equally protect people of all religions and beliefs, including non-belief and atheism.

Vilification of all non-believers is a difficult form of hatred to address within article 20, largely because such vilification is not necessarily targeted at particular non-believers, but rather at those who subscribe to any religion or belief that is different to that of the person or people inciting hatred. That is, the hatred may not be targeted at a distinct group but an amorphous, non-cohesive group. Neither General Comment 11 on article 20, nor HRC jurisprudence provide guidance on whether or not the prohibition of religious hatred extends to those with non-theistic and atheistic beliefs, and those who profess no religion or belief at all. Indeed it would seem that the broad understanding of religious freedom as protecting all religions and beliefs has been forgotten at this crossroads of freedom from hate and freedom of religion. And yet there are certainly religious expressions that direct hatred specifically towards non-religious and atheistic rights-holders. For example, the Bible instructs:

> Do not be yoked together with unbelievers. For what do righteousness and wickedness have in common? or what fellowship can light have with darkness?

103 Human Rights Council Resolution 17/19, Rep. of the Human Rights Council, 17th Sess., May 31–June 17, 2011, UN Doc. A/HRC/17/L.9/Rev.1 (15 June 2011); Human Rights Council Resolution 32/2, Rep. of the Human Rights Council, 27th Session, UN Doc. A/HRC/RES/27/32 (2 October 2014); and Human Rights Council Resolution 32/2, Rep. of the Human Rights Council, 32nd Sess., 30 June 2016, UN Doc. A/HRC/RES/32/2 (15 July 2016). It is notable that many states parties were against these resolutions; all three passed with an almost equivalent number of states in favour of the resolutions as there were states that abstained or were against them.

> ...What does a believer have in common with an unbeliever? Therefore come out from them and be separate, says the Lord. Touch no unclean thing, and I will receive you, and you will be my sons and daughters, says the Lord Almighty.[104]

Similarly, the Islamic Koran predicts a fiery finish for non-believers:

> Those who disbelieve, neither their wealth nor their offspring will avail them at all against God; they are fuel for the fire.[105]
>
> And kill them wherever you find them, and drive them out from whence they drove you out, and persecution is severer than slaughter, and do not fight with them at the Sacred Mosque until they fight with you in it, but if they do fight you, then slay them; such is the recompense of the unbelievers.[106]
>
> Let not the believers take the unbelievers for friends rather than believers; and whoever does this, he shall have nothing of (the guardianship of) Allah, but you should guard yourselves against them, guarding carefully; and Allah makes you cautious of (retribution from) Himself; and to Allah is the eventual coming.[107]

While domestic legislation in many countries is generally too narrow to explicitly protect non-believers against hatred, a wide interpretation has been made in some. One example is the UK *Racial and Religious Hatred Act 2006* which defines "religious hatred" as "hatred against a group of persons defined by reference to religious belief or lack of religious belief".[108] Tellingly, one of the concerns raised against this Act by religious groups was that it might imply that certain passages of the Koran or Bible would become illegal.[109]

Geert Wilders, a controversial right-leaning politician, made a film about jihadists who want to Islamise the West by force if necessary. His film *Fitna* was criticised for linking Islam with acts of terror and violence. After Dutch filmmakers refused to screen the film, the movie aired on the Internet as the only remaining medium available to it. Even in the free space of the World Wide Web, several hosts removed the film from their site in response to violent threats. Protestors, both Muslim and non-Muslim, took to the streets to express outrage at the views

104 *Bible*, 2 Corinthians 6:14–18.
105 *Koran*, Surah 3:10.
106 *Koran*, Surah 2.191.
107 *Koran*, Surah 3.28.
108 *Racial and Religious Hatred Act 2006* (UK) c.1, s 29A.
109 See for instance, Matthew Tempest, 'Religious hatred bill "will not harm free speech"', *Guardian*, 31 January 2006, http://www.guardian.co.uk/politics/2006/jan/31/immigrationpolicy.religion1?INTCMP=ILCNETTXT3487 and Polly Toynbee, 'What's at stake is the right to insult and cause offence', *Guardian*, 31 January 2006, http://www.guardian.co.uk/politics/2006/jan/31/religion.politicalcolumnists?INTCMP=ILCNETTXT3487 both accessed 22 March 2017.

Wilders expressed in the film.[110] However, no comparable protests arose over censorship of the film. Indeed, even the then UN Secretary General Ban Ki-moon added his condemnation of the film, saying there was no justification for hate speech inciting violence, and that "the real fault line is not between Muslim and Western societies, as some would have us believe, but between small minorities of extremists on different sides with a vested interest in stirring hostility and conflict."[111] Such criticism – expressed before the film was screened – was not aimed at people depicted in the film demanding death to non-Muslims – but at the filmmakers for making a film about them. The criticism also implies that causing offence to easily-offended people amounts to inciting violence: reasoning as tenuous as the suggestion that wearing revealing clothing provokes rape.

Regardless of whether the film is considered to be anti-Islamic or perhaps has valid points to make (an opinion about which could only be arrived at by viewing it), its suppression from discourse is disconcerting. LiveLeak.com, upon removing the film from its website out of concern for the safety of its staff, aptly summarised the triumph of violent threats by religious zealots over free speech:

> This is a sad day for freedom of speech on the net but we have to place the safety and well-being of our staff above all else. We would like to thank the thousands of people, from all backgrounds and religions, who gave us their support. They realise LiveLeak.com is a vehicle for many opinions and not just the support of one.
>
> Perhaps there is still hope that this situation may produce a discussion that could benefit and educate all of us as to how we can accept one another's culture. We stood for what we believe in, the ability to be heard, but in the end the price was too high.[112]

Since releasing the film, Geert Wilders has been living with heavy security, and in December 2016 was prosecuted for hate speech.[113] There have been calls for him to be murdered, including from Australian cleric Feiz Mohammed known for calling on Muslims to kill non-believers, and specifically to behead Wilders for

110 See for instance Foo Yun Chee, 'Dutch protest against Islam critic's Koran protest', *Reuters*, 22 March 2008, accessed 22 March 2017 http://uk.reuters.com/article/idUKL2243365220080322.

111 Secretary General Statement, 'No Justification for Hate Speech or Incitement, says Secretary-General in strong condemnation of Anti-Islamic Film', 28 March 2008, accessed 22 March 2017, http://www.un.org/News/Press/docs/2008/sgsm11483.doc.htm.

112 Thomas Claburn, 'Anti-Islamic Film Taken Offline Following Threats', *InformationWeek*, 28 March 2008, accessed 11 November 2009, http://www.informationweek.com/news/internet/showArticle.jhtml?articleID=207000505.

113 See Nina Siegal, 'Geert Wilders, Dutch far-right leader, is convicted of inciting discrimination', *New York Times*, 9 December 2016, accessed 7 March 2017 https://www.nytimes.com/2016/12/09/world/europe/geert-wilders-netherlands-trial.html?_r=0.

denigrating Islam.[114] The UN, though, has remained silent about such calls. It has also remained silent about comments calling the reputations of atheists into question. During a storm of controversy about paedophilia within the Catholic Church, Catholic Bishop Anthony Fisher, in his Easter address in Parramatta, Sydney in 2010 said:

> Last century we tried godlessness on a grand scale and the effects were devastating: Nazism, Stalinism, Pol Pot-ery, mass murder, abortion and broken relationships – all promoted by state-imposed atheism.[115]

Other than receiving widespread media coverage and criticism from the atheist and rationalist societies,[116] there was no particular response from NGOs or the state, or the international human rights community for this classification of atheism, nor was an apology forthcoming. It is hard to imagine that in 2010, this Catholic Bishop would credit any belief other than atheism with a century's mass murder without being met with accusations of vilification or at least discrimination. The question for international human rights law is whether atheists are truly respected equally alongside other non-believers who may subscribe to other religious beliefs.

The lack of concern expressed about vilification of atheists and defamation of their beliefs relative to the many statements made in favour of followers of major religions, shows that atheists are overlooked. It also may be symptomatic of the need to appease followers of major religions who are more demonstrative of criticisms of their beliefs than non-believers and atheists are. Non-religious people and atheists tend not to take to the streets in noticeable numbers or call for the deaths of those who slander their belief. But the practical and pragmatic reasons why religious people are favoured above non-religious people do not detract from the fact that they are: it adds credence to the fact of their unequal treatment. As yet there have been no complaints brought to the HRC by atheists alleging they are victims of hate speech. The lack of complaints brought by them is indicative of the blindness of international human rights law to their plight, and its underlying bias. The incitement to violence against atheists has manifested in several recent acts of violence and murder, including of Bangladeshi bloggers named on 'hit lists' and hacked to death in public or private spaces in the name of religion.[117] While the

114 See 'Aust Muslim calls for beheading: report', *SBS*, 4 September 2010, updated 24 February 2015, accessed 22 March 2017 http://www.sbs.com.au/news/article/2010/09/04/aust-muslim-calls-beheading-report.

115 Miles Godfrey, 'Atheists are believers who hate God, says Anglican Archbishop Peter Jensen', *News* 3 April 2010, accessed 22 March 2017, http://www.news.com.au/national/atheists-are-believers-who-hate-god-says-anglican-archbishop-peter-jensen/story-e6frfkvr-1225848927144?from=igoogle+gadget+compact+news_rss.

116 See for example, 'Atheists hit back at clergy for criticism of non-belief', *Sydney Morning Herald*, 2 April 2010, accessed 22 March 2017, http://www.smh.com.au/national/atheists-hit-back-at-clergy-criticism-of-nonbelief-20100402-rjmr.html

117 Among the victims are Nazimuddin Samad who was murdered in April 2016; Shafiul Islam in November 2015; Faisal Arefin Dipan in October 2015; Niloy Chatterjee in

Bangladeshi government condemned these acts, it has also ambiguously called for bloggers "not to cross the limits" of free expression.[118] While discrimination, hostility or violence is frequently incited against atheists on the basis of their antipathy towards, rejection of, or opposition to religion, the human rights community's defence of them has been relatively muted. And the apparatus of international law permits this neglect; article 20 prohibits "religious hatred" but not 'belief hatred', leaving those who are hated for their lack of religion, their non-religion, or their atheistic beliefs unprotected.

4. Conclusion: Curtailing incitement of violence against atheists

"Those who can make you believe absurdities can make you commit atrocities."
Voltaire

In accordance with the pluralism advocated in this monograph, the role of international human rights law is to determine when manifestation of a religion or belief must be limited for inciting violence, hostility or discrimination. The challenge the international rights community faces in pursuing this goal is to prohibit hate speech, while upholding freedom of religion and belief.

Despite several examples of hate speech in the name of religion targeting those who do not share the same belief, there is a reluctance to deem expressions that come from a religious point of view as 'hate speech' of the type which should be prohibited. The expressions most likely to be interfered with are those that criticise established religions. Those least likely to be interfered with are expressions that come from a religious point of view and target groups who are not defined by virtue of their religion or who are defined by virtue of their lack of religion, or another criteria not listed in article 20, such as sexuality. But even more telling than the hostility against atheists for their non-belief is the silence of the human rights community in defence of them and the lack of deliberation as to whether such attacks amount to hate speech.

August 2015; Oyasiqur Rahman in March 2015; Avijit Roy in February 2015; Washiqur Rahman Babu in March 2015; Ananta Bijoy Das in May 2015; Niladri Chatterjee in August 2015; Faysal Arefin Dipon in October 2015; and Ahmed Rajib Haider in February 2013. See Bangladesh Country Report, *Freedom of Thought Report* (International Humanist and Ethical Union, 2016); 'Secular activist who criticised Islamism killed in Dhaka', *Guardian*, 7 April 2016, https://www.theguardian.com/world/2016/apr/07/secular-activist-who-criticised-islamism-hacked-to-death-in-bangladesh, 'Bangladesh blogger Niloy Neel hacked to death in Dhaka', *BBC News*, 7 August 2015, http://www.bbc.com/news/world-asia-33819032, 'Bangladeshi professor Shafiul Islam hacked to death', news.com.au, 17 November 2014, http://www.news.com.au/world/asia/bangladeshi-professor-shafiul-islam-hacked-to-death/news-story/ea9038ef36d7a2ca82dd6f2ffadb9b0e, 'Knife attack kills Bangladeshi blogger Washiqur Rahman', *BBC News*, 30 March 2015, http://www.bbc.com/news/world-asia-32112433 all accessed 22 March 2017.

118 *World Report 2017: Events of 2016* (Human Rights Watch, 2016) 114–115; Heiner Bielefeldt, *Report of the Special Rapporteur on freedom of religion and belief on his mission to Bangladesh*, UN Doc A/HRC/31/18/Add.2, 22 January 2016 [53–54].

The key contention of this chapter is that the prohibition on hate speech should be applied to prohibit all incitement to discrimination, hostility or violence, regardless of the particular prejudices of the source, or the hated traits of its target. References to nationality, race and religion are not adequate to address the types of hatred advocated, including those emanating *from* religious points of view against those whose worldview is non-religious, irreligious or anti-religious. Human rights protection should be afforded on a non-discriminatory basis regardless of the nationality, race, religion, belief, gender, class, sexual orientation or any other trait or characteristic that can conceivably be the subject of hatred. Indeed, dwarves who become the target of hatred by a dwarf-hating new religion should not be left unprotected because the trait for which they are hated is not listed in article 20. From the perspective of those who are hated this is clear, and from the perspective of those espousing hatred, the fact that limitations to human rights are designed to protect individuals rather than religions or belief systems must be uncompromised.[119] The catalyst for intervention in respect of incitement to hatred, should be the fact that violence, hostility or discrimination is incited, regardless of who is inciting it or why.

In her final general report to the Human Rights Council, Special Rapporteur Asma Jahangir noted with regret that at the country level, "denunciation of human rights abuses is often selective; the religion of the victim and of the perpetrator, rather than the act itself, seems to be a determining factor as to who feels obliged to publicly condemn the incident."[120] The same should not be true at the level of international human rights law.

119 *Report of the Special Rapporteur on the promotion and protection of the right to freedom of opinion and expression, Ambeyi Ligabo*, UN Doc A/HRC/7/14 (28 February 2008) [65].

120 *Report of the Special Rapporteur on freedom of religion or belief, Asma Jahangir*, UN Doc A/HRC/13/40 (29 December 2009) [38].

5 Freedom from parents

Ideological and rights worldviews collide no more forcefully than in questions concerning the freedom of religion and belief of children. It is in the sacrifice of their rights on the altar of their parents' religion, that the human rights community has most failed in protecting individuals over ideologies.

There is no question that article 18 of the ICCPR strives to protect the right of children. The right belongs to 'everyone'; children do not have 'smaller' rights than their adult counterparts.[1] Yet where parental rights to bring their child up in conformity with their own belief conflicts with the child's own freedom of religion and belief, the bias towards religious rights-holders becomes evident. Sylvie Langlaude states that religious freedom of children has been conceived in international law as "the right of every child to be unhindered in their growth as an autonomous independent actor in the matrix of parents, religious community and society".[2] She opines that the Committee on the Rights of the Child has an "impoverished view of religion" that fails children by insisting too much on freedom not to have a religion.[3] This chapter conversely asserts that the international human rights framework affords children no such right, giving precedence to the rights of religious parents over the child's right to enjoy freedom from religion.

There is little guidance as to how article 18 rights of parents and the competing rights of their children are to be balanced in the event of collision.[4] In practice, the rights of parents to impose a religion or belief trump the rights of their children to be free from religion or belief. This lack of freedom from religion and belief will be illustrated in this chapter by looking to the article 18(4) liberty of parents to ensure the "religious and moral education" of their children in conformity with

1 See for instance, 'Using the CRC and Protocols for Children', UNICEF, accessed 22 March 2017, http://www.unicef.org/crc/index_using.html.

2 Sylvie Langlaude, *The Right of the Child to Religious Freedom in International Law* (Martinus Nijhoff Publishers, 2007) 116.

3 Sylvie Langlaude, 'Children and Religion under Article 14 UNCRC: A Critical Analysis' (2008) 16 *International Journal of Children's Rights* 475, 499.

4 Asma Jahangir, Speech delivered at the 25th Anniversary Commemoration of the adoption of the 1981 Declaration on the elimination of intolerance and discrimination based on religion or belief, Prague, 25 November 2006, accessed 22 March 2017, http://www.tolerance95.cz/1981declaration/download.php.

their own convictions. That liberty will be interrogated in relation to the upbringing and circumcision of children to ultimately conclude that in practice, parental freedom to manifest religion prevails over the child's rights to be free from the religion of others.

1. Balancing rights of parents and children

"*Anyone who curses his father or mother must be put to death.*"

Exodus 21:17

Everyone enjoys freedom to have a religion or belief of their choice free from coercion; that entitlement is not limited by age.[5] However, the developing capacity of children means they are not always able to exercise rights in the same way adults are. The response of international human rights law has been to bolster the role of the child's parents (or guardians) until such a time the child is able to make certain decisions independently. Avoiding rights violation here is no easy task; where the point is called too late, the child's freedom of religion and belief may be curtailed, but where it is called too early, the rights of parents to bring their children up according to their own convictions may be inappropriately interfered with.

That the manifestation of one person's religion or belief should not harm another person's human rights is an uncontroversial statement of law. Accordingly, a parent's manifestation of his religion or belief can and indeed must be limited where it would harm the rights of his child. While the state cannot be held liable for everything that happens in the complex relationship between parents and their children, it should be held to account where it fails to protect children from interferences that make their autonomous enjoyment of human rights – including freedom of religion and belief – meaningless.[6]

The point at which a parent's article 18 rights should be interfered with to protect a competing human right of his child is often difficult to determine. Killing a child for reasons of religious beliefs about possession or witchcraft would unequivocally fall outside any right of a parent vis-à-vis his child.[7] Similarly, religious practices that are tantamount to abuse or neglect should not be protected.[8] But

5 See for instance Human Rights Committee, *General Comment 17: Article 24 (Rights of the Child)* CCPR 35th Session (7 April 1989) [2]. Children have the right to freedom of religion and belief according to article 18(1) of the ICCPR and article 14(1) of the CRC.

6 Langlaude, above n 2, 93.

7 See Rex Ahdar and Ian Leigh, *Religious Freedom in the Liberal State* (Oxford University Press, 2013) 205, and 'National Action Plan to tackle child abuse linked to religion or belief' (The UK National Working Group on Child Abuse linked to Religion or Belief, 2012) which notes that parents have been key perpetrators of such abuse.

8 Consider, for instance, the death of a girl who had been banished to a shed while menstruating, in accordance with the Hindu practice of Chhaupadi. See: 'Nepal police investigate death of girl banished for menstruating' *BBC*, 20 December 2016, accessed 22 March 2017, http://www.bbc.com/news/world-asia-38384889.

when the right at risk is the child's non-derogable freedom of religion and belief, determining the point of interference is complicated by article 18(4) that affords parents the right to bring up their children in accordance with their own religion or belief.

1.1. The rights and liberties of parents over their children

Article 18(4) of the ICCPR reads:

> The States Parties to the present Covenant undertake to have respect for the liberty of parents and, when applicable, legal guardians to ensure the religious and moral education of their children in conformity with their own convictions.

While this provision can be read as referring to the child's own convictions or those of the parents, it tends to be interpreted as referring to the latter.[9] Here the risk is raised that in protecting the broad religious freedoms of parents, the child's own freedom of religion and belief is limited.[10] Article 14(2) of the 1989 Convention on the Rights of the Child (CRC) emphasises state respect for the "rights and duties" of parents and guardians to "provide direction" to the child in the exercise of that right in a manner consistent with the "evolving capacities" of the child. These CRC provisions positively act to reduce the control parents have in the upbringing of their child by explicitly referring to the child's own religion and belief in article 14(1). The ICCPR must be construed with the CRC in mind.[11] Comparing article 18(4) of the ICCPR with article 14(2) of the CRC that emerged 23 years later shows a shift in the emphasis placed on parental duties. While the ICCPR afforded parents the right to "ensure the religious and moral education of their children in conformity with their own convictions", the CRC protects the rights of parents to "provide direction to the child…in a manner consistent with the evolving capacities of the child", illustrating a shift from the primacy of parents' rights towards greater freedom granted to children in the exercise of their own.[12] However, the extent to which this shift has resulted in recognition of increased freedom for children is questionable. Indeed, among the provisions discussed here, only articles 14(1) and (2) of the CRC explicitly

9 Heiner Bielefeldt, Nazila Ghanea and Michael Weiner, *Freedom of Religion and Belief: An International Law Commentary* (Oxford, 2016) 205.
10 Throughout this chapter the term 'parents' denotes both 'parents' and 'legal guardians'.
11 Brice Dickson, 'The United Nations and Freedom of Religion' (1995) 44 *International and Comparative Law Quarterly* 327, 347.
12 This focus on the child's own rights and best interests can also be seen as a departure from equivalent article 13(3) of the International Covenant on Economic, Social and Cultural Rights and article 12(4) of the International Convention on the Protection of the Rights of all Migrant Workers and Members of their Families.

mention the rights of the child; other provisions concern the rights of parents in respect of their child's religion and belief.[13]

In affording rights and duties to parents to interfere with their child's religion and belief, international human rights law can again be seen to bolster religions over the rights to willingly adopt or reject them. In so doing, the rights framework reflects tenets of major religions over principles of human rights. A Christian view, for instance, may assert that the state should not interfere with the family and that parents have a "God-given mandate and responsibility (for which they will be accountable)" to raise their children as they are commanded to do.[14] Some major religions instruct obedience to parents. One of the commandments of the Hebrew Bible underscores obedience to parents:

> Honour your father and your mother, as the Lord your God commanded you, so that your days may be long and that it may go well with you in the land that the Lord your God is giving you.[15]

A challenge to strict obedience to the religious teachings of parents may arise where those teachings are anti-religious or differ from the dominant religion in question. For instance, a person attempting to obey parents who command Hinduism or atheism would be faced with a choice of failing in respect of the commandment to honour one's parents, or in respect of the first commandment to have no other god but the God of the Old Testament.[16] This notion of obeying parents only if parents command a particular ideology is also reflected in Islam, in which the notion of "obeying parents" as a means of justifying a non-believer's non-belief, has been rejected by the Koran.[17] Contrasted with this is another teaching of Islam that every Muslim from the age of maturity (a boy at fifteen years and a girl between nine and thirteen) should stand for the principles of his or her religion.[18] Yet it seems clear that that child is not free to stand for principles of a religion other than Islam given the prohibition of apostasy and another principle that a Muslim child is not allowed to choose a religion other than his father's, namely Islam.[19] The situation of a child who questions the beliefs of his

13 The preferences of parents in the religious upbringing of their child are even to be given consideration when the child is removed from them and placed in care. See article 20(3) CRC, noting that "due regard shall be paid to the desirability of continuity in a child's upbringing and to the child's ethnic, religious, cultural and linguistic background", listing "kafalah of Islamic law" as a potentially suitable care institution.
14 Rex J. Ahdar, 'Children's Religious Freedom, Devout Parents and the State' in Peter W. Edge and Graham Harvey (eds), *Law and Religion in Contemporary Society* (Ashgate, 2000) 102.
15 *Bible*, Deuteronomy, 5:16.
16 *Bible*, Exodus, 20:1–17; Deuteronomy 5:6–21.
17 Kamran Hashemi, 'Religious Legal Traditions, International Human Rights Law and Muslim States' (Martinus Nijhoff Publishers, 2008) 28, referring to *Koran* 2:170, 5:104, 7:28, 10:78, 21:54–54, 26:74–76, 31; 21; 43:22–23.
18 Ibid 28–29.
19 Ibid 242.

parents poses challenges for the well-meaning state that aspires to protect the child's human rights while simultaneously respecting the religious tenets and traditions of his parents. The child is faced with a predicament of disobedience to his parents and their religion, or disobedience to his own convictions, while the state is faced with the prospect of offending fundamental religious tenets (that children should follow the religion of their parents) in upholding fundamental rights (that children should be free to choose their own religion and belief).

To avoid this dilemma, declarations and reservations have been entered to article 14 of the CRC by several states, including Afghanistan, Algeria, Bangladesh, Belgium, Brunei Darussalam, the Holy See, the Islamic Republic of Iran, Iraq, Jordan, Kiribati, Kuwait, Malaysia, Maldives, Mauritania, Morocco, the Netherlands, Oman, Poland, Qatar, Saudi Arabia, Singapore, Syria and the United Arab Emirates.[20] Algeria entered an interpretative declaration underscoring that according to its Constitution, Islam is the state religion and that the Family Code stipulates that a child's education is to take place in accordance with the religion of its father. The Holy See emphasised that it interprets the articles in a way that safeguard the "primary and inalienable rights of parents" particularly concerning education, religion, association with others and privacy. Kiribati, Poland and Singapore all stressed respect for "parental authority" in interpreting article 14. Although article 14 does not clearly express the rights of children to choose their own religion or belief, and/or reject that of their parents, these reservations show that some states are concerned enough to take precautions against such an interpretation. Conversely, other states show a tendency to increase freedom of children; Belgium and Netherlands for instance declared that they understand article 14 to include the right of a child to choose his or her religion or belief.[21] Collectively these state responses illustrate the difficulty of reconciling international law with religious precepts and of disassociating a child's rights from those of his parents.

1.2. The rights and evolving capacities of the child

Article 14(1) of the CRC refers only to the child's freedom of thought, conscience and religion, omitting freedom to *have or to adopt* a religion or belief of his choice and the freedom to *manifest* his religion or belief. One interpretation of this

20 Other than Belgium, the Holy See, Kiribati, the Netherlands, Poland and Singapore, all of the states that entered reservations to article 14 were Islamic states entering general reservations on all provisions deemed incompatible with Islamic Sharia, sometimes making specific clarifications on the point of incompatibility. Several European states objected to reservations made by other states with regard to article 14 on the basis that they were vague or inappropriately evoked internal law to avoid treaty obligations, and that such reservations, as Sweden put it, "may cast doubts on the commitments of the reserving state to the object and purpose of the Convention and, moreover, contribute to the undermining the basis of international treaty law". See UN Treaty Series (online) accessed 22 March 2017, https://treaties.un.org/Pages/ViewDetails.aspx?src=IND&mtdsg_no=IV-11&chapter=4&clang=_en.

21 Ibid.

omission could be that article 14 intends only to protect the internal elements of the right, rather than external elements (in effect, allowing a child to believe anything he or she wants, but not to do so out loud).[22] Manifestation is mentioned in article 14(3), but only in the context of limiting it. The internal right afforded to children by article 14 is further weakened by the fact that the state is required only to "respect" the right of children, not to "protect" or ensure it.[23] The same respect is accorded to third parties in article 14(2), which gives parents "rights and duties" to direct their children in their enjoyment of this internal right. Finally, these parental rights and duties are not explicitly limited; the limitations provided for by article 14(3) work to limit the rights of children to manifest religion or belief (a right not explicitly set out elsewhere in the CRC), but not to limit the role played by their parents in "providing direction". The wording of these provisions may be owing to the controversy of including article 14 in the first place, disagreement about which compromised negotiations for the entire instrument.[24]

The child's freedom of thought, conscience and religion in the CRC is considered a 'participation' right.[25] Eva Brems asserts that the way parents exercise their right and duty to give direction in matters of conscience and religion in accordance with the CRC must be consistent with the CRC as a whole.[26] All provisions of the CRC are guided by the child's article 12 right to be heard and to have his or her views taken into account in all relevant matters in accordance with the child's age and maturity.[27] However, the extent to which the right to be heard includes a duty to empower the child to communicate views is unclear. Nor is it clear what is to be done with regard to the child's views once they have been heard.[28]

Irrespective of article 14 of the CRC, children also enjoy freedom of religion and belief in article 18 of the ICCPR. Yet, a pro-religious bias is evident in its approaches to resolving conflicts between article 18 rights of children and article 18(4) rights of their parents. A simple reading of article 18 ICCPR alongside article 14 of the CRC, determines that a parent's wishes can be disregarded when a child wishes otherwise and his or her capacity has evolved to make him or her capable of fully exercising his or her rights.[29] This notion of 'evolving capacities'

22 Ursula Kilkelly, 'The Child's Right to Religious Freedom in International Law: The Search for Meaning', in Martha Alberson Fineman and Karen Worthington (eds), *What is Right for Children? The Competing Paradigms in Religion and Human Rights* (Ashgate, 2009) 247–248.

23 Eva Brems, 'Article 14: The Right to Freedom of Thought, Conscience and Religion', in A. Allen, J. Vande Lanotte, E. Verhellen, F. Ang, E. Berghams and M. Verheyde (eds), *A Commentary on the United Nations Convention on the Rights of the Child* (Martinus Nijhoff Publishers, 2006) 3 and 10.

24 See Ahdar and Leigh, above n 7, 482–486.

25 Kilkelly, above n 22, 244.

26 Brems, above n 23, 31.

27 *United Nations Convention on the Rights of the Child*, opened for signature 20 November 1989, 1577 UNTS 5 (entered into force 2 September 1990), article 12.

28 Kilkelly, above n 22, 248.

29 *CRC*, article 5 and article 14(2).

was introduced by the CRC to determine the point at which a child's religious and belief rights are her own to exercise.[30] The principle recognises that parents have a right to guide their child in the exercise of her rights, but as the child's capacity increases, she has more influence on her own religion and belief, and her parents less.[31] Though it offers such a framework, article 14(2) of the CRC provides little guidance as to how or when this transfer takes place.[32]

This notion of a child being entitled to make her own choice of religion or belief according to her ability to do so is referred to as a 'sliding scale' that tilts according to the child's evolving capacity.[33] Here, a case-by-case basis has been asserted over fixed aged limits.[34] It is clear that such a scale must slide rather than be marked with indicators of requisite capacity; the different rates at which individuals evolve and the ethereal nature of some religions and beliefs make absolute criteria impossible. Therefore, as Cornelis D. de Jong asserts, a sliding scale "does not provide absolute guarantees, but taking into account the sensitivity of the issue it seems to be the best possible solution".[35] But de Jong agrees that the international rights framework applies the consideration in a way that is heavily biased in favour of parental rights.[36] Measuring the evolving capacities of a person in relation to spiritual matters is objectively impossible. At a certain point a child develops the capacity to question the existence of Santa Claus or the tooth fairy and his continued belief in either into adulthood would raise concerns about his capacity. However, where a child continues to believe in a religiously sanctioned supernatural being, it would be wholly inappropriate to draw a connection between his continued belief and his capacity. Indeed for many parents, a child who questions the existence of a Supreme Being may be the cause of far greater concern.[37]

Another criticism of the evolving capacities approach is that it oversimplifies and undervalues how a child is religious or believing. Langlaude has criticised international law for catering to adult understandings and not reflecting how children engage with religion and belief.[38] She suggests that holders of a particular religious belief are generally required by human rights law to have an appropriate

30 *CRC*, article 14(2) and article 5. Also see Bielefeldt, Ghanea and Weiner, above n 9, 67, 422.
31 Kilkelly, above n 22, 246. Also see Geraldine Van Bueren, 'The Right to be the Same, The Right to be Different: Children and Religion' in T. Lindholm, W. Cole Durham and B. G. Tahzib-Lie, *Facilitating of Freedom of Religion or Belief: A Deskbook* (Martinus Nijhoff, 2004), 563.
32 Langlaude, above n 2, 102.
33 Cornelis D. de Jong, *The Freedom of Thought, Conscience and Religion or Belief in the United Nations (1946–1992)* (Intersentia, 2000), School of Human Rights Research Series, Vol. 5, 54 and 69.
34 Bielefeldt, Ghanea and Weiner, above n 9, 67–68, 438.
35 de Jong, above n 33, 54
36 Ibid 587.
37 This point is not made to suggest that the existence of God, Ganesha or any other religious figure is as implausible as Santa or the tooth fairy, but to highlight the difficulty of measuring a person's capacity against intangible beliefs.
38 Langlaude, above n 2, 201.

understanding of the doctrines of that religion or belief.[39] This requirement was questioned in Chapter 3 on proselytism where it was suggested that a threshold of understanding of religious doctrines should not be a prerequisite for espousing a particular religion.[40] The same is true for children. Langlaude makes the telling point that "children's religious beliefs may be less coherent than those of adults..." but "[f]rom a religious perspective, of course, children may be better able to 'connect' with spiritual matters than adults."[41] That children may be able to connect better with spiritual matters may be *because* of their lower capacity; they may not yet have been exposed to viewpoints which challenge the 'truths' of the religion in which they are brought up, nor have developed analytical capacity to question doctrines. However, it should not follow from a religious or a legal perspective that the lower capacity of a child relative to that of an adult should mean his freedom of religion of belief is entitled to less protection.

The situation of Amish children is enlightening in considering the challenges young people face in decisions that diverge from the religion in which their parents raised them. The Amish are a strict group of Christian Mennonites based largely in eastern parts of the United States.[42] Though religious practices permeate every aspect of Amish lifestyle, some subgroups allow young members 'rumspringa', a period of grace from the high standards of behaviour demanded by their faith. During this period, youth between sixteen and eighteen years old may live for a period of time within non-Amish communities, after which time they must choose to be baptised into the faith and live according to its doctrines for the rest of their lives, or leave the faith and their community.[43] The fact that most return can be considered a free choice that reflects positively on the appeal of the religion, but the alternative of leaving and being shunned by one's community, may not present a meaningful choice to a teenager. The activities engaged in during the period of rumspringa (including experimentation with or exposure to previously forbidden modern clothes, alcohol, cigarettes, drugs, pre-marital sex, motor vehicles and gadgets)[44] cannot be considered to provide meaningful insight into alternative belief systems; such activities are engaged in because they are prohibited by the Amish, not because they are part of other religions or beliefs. Though the choice between complete submission or complete separation from family and friends may not be a 'free' one, it is still a choice that many children of religious parents do not have. Indeed, the idea that an Islamic teenager could be given 'time off' to decide whether she wants to commit to being a Muslim is

39 Ibid 201–202.

40 See Chapter 3, on attributes of the target of proselytism.

41 Langlaude, above n 2, 202.

42 John Bowker (ed.), *The Concise Oxford Dictionary of World Religions* (Oxford University Press, 2005) 35; Donald B Kraybill (ed.), *The Amish and the State* (Johns Hopkins University Press, 2nd edn, 2003) 5–8.

43 *The Devil's Playground*, film, directed by Lucy Walker, Stick Figure Productions, 2002.

44 Ibid.

unthinkable in parts of the world where significant duties may already be imposed upon her while she is still a child (such as marriage and motherhood).[45]

Ursula Kilkelly criticises the 'evolving capacity' approach for overlooking the heavy influence parents have, some supporting their child's independence and others retaining control well beyond the time a child is capable of exercising rights independently.[46] While the 'evolving capacities' approach may be a pragmatic suggestion to resolve conflicts between parents' and childrens' rights, Kilkelly ultimately finds that "…there is no remedy to the totalitarian exercise of parental authority."[47] In short, a child obtaining the capacity to exercise her rights autonomously is not tantamount to her parents granting her the freedom to do so. Determining when the state should intervene where they do not is complex. Article 19 of the CRC allows the state to intervene where parents try to impose their ideas onto their child through mental or physical violence.[48] The nature of the message has significant impact on whether it can be considered improperly coercive. Baptising a baby into a particular religion, for instance, would not trigger the same concern as interference with that baby's bodily integrity for religious reasons.[49] Similarly, deciding that a child should take part in a kindergarten nativity play would seem to have no implications on the long-term religious or belief choices of the child, whereas presenting her on a daily basis with the 'truth' and horror of hell may hinder her capacity to consider alternative ideologies, or be so injurious as to require intervention.[50] Consideration must therefore be given to the way in which a child is brought up in a particular religion or belief, and the extent to which that upbringing supports his capacity to choose his own religion or belief. It is suggested here that there should be a presumption in favour of the child, so that the sliding scale tilts in her favour, for it is she whose long-term

45 See for instance *Early Marriage, A Harmful Traditional Practice* (UNICEF, 2005) 26, and *Combating trafficking in persons in accordance with the principles of Islamic law* (UNODC, 2010) 11. Also see Anthony Bradney, *Islam and European Legal Systems* (Ashgate, 2000) 185 in which the author notes that in some branches of Islamic law females (of any age) are have no capacity to contract marriages.

46 Kilkelly, above n 22, 246.

47 Ibid.

48 Article 19 of the CRC reads: 1) States Parties shall take all appropriate legislative, administrative, social and educational measures to protect the child from all forms of physical or mental violence, injury or abuse, neglect or negligent treatment, maltreatment or exploitation, including sexual abuse, while in the care of parent(s), legal guardian(s) or any other person who has the care of the child; 2) Such protective measures should, as appropriate, include effective procedures for the establishment of social programmes to provide necessary support for the child and for those who have the care of the child, as well as for other forms of prevention and for identification, reporting, referral, investigation, treatment and follow-up of instances of child treatment described heretofore, and, as appropriate for judicial involvement.

49 See, for instance, Manfred Nowak, *CCPR Commentary* (NP Engel Kehl, 2nd edn, 2005) 417.

50 The extent to which threats of a religious nature, for instance, to a person's soul, can be considered to constitute mental violence was considered in Chapter 3 on proselytism.

freedom is affected. The hesitancy to date in applying this reasoning is arguably due to the inconvenient fact of how many children around the world would be considered improperly coerced by their parents.

Article 3(1) of the CRC emphatically clarifies that the best interests of the child shall be the primary consideration in all actions concerning children, yet offers no explanation of what those best interests are: a particularly challenging question in the context of religious and belief interests. The best interests of the child as pursued by the ICCPR and CRC "do not necessarily correspond with that which might be shown empirically to be the best for the child's physical development, psychological disposition, social well-being, education advancement, economic prosperity, or religious salvation".[51] This is so, Van der Vyver explains, because legal decisions as to what is in a child's best interests must be cognisant of non-legal factors such as social realities and the religious convictions of local populations.[52]

As with the sliding scale, assessing best interests in matters of religion and belief is also rife with complexity and disparate views.[53] While the rights framework is concerned with the interests of the child in the tangible world, a religious viewpoint may also be concerned with the child's posthumous spiritual wellbeing. There is no objective way of ascertaining which consideration should prevail where they conflict. Secular courts of law are not qualified to decide upon religious doctrine, but where the best interests of the child are at stake, legal reasoning may be required to consider implications of a given religion or belief on the child brought up in accordance with it.[54] As Van der Vyver notes, "[t]he law operates alongside a conglomerate of other non-juridical structures, each with its own vital function in human society and a typical set of values that contribute, each in its own way, to the best interests of the child."[55] Whatever the best interests of a child are determined to be in a given scenario, consideration must be given to her participation rights, in accordance with her evolving capacity to determine her own best interests.

2. Freedom from coercive religious or moral education

> "*Let the little children come to me, and do not hinder them, for the kingdom of God belongs to such as these.*"
>
> Mark 10:14

51 Johan D. van der Vyver, 'Limitations on Freedom of Religion or Belief: International Law Perspectives' (2005) 19 *Emory International Law Review* 499, 517.

52 Ibid.

53 See generally, Van Bueren, above n 31.

54 There are no illustrative HRC cases to explore this point, but the European Court of Human Rights has evinced reasoning discriminatory towards minority religions. See *Ismailova v Russia*, Application No 37614/02 (8 November 2007); *Hoffmann v Austria*, Application No 12875/87 (3 June 1993); *Palau-Martinez v France*, Application No 64927/01 (16 December 2003); and *Vojnity v Hungary*, Application No 29617/07 (12 February 2013).

55 van der Vyver, above n 51, 517.

Significant attention has been given to assertions of article 18(4) by parents against school authorities to stop proselytism through education. However, little consideration has been given to how this provision would apply where children resist the religious and moral education provided by their parents.[56] This tension – between a child's right to freedom of religion and belief and her parents' rights with respect to her upbringing – is the subject of this section.

It is well established that students should be able to opt out of religious instruction classes and have access to alternative courses in state-funded schools.[57] Further, a body of literature promoting intercultural education based on pluralism of religious and non-religious belief is emerging.[58] However, it is less clear *who* decides whether or not the student participates in religious education.[59] Eva Brems asserts that the choice cannot be left in the hands of parents until the child reaches the age of majority, arguing that a child should be given the responsibility for this decision earlier than he should be entitled to decide his membership of a religion, given that the choice of religious education is 'less radical' than membership of a religion.[60]

The freedom of an individual to choose what he or she thinks and believes should guide rights-based approaches to religious education. Richard Dawkins urges parents to "[l]et children learn about different faiths, let them notice their incompatibility, and let them draw their own conclusions and consequences about that incompatibility. As for whether any are 'valid', let them make up their own minds when they are old enough to do so."[61] Indeed, while the incompatibility of different faiths is arguably something that is taught from many religious perspectives, it is allowing children to draw their own conclusion that is the difference between educating and coercing. From a rights-based perspective anchored on the principle of pluralism, it is desirable that children "be taught that their own religion is one out of many and that it is a personal choice for everyone to adhere to the religion or belief by which he or she feels most inspired, or to adhere to no religion or belief at all".[62] However, article 18(4) gives parents a countervailing

56 See for instance, *Report of Special Rapporteur on Freedom of Religion and Belief, Heiner Bielefeldt*, UN Doc A/HRC/16/53, 15 December 2010 [25].

57 Ibid [50].

58 Most notably at the European level: see Robert Jackson, *Signposts – Policy and Practice for Teaching about Religions and Non-religious Worldviews in Intercultural Education* (Council of Europe, 2014); *Toledo Guiding Principles on Teaching about Religions and Beliefs in Public Schools* (OSCE, 2007)

59 See for instance Bielefeldt, above n 56 [40]. Bielefeldt leaves the decision with students *or* their parents, without offering guidance as to whose decision trumps in the event of conflict.

60 Brems, above n 23, 30.

61 Richard Dawkins, *The God Delusion* (Bantam Press, 2006) 340. See Trigg's critique of Dawkins for not allowing for the possibility of a religion being true. Roger Trigg, *Equality, Freedom and Religion* (Oxford University Press, 2012) 136–137.

62 Mr Piet de Klerk, Ambassador at Large of the Netherlands on Human Rights (Speech delivered at the 25th Anniversary Commemoration of the adoption of the 1981 Declaration on the elimination of intolerance and discrimination based on religion or

right to bring their children up in accordance with their own religious and moral convictions. The question reasonably posed, then, is why a parent concerned about the spiritual wellbeing of his child would offer options to the child that could lead away from the 'one true faith' that offers salvation?[63] It may be unreasonable to expect parents who take their child with them to church on Sunday to explain before each service that Christianity is but one of many options, which he has been baptised into, but is free to opt out of as soon as he has the capacity to decide to. But it is also unreasonable to allow a child to be so coerced into one way of thinking that his capacity to discover and decide his own beliefs is blunted. It can be argued, then, that an upbringing that leads a person to one option and denies her others is contrary to the 'freedom' envisaged in article 18, as one of meaningful choice.[64]

2.1. The liberties of the parent

Kilkelly argues that the parental duty is merely to provide direction (CRC article 14(2)) in a way that does not involve physical or mental violence, and takes into account the child's views in accordance with his age and maturity.[65] She goes on to say that while there is no clear solution in resolving conflicts between a child and his parents in relation to religious matters, "a more positive interpretation of article 14(2) may reflect the reality that in most cases such conflict would not exist, given that most children will share their parents' religious beliefs."[66] That fact is no coincidence. Dawkins makes a telling point in relation to the legitimacy of a child's religious 'choice' when he argues that it is just as erroneous to label a child a Muslim child or a Christian child as it would be to label him or her a Keynesian child, Marxist child or a secular humanist child.[67] Nonetheless, many are baptised or otherwise initiated into the religion of their parents before they are cognisant of that event and its implications. The fact that 'most' children share the religion of their parents says little, then, about the extent to which they enjoy freedom of religion or belief. More convincing would be a situation in which 'most' children were practising a different religion to that of their parents, for such a situation would show that those children had made an active choice and that

belief, Prague, 25 November 2006), accessed 22 March 2017, http://www.tolerance95.cz/1981declaration/download.php.

63 See Ahdar and Leigh, above n 7, 249–250 on the Christian perspective of the purpose of education.

64 See Joel Feinberg, 'The Child's Right to an Open Future' in William Aiken and Hugh LaFollette (eds), *Whose Child? Children's Rights, Parental Authority, and State Power* (Rowman and Littlefield, 1980). Feinberg argues that parents and the state have a duty to safeguard the child's right to an 'open future'. Also see Myriam Hunter-Henin, 'Law, Religion and the School' in Silvio Ferrari (ed.), *Routledge Handbook of Law and Religion* (Routledge, 2015) 262 and Bielefeldt, Ghanea and Weiner, above n 9, 215–219.

65 Kilkelly, above n 22, 250.

66 Ibid.

67 Dawkins, above n 61, 337–338.

their parents had allowed them freedom to act upon it. Article 14(2) would serve no purpose as far as the child is concerned if it serves only, as Kilkelly suggests, to reflect the duty of the state to "respect the integrity of the family and its collective beliefs and convictions".[68] Were it so, international human rights law would simply serve to elevate parents' rights above those of their children, quieting the already hushed voices of children in contravention of their article 12 right to be heard. But at the same time, assuming that a child shares the religion or belief of his parents simply because he does not say otherwise, is to overlook the relationship of the child with his parents and whether coercion has taken place.

Article 13(1) of the ICESCR provides that education should "strengthen the respect for human rights and fundamental freedoms". A religious education that promotes superiority of worldviews and the inferiority of others may undermine human rights. However, an education that promotes respect for all religions may conflict with parents' wishes to bring their child up with the belief in the superiority of one over others.[69] The same conflict may arise in respect of the CRC, article 29 of which directs education to the development of the child to his or her full potential. Such potential may not be reached where a parent exercises his or her right to 'provide direction' to a child in the exercise of his freedom of religion by directing her against such education. The HRC clearly adopts a strict approach to ICCPR article 18(4) in respect of religious education at schools and is protective of parental rights in educating of their children.[70] Several general comments underline the importance of respect for parents in the education of their children, but are silent on the approach to be taken where parental rights clash with the child's.[71]

Parents are granted a seemingly unqualified right to determine the religious education their child receives, often manifesting as the right for the child *not* to participate in religious education at school where it would be contrary to the parent's wishes.[72] Here the situation of atheist parents and children can be considered. In the HRC case of *Hartikainen et al v Finland*, the author claimed that

68 Kilkelly, above n 22, 250.

69 Asma Jahangir, *Report of the Special Rapporteur on freedom of religion or belief to the Human Rights Council*, UN Doc A/HRC/4/21 (26 December 2006) [49–50]. Jahangir notes that several schoolbooks encourage lack of respect for non-traditional religious minorities or religions differing from the predominant religion in the country.

70 Langlaude, above n 2, 91; Bielefeldt, above n 56 [53]; *Interim report of the Special Rapporteur on Freedom of Religion and Belief, Heiner Bielefeldt*, UN Doc A/70/286 (5 August 2015) [48].

71 Human Rights Committee, *General Comment 22: The right to freedom of thought, conscience and religion (Article 18)*, UN Doc CCPR/C/21/Rev.1/Add.4 (27 September 1993) [6]; *General Comment 13*, UN Doc E/C.12/1999/10 [9], and *General Comment 1*, UN Doc CRC/GC/2001/1 [7].

72 This principle of providing for a non-discriminatory exemption from participation in religious education is protected by article 13(3) of the ICESCR and article 18(4) of the ICCPR. See *General Comment 22*, above n 71 [6] and Human Rights Committee, Communication No. 40/1978; *Hartikainen et al v Finland*, Human Rights Committee, UN Doc CCPR/C/12/D/40/1978 (1981).

Finnish law stipulating obligatory attendance of children of atheists in classes on the history of religion and ethics, was in violation of article 18(4). The HRC found no violation, and did not consider such a requirement objectionable if the course was taught in a neutral and objective way respecting the convictions of parents who did not adhere to any religion.[73] In *Leirvåg et al v Norway*, humanist parents objected to the compulsory education of their children in a subject called 'Christian Knowledge and Religion and Ethical Education', which they argued emphasised Christian tenets. The HRC agreed with the authors that the course was not neutral and objective, and concluded that the exemption arrangements did not protect the liberty of parents to ensure the religious and moral education of their children in conformity with their own convictions, thereby violating article 18(4).[74] Again the rights at stake were those of the parents, not their child. It is unclear what would have happened if the child wanted to attend those classes in contravention of her parents' wishes.

2.2. The best interests of the child

De Jong makes the point that if a Convention on religious freedom was to be drafted, it should contain a distinct section on education in matters relating to religion and belief, and in so doing, clarify that education should accord with minimum standards, and be led by the principle of the "best interests of the child" both within and outside the family. He stresses that the application of that principle requires clarity particularly in cases where the views of parents diverge from those of the child.[75] An example of such conflict could arise, for instance, where religious parents opt for prayer and theological study aimed at the child's salvation, over secular education that can empower her to participate in the community and secure a livelihood for herself.[76] Thus far, however, no such Convention exists, leaving the article 18(4) rights of parents to trump the child's own freedom of religion and belief under article 18.

73 *Hartikainen et al v Finland*, UN Doc CCPR/C/12/D/40/1978 [10.4]. Also see *Angelini v Sweden*, European Court of Human Rights, Application No. 10491/83 (1988) in which the state found no violation in the state's refusal to exempt an atheist from religion teaching, considering the classes at issue to be teaching about religion rather than teaching religion.

74 See *Leirvåg et al v Norway*, Human Rights Committee, Communication No. 931/00, UN Doc CCPR/C/82/D/1155/2003 (2004) [14.2–14.7] and the similar European case of *Folgerø and Others v Norway*, European Court of Human Rights, Grand Chamber Judgment, Application No 15472/02 (29 June 2007) in which the Court found a violation of article 2 of Protocol No. 1 on the right to education, on similar facts. See also *Hasan and Eylem Zengin v Turkey*, Application No 1448/04 (9 October 2007), *Grzelak v Poland* (Application No 7710/02) and *Appel-Irrgang v Germany*, Application No 45206/07 (6 October 2009).

75 de Jong, above n 33, 587.

76 Such a scenario was at issue in *Çiftçi v. Turkey*, European Court of Human Rights, Application 71860/01 (17 June 2004), in which national authorities refused permission for a father to enrol his son in a course exclusively dedicated to study of the Koran. Though the case was found inadmissible, the Court suggested that a purely Koranic religious education might be indoctrinating, and therefore not in the best interests of the child.

It is argued here that in the event of conflict between these rights, the child's right to enjoy her own religion or belief should rather trump the parent's right to dictate the child's religion or belief to her. The grounds for justifying state interference should be the best interests of the child. Such grounds should of course not be misused to justify state actions aimed at undermining the continuity of the religion or belief itself, but if such interference were not possible, the child's rights would be reduced in the private domain. In practice it is of course difficult to determine the point where religious and moral parental guidance undermines the child's rights to freely practise religion and belief. As noted above, spiritual perspectives may complicate and cloud best interest determinations; where parents place posthumous interests of children above their educational interests, the parents and the state may disagree on what best interests are.

The interrelationship of religion with all spheres of life for many rights-holders is understood to mean that the right to have, adopt, or change religion or belief does not presuppose a right of the child to a religiously 'neutral' upbringing.[77] The balance between the parents' rights in respect of the upbringing of their children and the child's right to freedom of religion and belief, is seemingly tipped in favour of the parents, notwithstanding the greater vulnerability of the child. This vulnerability is evident in the fact that no cases have been brought before human rights bodies by a child applicant seeking state assistance to assert his own religion or belief against the wishes of his parent. Thus far, ICCPR article 18(4) of ICESCR article 13(3) has been used by parents against school authorities, it has not been asserted by a parent in response to an ideologically or theologically dissenting child, nor by a child in response to a coercive parent.[78]

The particular vulnerability of children to the influence of their parents should ensure the state's vigilance in protecting them. Despite the challenge posed by having to navigate through complex parental, family, privacy and religious rights landmines, the state cannot simply abandon the child to whatever ideological or theological hand he was dealt. Religious education mandated by parents should be limited where it reaches a level of coercion that undermines the child's enjoyment of his own freedom to adopt, maintain, reject or change his or her religion or belief. Or, at the very least, the attempt to do so should be made.

3. Freedom from religious circumcision

> "*By all means let an observant Jewish adult male have his raw-cut penis placed in the mouth of a rabbi…By all means let grown women who distrust their clitoris or labia have them sawn away by some other wretched adult female…But the conscription of*

77 *Interim report of the Special Rapporteur on Freedom of Religion and Belief, Heiner Bielefeldt*, UN Doc A/70/286 (5 August 2015) [35–38].

78 Here it must be noted that the mechanism to bring complaints in relation to article 13 (3) of the ICESCR is relatively recent; the *Optional Protocol to the International Covenant on Economic, Social and Cultural Rights*, opened for signature on 24 September 2009, GA Resolution A/RES/63/117, entered into force on 5 May 2013.

the unprotected child for these purposes is something that even the most dedicated secularist can safely describe as a sin."[79]

Christopher Hitchens

Circumcision involves removing the loose fold of skin (prepuce) that covers the head of the penis.[80] When performed for religious reasons the practice often takes place before the infant has the mental capacity to refuse or the physical capacity to resist.[81] Rather than being treated as a threat to the child's rights, the HRC asserts that "male circumcision of children who have not yet reached religious maturity should generally be respected as falling within the freedom to manifest one's religion or belief, which includes ritual initiation of children into religious life."[82] The practice then is not considered a violation of the rights of the child, but a protected manifestation of his parents' rights under article 18(4) of the ICCPR.

By allowing harmful religious practices of major religions to be meted out on people particularly vulnerable to them, the bias of human rights law towards major religions is highlighted. Here it asserted that there should be no 'right' to cut off another person's foreskin but that this manifestation of religion should be limited on the basis of the rights of others, namely the child's right to health and to freedom of religion and belief that should include the right to be free from the irreversible mark of another person's religion on one's body. Simply put, it should be for the owner of the foreskin to determine whether to remove it for religious reasons or not, in accordance with his best interests and his evolving capacity to autonomously enjoy freedom of religion and belief.

3.1. The child's right to health

In academic discourse, female circumcision often falls into a different category of consideration to male circumcision. Widely known as female genital mutilation (FGM), female circumcision is practised for both cultural and religious reasons,[83] though in rights discourse tends to be classified as a 'cultural' rather than a 'religious' practice.[84] Though some supporters of female circumcision consider that

79 Christopher Hitchens, *God is not Great* (Allen & Unwin, 2007) 51–52.

80 Thoai D. Ngo and George Obhai, Marie Stopes International, *At the Cutting Edge: Delivering Male Circumcision through Marie Stopes' Reproductive Health Mobile Outreach Programmes in Kenya* (2009) 4.

81 In many instances of ritual or customary circumcision, the person being circumcised is not an infant but a child.

82 *Interim report of the Special Rapporteur on Freedom of Religion and Belief, Heiner Bielefeldt*, UN Doc A/70/286 (5 August 2015) [73]; Bielefeldt, Ghanea and Weiner, above n 9, 424–425. See, however, John Tobin, 'The International Obligation to Abolish Traditional Practices Harmful to Children's Health: What Does it Mean and Require of States?' (2009) 9 *Human Rights Law Review* 272, 382–383.

83 For example, see 'Egypt girl's death puts spotlight on genital mutilation', *BBC News*, 19 June 2013, accessed 22 March 2017, http://www.bbc.co.uk/news/world-middle-east-22975400.

84 OHCHR, *Fact Sheet 23, Harmful traditional practices affecting the health of women and children*, accessed 22 March 2017, http://www.ohchr.org/Documents/Publica

the practice has some health benefits,[85] medical professionals generally agree that the practice offers no benefits for the circumcised person.[86] Female circumcision is recognised as breaching several human rights of the girl who is mutilated, including her right to health and her right not to be subjected to torture or cruel and degrading treatment.[87] Male circumcision is similarly practised for cultural, religious and health reasons, but is not considered to be a violation of the health rights of the child in the way that female circumcision is, nor is it equivalently labelled as 'male genital mutilation'. The caveat that the former Special Rapporteur on freedom of religion and belief offers in condoning male circumcision is that it be "performed by trained practitioners, in sanitary conditions and with the clearly expressed consent of parents or guardians" and other measures to avoid risks of physical and psychological damage, pointing to discussions about postponing the practice until the concerned child can make his own decision.[88] This same proviso is not offered for ritual female circumcision, which, he says, can never be justified by the invocation of freedom of religion and belief.[89]

Female circumcision is not recognised as part of major religions in the same way that male circumcision is, but it must be considered whether its condemnation would be so uncontroversial if it were. Among the religions that prescribe male circumcision, Judaism and Islam are the largest. In Judaism circumcision is a sign of the covenant between God and mankind known as B'rit Milah, which takes place on the eighth day after the baby is born.[90] The religious prescription for this practice is found in Genesis 17 of the Torah, which prescribes that every male be circumcised.[91] Of the 30% of the world's males who are believed to be circumcised, around two-thirds are believed to be Muslims,[92] though there is no

tions/FactSheet23en.pdf and Human Rights and Equal Opportunity Commission, *Article 18 Freedom of Religion and Belief* (Commonwealth of Australia, 1998) 59.

85 Some supporters of female genital mutilation are of the view that reduced sexual arousal is a health benefit; see Dr Trisha Macnair, 'Female Genital Mutilation', *BBC* (online) January 2011, accessed 4 May 2011, http://www.bbc.co.uk/health/physical_health/conditions/female_genital_mutilation.shtml; Olga Khazan, 'Why some women choose to get circumcised', *The Atlantic*, 8 April 2015, accessed 22 March 2017, https://www.theatlantic.com/international/archive/2015/04/female-genital-mutilation-cutting-anthropologist/389640/.

86 World Health Organization, *Fact Sheet: Female Genital Mutilation* (February 2017), accessed 22 March 2017, http://www.who.int/mediacentre/factsheets/fs241/en/.

87 OHCHR, *Fact Sheet 23: Harmful traditional practices affecting the health of women and children*, http://www.ohchr.org/Documents/Publications/FactSheet23en.pdf accessed 22 March 2017 and Human Rights and Equal Opportunity Commission, *Article 18 Freedom of Religion and Belief* (Commonwealth of Australia, 1998) 59.

88 *Interim report of the Special Rapporteur on Freedom of Religion and Belief, Heiner Bielefeldt*, UN Doc A/70/286 (5 August 2015) [72–73].

89 Ibid [14], [67], [69], [77].

90 Philip Wilkinson, *Religions* (Dorling Kindersley, 2008) 78.

91 *Bible*, Genesis 17:10.

92 *Male Circumcision: Global trends and determinants of prevalence, safety and acceptability* (World Health Organization and Joint United Nations Programme on HIV/AIDS, 2007) 7.

specific mention of the practice in the Koran. In Judaism the practice is considered to confirm the relationship between man and God. There is no prescribed age at which a person should undergo the ritual in Islam, which generally takes place between the child's seventh day of life and puberty.[93] While international organisations are clear on the urgent need to eradicate FGM due to the danger it poses to health,[94] male circumcision is often promoted for its contribution to reducing HIV prevalence.[95] Research has found that male circumcision can (in combination with other measures) reduce contraction of HIV among sexually active males by up to 60%.[96] However, the medical pros and cons of the procedure are beyond the scope of this monograph, and are very much beside the point. Alleged benefits of circumcision do not absolve flawed legal reasoning to justify the practice on the basis of the religious motivations of parents. A neutral understanding of human rights law that does not elevate some religions over others, would consider that the decision to be circumcised to guard against HIV contraction is best left to adults at risk, or children with the requisite capacity to decide on that basis.

Male circumcision is also a custom widely accepted in many societies often for social rather than religious reasons.[97] Studies have found that a key determinant in parental decisions to circumcise sons is the desire of parents for their child not to look 'different' and to ensure that their son conforms to what is 'normal'.[98] In some societies the practice is so widespread that it is the norm: in the United States 75% of males are circumcised for non-religious reasons.[99] A desire in fathers that their son's penis resembles their own has been noted: a study in the US showed that 90% of circumcised men chose to circumcise their sons compared to 23% of non-circumcised fathers.[100] In other parts of the world, circumcision is a rite of passage into manhood that is associated with factors such as courage and masculinity.[101] Setting aside health and social reasons for circumcision that are

93 Ibid 3–4.
94 World Health Organization, above n 86.
95 See for instance, World Health Organization, *Male circumcision for HIV prevention*, http://www.who.int/hiv/topics/malecircumcision/en/, accessed 22 March 2017 and Ngo and Obhai, above n 80.
96 Ibid. Some medical opinions stress that HIV transmission is more concerned with sexual behaviour than it is with genital anatomy or the best interests of the child, and that decisions to undergo the procedure should be made by the person when he is old enough to make an informed decision. See for instance, Geoff Hinchley, 'Head to Head: Is Infant Male Circumcision an Abuse of the Rights of the Child?' (2007) 335 *British Medical Journal* 1180.
97 World Health Organization and Joint United Nations Programme on HIV/AIDS, above n 92.
98 Ibid 5.
99 Ibid 11. Here it should be noted that in some societies the practice of FGM is also so widespread as to be considered 'normal'.
100 Ibid 5.
101 Ibid 4. For instance, as a member of the Themba people of the Xhosa nation, Nelson Mandela recalls his circumcision ceremony, during which he had to shout 'I am a man!' at the moment his foreskin was severed. See Nelson Mandela, *Long Walk to Freedom* (Abacus, 1994) 30–34.

beyond the scope of this monograph, it is asserted that *religious* motivations of parents do not lessen the implications of that act for the child, and do not amount to a universally acceptable practice that human rights law should protect. From a criminal law point of view, the *actus reas* (cutting off a part of an infant's genitalia) could not be excused by the *mens rea* (entering that infant into a covenant with God) any more than other assaults (for instance, whipping the child) could be excused by religious reasons (to excise the devil from the infant's body).[102] But in practice, human rights law reveals a pro-religious bias by reasoning towards a conveniently permissive conclusion for majority religions that favours the rights of parents over those of their children.

As an example, in New York in 2005, the Jewish practice performed by mohels of sucking the penises of circumcised baby boys was found to have caused genital herpes to some babies resulting in some deaths.[103] Though physicians argued against the practice, New York's mayor (during election time) publicly defended freedom of religion (of the mohel and the child's parents) over the health and rights of children.[104] Yet the best interests of the child are supposed to be the overriding consideration in all decisions relating to him. It is posited here that an irreversible procedure carried out for ritual rather than medical reasons, with both short- and long-term implications for the individual concerned, cannot be considered in the child's best interests. Indeed, the fact of potential risks, not only in the course of the procedure itself (particularly where that procedure is performed by someone not medically trained), along with the long-term impact the procedure may have on the individual's sexual life, are strong arguments to suggest that the procedure is *not* in his best interests.

Attempts to challenge the practice in defence of the interests of children have been attempted in some secular states. In San Francisco in May of 2011, child rights advocates managed to put the issue of banning circumcision on the voter's ballot. Legal challenges to the referendum alleged that the proposed ban was anti-Islamic and anti-Semitic, and an assault on ancient religious practices. In July 2011 Judge Loretta Giorgi struck the issue from the ballot on the grounds that the ban would violate religious freedom, and because the city of San Francisco had no authority to regulate what she termed to be 'medical' procedures.[105] Her decision

102 In the instance of whipping a child, it should be noted that depending on the severity of the assault, the child is capable of physically recovering.

103 See Howard Markel, 'Circumcision, Religious Freedom, and Herpes Infections in New York City', *Medscape*, 17 October 2006, http://www.medscape.com/viewarticle/545756 and Andy Newman, 'City Questions Circumcision Ritual after Baby Dies', *New York Times*, 26 August 2005, http://www.nytimes.com/2005/08/26/nyregion/26circumcise.html both accessed 22 March 2017.

104 Hitchens, above n 79, 50.

105 See for instance Carolina Madrid, 'Jews, Muslims sue to block referendum on circumcision', *Reuters*, 22 June 2011, http://www.reuters.com/article/2011/06/23/us-circumcision-sanfrancisco-idUSTRE75M05120110623; Anna Holligan, 'Dutch Jews and Muslims fight for circumcision right', *BBC News*, 3 November 2011 http://www.bbc.co.uk/news/world-europe-15486834 and 'San Francisco circumcision ban

was based on consideration of the impact the proposed ban would have had on the rights of parents, rather than on the children being circumcised by them.

Yet some decisions made by parents in accordance with their religious beliefs are limitable where those decisions impact on his child. Kilkelly argues that situations where a parent seeks to deny a life-saving blood transfusion from his child for religious reasons, or seeks to rely on religious grounds to inflict corporal punishment, would be captured by limitations in the relevant human rights instruments.[106] She does not comment on whether such a limitation should act to stop parents from removing their child's foreskin. Limitations on the 'rights' of parents to circumcise their infants on grounds of health are not to be confused with apparent long-term benefits, namely the reduced risk of HIV transmission among circumcised males.[107] The health consideration at issue rather concerns the risks posed to infants through the *procedure* of circumcision. Article 12 of the ICESCR recognises the right of everyone to the "highest attainable standard of physical and mental health".[108] Steps taken by states parties to fully realise such a standard include those necessary to reduce infant mortality and for the healthy development of the child.[109] Article 24(3) of the CRC requires states parties to "take effective and appropriate measures with a view to abolishing traditional practices prejudicial to the health of children".[110]

Relative to FGM, it is generally conceded that male circumcision does not result in the same level of trauma, physical injury and long-term health and sexual problems, but this relativity is of little comfort to the boy concerned. Nor does it mean that the same reasoning should not apply in considering the impact that the practice has on those who it is performed on. Where FGM is performed in a way that carries no short- or long-term risk to the girl concerned (for instance, by cutting the hymen or symbolically cutting or merely touching the labia in a way that completely heals and does not interfere with the sexual functioning of her genitalia), the procedure would still likely raise human rights concerns on principle.[111] Indeed, many scholars argue that the distinction drawn between male and

struck from ballot', *BBC News*, 28 July 2011 http://www.bbc.co.uk/news/world-us-canada-14335715 all accessed 22 March 2017.

106 Kilkelly, above n 22, 249.

107 Ngo and Obhai, above n 80, 3.

108 *ICESCR* article 12(1).

109 *ICESCR* article 12(2)(a).

110 Additionally article 5(5) of the 1981 Declaration provides that practices of a religion or belief in which the child is brought up must not be injurious to his physical or mental health or full development.

111 At the time of writing, defence lawyers in Detroit were preparing to argue religious freedom in a case concerning circumcision of two seven-year-old girls in Minnesota by three members of the Dawoodi Bohra Muslim community. Several scholars consider the argument unlikely to succeed, pointing to the fact that the parental right to practise religion does not permit them to inflict harm on others. The lawyers will argue that the acts were done in accordance with their religion and involved non-harmful genital scraping rather than actual cutting. See Tresa Baldas, 'Religious defense planned in landmark Detroit genital mutilation case', *Detroit Free Press*, 21 May 2017,

female genital mutilation amounts to discrimination on the basis of sex that detracts from a clear and objective approach to the issue of mutilating genitalia of infants.[112] It also reveals the hierarchy of religions at play that serves to 'normalise' some religious practices. Though we are urged to consider the practice of male circumcision as being quite separate from FGM,[113] there are risks posed to the infant's health that should be weighed in decisions to allow parents to remove his foreskin for religious reasons. Risks to infants include anaesthetic risks (where anaesthetic is used, which is not always the case),[114] as well as short-term risks of bleeding and infection. Potential long-term risks may include pain on erection and penile disfigurement, and psychological harm resulting from the operation.[115] Though the World Health Organisation encourages use of circumcision to reduce HIV transmission, it acknowledges risks including pain, bleeding, infection, injury to the penis, urethra, glands and scrotum, disfigurement and scarring, and reactions to anaesthetic agents.[116] Indeed, there have been instances of babies bleeding to death as a result of circumcision.[117] Though the risk of complications is low when performed by well-trained, adequately equipped and experienced healthcare practitioners, the absence of those factors is acknowledged to increase the risk of complications by up to 20%.[118] In fact, the complication rate for infant circumcision is essentially unknown because most operators are unregistered.[119] Lack of information and a failure to register the people commissioned to bring a knife to an infant's genitals should act as a caution against allowing the practice to continue

accessed 26 May 2017, http://www.freep.com/story/news/2017/05/21/female-genital-mutilation-religious-freedom/319911001/.

112 See Ranipul Narulla, 'Circumscribing Circumcision: Traversing the Moral and Legal Ground around a Hidden Human Vights violation' (2007) 12, *Australian Journal of Human Rights* 89; Robert Darby and J. Seven Svboda, 'A Rose by Any Other Name: Rethinking the Similarities and Differences between Male and Female Genital Cutting' (2007) 21 *Medical Anthropology Quarterly* 301; Christine Mason, 'Exorcising Excision: Medico-legal Issues Arising from Male and Female Genital Surgery in Australia' (2001) 9 *Journal of Law and Medicine* 58.

113 See Kirsten Patrick, 'Head to Head: Is Infant Male Circumcision an Abuse of the Rights of the Child?' (2007) 335 *British Medical Journal* 1181.

114 Hinchley, above n 96, 1180.

115 See D. Bollinger and R. Van Howe, 'Alexithymia and Circumcision Trauma: A Preliminary Investigation' (2011) 10 *International Journal of Men's Health* 184 and R Goldman, 'The Psychological Impact of Circumcision' (1999) 83 (Supplement 1) *British Journal of Urology International* 93, accessed 22 March 2017, http://www.cirp.org/library/psych/goldman1/.

116 *Manual for early infant circumcision under local anaesthesia* (World Health Organization, 2010) 7.

117 In Canada one-month-old Ryleigh McWillis bled to death despite being circumcised at a hospital. See 'Baby bleeds to death after circumcision', *Miami Herald,* 26 June 1993; 'B. C. parents lobby against circumcision' *CBC News,* accessed 22 March 2017, http://www.cbc.ca/news/canada/b-c-parents-lobby-against-circumcision-1.513363.

118 World Health Organization, above n 115, 7.

119 Patrick, above n 113, 1181. Patrick argued in the negative (that male circumcision is not an abuse of the rights of the child) and presented the lack of data to support her contention that there is no significant harm caused to the child.

without subjecting it to greater scrutiny.[120] The same risks have been acknowledged in international law: in 2013 the Committee on the Rights of the Child expressed concern about short- and long-term complications arising from some traditional male circumcision practices in Israel.[121]

Circumcision also poses risks to sexual health. There is evidence that the non-circumcised adult penis is more sensitive, given that the five most sensitive areas of the penis are removed during circumcision, implying reduced sexual sensitivity for the circumcised male.[122] One of the key reasons for opposing FGM is the reduced sexual pleasure the victim will experience upon becoming sexually active. While the degree to which this is the case may be significantly higher than for her male counterpart depending on the extent of the circumcision (often resulting in pain during sex as opposed to reduced pleasure), the fact of this relativity should not exempt male circumcision from scrutiny. Consider for instance the position of a doctor rendered objective by having been isolated from exposure to the widespread acceptance and 'normalisation' of the practice. Were this doctor asked to decide upon the ethics of cutting off an infant's foreskin in accordance with the religious convictions of his parents, she would consider both questions of consent and the Hippocratic Oath which compels her to "do no harm", and arguably decide that "the irreversible, invasive and painful removal of any neurologically complex external organ of a powerless patient at the request of a third party is an ethical travesty."[123]

Christopher Hitchens (an atheist who was himself ritually circumcised as an infant and said in an interview the year before he died, that he sometimes "broods about the missing bit"[124]) was firm in his belief that the health risks posed to the baby should outweigh the religious preferences of his parents:

> who can bear to read the medical textbooks and histories which calmly record the number of boy babies who died from infection after the eighth day, or who suffered gross and unbearable dysfunction and disfigurement? The record of syphilitic and other infection, from rotting rabbinical teeth or other rabbinical indiscretions, or of clumsy slitting of the urethra and sometimes a vein, is simply dreadful…If religion and its arrogance were not

120 For this reason it is recommended that appropriate sanitary conditions and professional performance should be ensured in ritual circumcisions. See: *Interim report of the Special Rapporteur on freedom of religion and belief, Heiner Bielefeldt*, UN Doc A/70/286 (5 August 2015) [78].

121 CRC/C/ISR/CO/2–4 [41–42].

122 See for instance, Hinchley, above n 96. However, the World Health Organization disagrees with this finding, arguing that reduction of sexual satisfaction is unlikely to result from male circumcision. See World Health Organization, above n 116, 8.

123 Paul Mason, Commissioner for Children, Hobart, Tasmania, Australia, Letter to the Editor, *Sydney Morning Herald* (online), 6 June 2009, accessed 22 March 2017, http://www.smh.com.au/national/letters/stopping-circumcision-a-matter-of-human-rights-20090605-byf4.html?page=6.

124 Paul Holdengraber interview with Christopher Hitchens (in conversation at the New York Public Library), 4 June 2010.

> involved, no healthy society would permit this primitive amputation, or allow any surgery to be practiced on the genitalia without the full and informed consent of the person concerned.[125]

Objectively scrutinised with reference to medical findings over religious reasons, continued circumcision of infant males compromises the child's right to health and also may raise issues under article 7 of the ICCPR, stating that "[n]o one shall be subjected to torture or to cruel, inhuman or degrading treatment or punishment."[126] The right of children to be protected from such treatment is reinforced by article 37(a) of the CRC.[127] It is submitted here that the removal of the foreskin, often without anaesthetic,[128] from an infant who does not have the capacity to consent or resist not only risks violating his right to health, but could even amount to degrading and inhuman treatment.

3.2. The child's freedom of religion and belief

Male circumcision is of fundamental religious importance to those who perform it. Considered by some as a command from God necessary to enter a given faith,[129] a human command not to circumcise is understandably less compelling. In the book of Genesis it is commanded:

> Whether born in your household or bought with your money, they must be circumcised. My covenant in your flesh is to be an everlasting covenant. Any uncircumcised male, who has not been circumcised in the flesh, will be cut off from his people; he has broken my covenant.[130]

For some Jews, circumcision is considered essential to Jewish identity and a key commandment of Judaism.[131] Therefore the negative consequences of not being circumcised from a religious point of view may be so grave as to outweigh negative considerations from a rights point of view. As a result, were the practice to be prohibited in international law, many people would simply be compelled to contravene prohibitions in order to practise their faith. Rather than acknowledging the simple fact of the limits of the law and the incompatibility between religion and rights,

125 Hitchens, above n 79, 226.
126 *ICCPR*, Article 7.
127 *CRC*, Article 37(a).
128 See for instance, Hinchley, above n 96.
129 See for instance, Jack Ewing, 'Some Religious Leaders See a Threat as Europe Grows More Secular', *New York Times*, 19 September 2012, accessed 22 March 2017, http://www.nytimes.com/2012/09/20/world/europe/circumcision-debate-in-europe-reflects-deeper-tensions.html?pagewanted=all&_r=0.
130 *Bible*, Genesis, 17:13–14.
131 See for instance, 'Why do Jews circumcise their children? Dossier of the Central Council of Jews in Germany on the issue of circumcision', Zentralrat der Juden in Deutschland, accessed 22 March 2017, http://www.zentralratdjuden.de/en/article/3734.html.

the latter has been interpreted to condone the practice on the basis of the parent's religious freedom, notwithstanding that doing so subordinates the child's freedoms.

Wide acceptance of religious circumcision globally, implies that rationally and objectively approached rights perspectives play little role. Indeed, no simple question has been raised by human rights bodies about whether parents have a right over their son's penis for this purpose.[132] Yet, circumcision of an infant amounts to manifestation of the religion of one person upon another person's penis. The child's own article 18 rights are at issue; where circumcision represents a covenant with God, it is ostensibly the child who is entered into such a covenant. In the matter of cutting off the foreskin of an infant's penis, while the protection of the practice under international human rights law is based on a parent's religious rights vis-à-vis his child, there must also be countervailing human rights that intervene to protect his freedom not to permanently bear the mark of another person's religion. Yet on male circumcision human rights scholars have noted that

> the child's freedom *from* religion or the alleged right of the child to 'an open future' largely uninfluenced by any religious socialization…cannot count as a persuasive argument for limiting religious initiation ceremonies undertaken with the free consent of the parents of a child who has not yet reached religious maturity.[133]

A 2012 decision of the Cologne regional court in Germany reached a different decision, finding that the child's rights to not be subjected to bodily harm and to make religious choices for himself later, trump the religious rights of parents. That case involved medical complications resulting from the circumcision of a four-year-old. The surgeon who performed the procedure at the request of the child's parents was acquitted on charges of criminal battery, but the court nonetheless found that circumcision of a boy unable to consent, if not medically necessary, could constitute criminal battery even if performed with the consent of both parents. The court noted that such circumcision was not in the best interests of the child given the irreparable and permanent change that results from the procedure, which is counter to the child's interest to decide about his religion later. Here, it did not consider the rights of the parents to be unduly interfered with, as the child could later decide to be circumcised when capable of doing so. The child's right to bodily integrity and determination of his own religion were thus found to trump the rights of parents.[134]

132 A search for 'male circumcision' of the 'Universal Human Rights Index of United Nations Documents' (http://www.universalhumanrightsindex.org/en/index.html) 22 March 2017 yielded nine results which raise concern about the health risks of male circumcision carried out in unsafe conditions, but none questions that the practice should be allowed.

133 Bielefeldt, Ghanea and Weiner, above n 9, 425. This same reasoning is not applied to female circumcision.

134 Landgericht Köln, Beschneidung, Judgment of Monday, 7 May 2012, No. 151, Ns 169/11, Neue Juristische Wochenschrift (NJW), http://www.justiz.nrw.de/nrwe/

The reactions to this decision of the Cologne regional court offer insight into the profound significance of the practice for many. While the case concerned the child of Muslim parents, an enraged response came also from the Jewish community: the head of the Orthodox Conference of European Rabbis in Berlin referred to the decision as the "worst attack on Jewish life since the Holocaust".[135] It also attracted the chagrin of scholars who pointed out the failings of decision-makers to adequately consider established literature on the importance of the practice in religion, and for failing to adequately consider the rights of parents.[136] The negative response to the decision was so vehement (and politically charged) that the German government amended its Civil Code in December of 2012 to clarify that circumcision for religious reasons remained legal in Germany.[137] This case highlights the complexity of ritual circumcision from a human rights perspective. For the non-religious or otherwise objective observer, the practice may amount to bodily harm inflicted against a non-consenting minor. But for the religious parent, prohibiting the practice may amount to something much worse, preventing them from establishing the child's place in their community and religion.

Applying the evolving-capacities consideration to the circumcision scenario reveals the flaws in human rights law as it operates in respect of children. The point at which the child evolves to have adequate capacity to decide on the fate of his penis, operates not to enable that child to choose to have a part of it removed, but rather becomes the point at which the child is capable of refusing consent. In other words, parents are given the advantage of this decision simply because the child is powerless against them. The fact that the child has no capacity to give or refuse consent or bring a complaint accounts for why parents are able to remove foreskins unchallenged, yet a necessary principle of international human rights law is that all people should enjoy human rights, regardless of their capacity to do so. The consequences were this not the case would result in respect for rights being tempered by degrees relative to the capacity of rights-holders, such that torture, for instance, would be considered less abhorrent where meted out on a person with low mental capacity to understand or experience it.

lgs/koeln/lg_koeln/j2012/151_Ns_169_11_Urteil_20120507.html in German. An unofficial translation is available at http://www.scribd.com/doc/98810698/Cologne-Circumcision-Decision-Translated-6-12.

135 Quoted in 'The World from Berlin: Circumcision Ruling is a "Shameful farce for Germany"', *Spiegel Online,* 13 July 2012, accessed 22 March 2017, http://www.spiegel.de/international/germany/german-press-review-on-outlash-against-court-s-circumcision-ruling-a-844271.html.

136 See for instance, Angelika Günzel, 'Nationalisation of Religious Parental Education? The German Circumcision Case' (2013) 2 *Oxford Journal of Law and Religion*, 206, 208 and Bijan Fateh-Moghadam, 'Criminalizing male circumcision? Case Note: Landgericht Cologne, Judgment of 7 May 2012 – No. 151 Ns 169/11', (2012) 13 *German Law Journal* 1131, 1136.

137 See §1631d of the German Civil Code and reasoning offered for the amendment, including the significance of the practice to several religions, notably Judaism and Islam (available in German at http://dipbt.bundestag.de/dip21/btd/17/112/1711295.pdf). Also see Günzel, above n 136, 209.

In his *Study of Discrimination in the matter of Religious Rights and Practices* written before the text of the human rights Covenants had been finalised, Arcot Krishnaswami issued guidance to legislators in the form of 16 "basic rules" towards achieving the goals outlined in the UDHR. Relevant for present discussions, Rule 16(4)(c) states simply that:

> In case of conflict between the requirements of two or more religions or beliefs, public authorities should endeavour to find a solution assuring the greatest measure of freedom to society as a whole, while giving preference to the freedom of everyone to maintain or to change his religion or belief over any practice or observance tending to restrict this freedom.[138]

Valuing pluralism can be seen as a reply to Krishnaswami's request for an approach that serves society as a whole. Where the religious freedoms of an individual or a group of persons must be limited in defence of the rights of others, the limitation is ultimately issued in service of the religious freedom of society as a whole. In resolving conflict between a parent's right to manifest their religion and the child's right to be free from that manifestation, the weight of decision would come down in favour of the child. To echo the words of the UN High Commissioner for Human Rights, Ms Navi Pillay, "the balance between tradition and culture, on one hand, and universal human rights, on the other, must be struck in favour of rights" such that "[n]o personal opinion, no religious belief, no matter how deeply held or widely shared, can ever justify depriving another human being of his or her basic rights."[139]

When religious circumcision is performed on an infant or young child he is unaware of what is happening and the reasons why, and unable to articulate his viewpoint or describe the nature and gravity of his pain. He does not enter willingly into a covenant or understand the implications and risks of doing so. The choice then to circumcise infants takes advantage of the fact that their capacity has not yet evolved to let them exercise their own religious or belief choices. Subjecting this particular religious practice to the evolving-capacity consideration would operate to allow a child to assume his own religious identity when he has the capacity to do so. The fact that a practice is a religious practice should not immunise it from scrutiny, particularly where it is manifested by an adult on a powerless infant. Prohibiting male circumcision of infants for religious reasons would not result in lost medical benefits or lost religious significance; an individual would be free to choose to undergo the procedure when he has the capacity to consent to its associated risks and religious connotations. The decision of

138 Arcot Krishnaswami, *Study of Discrimination in the matter of Religious Rights and Practices*, UN. Doc. E/CN.4/Sub.2/200/Rev.1 (1960), UN. Pub. No 60.XIV.2, 66.

139 Statement by UN High Commissioner for Human Rights Navi Pillay to the Panel on ending violence, discrimination against people because of their sexual orientation, Geneva, 7 March 2012, accessed 22 March 2017, http://acnudh.org/en/pillay-presents-groundbreaking-un-study-on-violence-discrimination-against-people-because-of-their-sexual-orientation/.

parents to circumcise their son before he has capacity to participate in the decision, robs him of the choice to be circumcised or not in accordance with his religion or belief.

4. Conclusion: The need to protect children from their parents

The international human rights framework views the religion of children through the lens of their parents, and there is scant guidance on how conflicts between rights of parents and children can be resolved.[140] Rex Ahdar acknowledges that a child's religious and belief wishes may conflict with the wishes his parents have for him, but ultimately argues against recognising an autonomous right of children because its practical operation would undermine family integrity and call upon secular decision-makers to adjudicate on matters they are ill-qualified for and may be biased in relation to.[141] He notes that in bringing up their children, parents are wise to respect the eventual freedom that a child will have in relation to his or her religion and belief, but in the meantime considers that the danger of parents occasionally abusing their authority are outweighed by the harm that would result from granting children religious autonomy, and that the parent should be given the benefit of the doubt unless he "is commanding something patently objectionable or immoral".[142]

Nowak and Vospernik express a different view, pointing out that forcing a baby or small child to become a member of a political party or trade union would likely be considered an unjustified interference with his privacy or freedom of association, while such interferences are generally accepted when they become members of religious organisations. They go on to note that even parental rights to bring up children in accordance with their own religion or belief have limits, referring to interventions that they believe should take place to protect the life and health of children.[143] The reasoning they offer relating to blood transfusions is asserted here as applying to male circumcision. The fact that children currently do not enjoy meaningful freedom from the religion of their parents raises the question of what their article 18 rights practically mean if they have no autonomous recourse to protection from bodily interference. As one activist said about female circumcision, "It's the first sign to a child that her body is not hers, it's the community's."[144] The same is true with male circumcision that claims a boy's body for the religious community.

140 See General Assembly, *Elimination of all forms of religious intolerance*, UN Doc A/67/303 (13 August 2012) [48–50].

141 See Ahdar above n 14, 93–114, and Ahdar and Leigh, above n 7, 241.

142 Ahdar, above n 14, 108.

143 Manfred Nowak and Tanja Vospernik, 'Permissible Restrictions on Freedom of Religion or Belief' in T. Lindholm, W. Cole Durham and B. G. Tahzib-Lie, *Facilitating of Freedom of Religion or Belief: A Deskbook* (Martinus Nijhoff, 2004) 170.

144 Yvette Tan, 'Why female genital mutilation still exists in modern Singapore', *BBC News*, 21 November 2016, accessed 22 March 2017, http://www.bbc.com/news/world-asia-37819753.

The pro-parental, pro-religious bias inherent in international law is acutely apparent in the fact that religious interests and preferences of the parent trump any claim the child may have to a contrary outcome. Indeed, the primacy accorded to the wishes of parents over the individual rights and interests of their child in respect of circumcision reveals the bias shown towards major religions in international law, despite the fact that rights attach to people, not their religions or beliefs. Indeed, if a new religion could be manifested by slapping a person in the face, the law would likely intervene to prohibit the slapper from interfering with the bodily integrity of the slappee, irrespective of the mildness of the harm done. Similarly, challenges would likely be mounted against new religious movements that encouraged tattooing or otherwise branding infants as a mark of their membership, perhaps particularly where sexual organs were involved. The same is not true where major religions practise circumcision. The bias of international human rights law in favour of major religions is borne out no more blatantly, than in its protection of the cutting of infant genitals, as a manifestation of religion and belief.

It has been stated that "[h]armful practices can never be justified as manifestations of freedom of religion or belief, whatever their underlying reasons may be."[145] The logic that excludes male circumcision from this principle is not sound. Determining what amount to harmful practices in matters of religion and belief is complicated, and must be done in a way that is ideologically impartial and guided by the principle that at some point, the child acquires the right and capacity to enjoy his non-derogable article 18(1) right to freedom of religion and belief. Human rights bodies are reticent to define the outer limits of parents' article 18(4) rights for the pragmatic reason that interfering with all instances in which parents improperly coerce their children would result in an unmanageable number of human rights violations. Indeed, approaching circumcision as a violation of article 18 would simply result in an untenable number of abuses; parents would continue the practice and states would continue to allow it.

Practical implementation challenges notwithstanding, it must at least be conceded that objective reasoning has been relinquished in deference to religious sensibilities, resulting in what is *prima facie* a violation of rights being artfully morphed into a skewed form of permissible manifestation. If the right of the child to reject the religion of his parents were protected equally alongside his right to maintain the religion he was born into, the conclusion would be that not circumcising a child in accordance with the religion of his parents, would grant him the choice to be circumcised – or not to be – in accordance with his own convictions. Abandoning children to the harmful religious practices of their parents is the moral equivalent of denying human rights to rights-holders who are the most vulnerable among us, because they are vulnerable.

145 Bielefeldt, Ghanea and Weiner, above n 9, 435.

6 Conclusion

Preceding case study chapters underline the pro-religious bias in the practice of international human rights law, and the presence of a hierarchy of religion and belief that privileges followers of some major monotheistic religions and disadvantages atheists and non-believers. This chapter asserts that this hierarchy is unjustified and must be levelled by ensuring that freedom of religion and belief equally protects freedom *from* religion and belief.

1. Indefensibility of pro-religious bias of human rights law

> *"I am a deeply religious nonbeliever."*[1]
>
> Albert Einstein

Having established that a pro-religious bias exists in the practice of international human rights law, it becomes necessary to consider whether such bias is justified. Perhaps it is appropriate to accord more respect to followers of established, time-tested religions over others and over non-religion and atheism. Simply put, perhaps some religions and beliefs are more deserving of respect than others.

1.1. Relevance of the inherent value of religion and belief

An argument could be made that pro-religious bias at international law is justified because of the inherent value of some religions and beliefs relative to others. This proposition raises questions as to who is to judge what is inherently valuable, and what the implications of doing so are. Legal bodies are tasked to determine what is and is not permissible according to the laws they are mandated to interpret and apply, not to judge whether a religion or belief is inherently 'good' or 'bad'. Even if they did attempt to determine whether some religions or beliefs are inherently more valuable than others, there would be no objective grounds for doing so. Some potential grounds are raised and dismissed below to show the impossibility of this task.

1 Albert Einstein, 'Selected Writings on Religion' in Christopher Hitchens, *The Portable Atheist* (De Capo Press, 2007) 157.

Longevity

Temptation may be to accept the privilege that established religions enjoy on the basis that it has always been thus. History shows that followers of almost every religion have had to survive significant persecution before becoming respected. One can speculate, then, that their endurance through turbulent times somehow bestows them with value. However, a consequence of this approach would be that Judaism would gain more esteem than relatively newer religions like Christianity and Islam. The approach also must contend with the fact that atheists have existed for as long as there have been religions for them to reject.

While this approach may be acceptable from a religious or cultural point of view, from a rights perspective, the extent to which a religion or belief has endured does not justify discriminatory treatment of others.[2] Indeed, the very reason that some religions and beliefs have *not* endured is due to rights violation and eradication of their adherents. Followers of now extinct indigenous religions who perished refusing attempts by invaders to convert them, cannot be said to be have been less entitled to freedom of religion and belief. Further, if longevity is considered a factor justifying a particular place on the hierarchy, how long would a religion or belief be expected to endure and in what form? Longevity, no matter how hard won, remains a sketchy criterion and is irrelevant to the individual who sincerely adheres to a religion or belief.

Popularity

Another approach may be to assert a utilitarian proposition that the greater number of adherents a religion or belief has, the greater the respect it is entitled to. Major religions would therefore have higher standing than those with only a handful of adherents.

In 2010, the Pew Research Centre estimated that there are 5.8 billion religiously affiliated adults and children around the globe, representing 85% of the world population of 6.9 billion. Of these, 2.2 billion (32%) are Christian and 1.6 billion (23%) are Muslim, making up more than half the global population.[3] These numbers could justify the higher place of Christians and Muslims, relative to the significantly less practised Cao Dai, for instance.[4] The implication of such numbers is that their adherents have a collective voice that is comparatively louder than that of members of minority religions or beliefs beside them. Almost three-quarters of people in the world (73%) live in countries in which their religion is the majority

2 Manfred Nowak and Tanja Vospernik, 'Permissible Restrictions on Freedom of Religion or Belief' in T. Lindholm, W. Cole Durham and B. G. Tahzib-Lie, *Facilitating of Freedom of Religion or Belief: A Deskbook* (Martinus Nijhoff, 2004) 165.

3 The Pew Forum on Religion and Public Life, 'The Global Religious Landscape; A report on the size and distribution of the world's major religious groups as of 2010', December 2012, 9.

4 There are an estimated 8 million followers of Cao Dai. See Philip Wilkinson, *Religions* (Dorling Kindersley, 2008) 279.

religion,[5] begging the question of how the other 27% fares. This question points to the obvious weakness of popularity as a criterion; the vulnerability of minority groups would be entrenched merely because they lack strength of numbers. The result would be that heavily persecuted Baha'i would be sidelined to their persecutors. 'Rankings' would also be ever changing as the popularity of one religion or belief rose and another fell out of favour, potentially providing an incentive for believers to more aggressively recruit additional adherents in a bid to increase their respectability. Islam and Christianity could be ranked against each other on the basis of which had more adherents,[6] and different denominations within a religion would be pitted against each other. The result would be that more respect would be given to more popular religions, rather than to the individuals who most need protection. It would mean that Jews, who account for only 0.2% of the global population (approximately 14 million people), would be ranked low in the new hierarchy,[7] but it is their particular history of persecution resulting in tragically depleted numbers of adherents, that stands as a compelling argument against measuring the worth of a religion on the basis of its popularity. Indeed, it may be for the very reason of their small numbers and minority status that some adherents of religion or belief are in particular need of rights protection. Further, members of the dominant religion may remain members for want of a meaningful choice to leave.

In the final analysis, then, numbers speak to the extent to which a given religion is followed around the world, but say nothing of the methods used to bring that adherence about or of the rights enjoyed by individuals who belong to that religion or do not. The popularity of a religion, whether high or low, should be irrelevant in determining individual rights entitlements.

Content or plausibility

Another approach that could justify the existence of a hierarchy could be found in considering the content of the beliefs in question. But attempting to establish which beliefs are more valid, correct or plausible is to misunderstand the nature of religion and belief. Any attempt to identify elements within belief sets that are 'good', 'bad', 'better' or 'worse' than others, begs questions of who has authority to decide and how decisions are made. As discussed in Chapter 2, the ingredients of relatively new religions, such as Scientology, are met with less respect than those of more established religions. But the Dianetics of Scientology may be as ridiculous to a Protestant as baptism is to a Scientologist. As Jeremy Gunn explains:

5 The Pew Forum on Religion and Public Life, above n 3, 11. This figure does not include sub-groups of major religions, for instance Shia Muslims living in Sunni-majority countries or Catholics living in Protestant-majority countries.
6 Pew predicts that the number of Muslims will equal the number of Christians by the year 2050. See The Pew Forum on Religion and Public Life, 'The Future of World Religions: Population Growth Projections, 2010–2050,' April 2015, 5.
7 Ibid 9.

> Whether the E-Meter is a mechanical gimmick or is a sophisticated piece of equipment that provides spiritual information is not the question. For a court or a government to presume that it knows the answer to that question, and to impose restrictions accordingly, is to ignore rights of conscience.[8]

Reincarnation may be as implausible to a Catholic as transubstantiation is to a Hindu. The ideas contained in different branches of Islam may be vital to some Muslims and offensive to others. If an international tribunal was to rank Sunni or Shiite branches of Islam against each other, doing so would inevitably discriminate against those who adhered to whichever branch was decided to have less inherent value or verisimilitude than the other.

The respect that different religions and beliefs are afforded must be acknowledged as time and culture bound; what is respectable now was not always so. Indeed, Jesus Christ and Joseph Smith are examples of past prophets who were persecuted for controversial claims that are now accepted as 'respectable' religious beliefs. Belief in flesh and blood prophets of the present is met with more scepticism than is commitment to prophets of the past that do not have (and may never have had) flesh and blood presence to vouch for their credibility. This is so despite the fact that claims of 'new' prophets are not necessarily any more supernatural, intangible or lacking in proof than claims made by past prophets.[9]

Human rights law cannot and should not define religion or belief, nor engage in questions as to the verisimilitude of their various precepts. The consequence for non-religious or atheistic rights-holders, would be that they would be compelled to disprove the existence of the God or gods they do not believe in in order for their non-belief to be accorded protection, while followers of those religions scurry to counter those claims in a bid to maintain theirs. This scenario is untenable, and would catastrophically undermine human rights protection. A religion or belief is valuable and important and true to its adherents in a way that is unchanged by the absence of proof.

Purpose

Finally, there may be an argument that some religions pursue genuine religious or spiritual purposes, while others have questionable or even rights-antithetical

8 Jeremy Gunn, 'Adjudicating Rights of Conscience under the European Convention on Human Rights', in Johan van der Vyver and John Witte (eds), *Religious Human Rights in Global Perspective: Legal Perspectives* (Martinus Nijhoff Publishers, 1996) 327.

9 Consider the people of the island of Tanna in Vanuatu whose belief that Prince Philip, the Duke of Edinburgh, is a deity was strengthened by an in-person meeting with him in the mid-1970s and the gifts and the Prince subsequently sent them. Amos Roberts, 'Waiting for Philip', *Dateline Report* (SBS Australia), 8 August 2010 http://www.sbs.com.au/dateline/story/about/id/600662/n/Waiting-for-Philip; Paul Chapman 'Why a tribe in Vanuatu believes their god Prince Philip is set to visit', *The Telegraph*, 25 April 2015, http://www.telegraph.co.uk/news/worldnews/australiaandthepacific/vanuatu/11563091/Why-a-tribe-in-Vanuatu-believes-their-god-Prince-Philip-is-set-to-visit.html, both accessed 2 May 2017.

aspirations. The loaded terminology used to distinguish between 'cults' or 'sects' and more prevalent and widely accepted 'new religious movements' is emotive and can generate intolerance of some beliefs and practices, for instance where the state takes measures to counteract the influence of 'sects' but not of 'religions'.[10] Irrespective of terminology, the true challenge in determining whether spiritual or religious motives are genuine or not, starts at the point of determining what a 'genuine' religious aspiration is. Genuineness measured by plausibility is a problematic endeavour: for some, it is the absence of proof that makes their belief more sacred and sincere. A cult that ends in a mass suicide may, from a spiritual point of view, have achieved its religious purpose and transported its adherents to an afterlife of sorts, in the same way that some monotheists believe they are bound for eternal life after death.

Sincerity of belief cannot be measured by the purposes of its religious (or belief) leaders. A 'cult' leader may rally followers for the purpose of his own sexual gratification or financial gain, or simply be insane, but his motivation may not make the devotion of his followers any less sincere. Respected leaders of major religions may also promote practices that are criminal in nature or subvert justice. What happens at the higher levels of a religious or belief organisation, or what the motivations of its leaders are, should not detract from the religious freedoms of the people who adhere to that religion or belief. If this were so, changed leadership could result in reduced rights protection. Regardless of the fact that leaders of a given Church may have questionable and non-religious motives, the sincerity of the beliefs of their followers may remain undiminished and it is this sincerity of belief that is an essential component of article 18. By way of illustration, the Unification Church (referred to derogatorily as the 'Moonies' after its self-proclaimed messiah, the late Sun Myung Moon, and known for its mass wedding ceremonies) continues today, and is generally recognised as a religion despite several scandals and significant financial interests of the 'true family' who leads it.[11] The fact that the Church of Scientology may be driven largely by the financial thirst of its upper echelons does not detract from the rights of Scientologist to practise Scientology. In the same way that some Catholics have stepped out of the Catholic Church in protest against its mishandling of child abuse but remain believing Catholics, so too are many Scientologists leaving the establishment, disillusioned by its exploitation and mistreatment of members, but continuing to practise Scientology outside the 'official' Church.[12] In short, it is impossible to judge the 'purpose' of religions and

10 Natan Lerner, *Religion, Beliefs, and International Human Rights* (Orbis Books, 2000) 7–8.

11 For more on the Unification Church, see John Bowker (ed.), *The Concise Oxford Dictionary of World Religions* (Oxford University Press, 2005) 384 and 'Rev. Sun Myung Moon, Self-proclaimed messiah who built religious movement, dies at 92', *New York Times*, 2 September 2012, accessed 22 March 2017, http://www.nytimes.com/2012/09/03/world/asia/rev-sun-myung-moon-founder-of-unification-church-dies-at-92.html?pagewanted=all&_r=0.

12 See for instance, Lawrence Wright 'The Apostate: Paul Haggis v the Church of Scientology' *The New Yorker* (online), 14 February 2011, accessed 22 March 2017, http://www.newyorker.com/reporting/2011/02/14/110214fa_fact_wright.

beliefs from a rights-based point of view, and doing so remains beside the point as far as adherents are concerned.

Bias is unjustified

Ultimately, whatever inherent value religions or beliefs may or may not have is irrelevant for human rights law and cannot be determined by it. A religious perspective may be that a given religion is intrinsically 'good' and represents the only correct way for humans to live and organise themselves. The same cannot be true from a human rights point of view for which pluralism of religion and belief is a 'good', because it represents diverse individuals exercising and enjoying freedom of religion and belief. Religions and beliefs are important to individuals who hold them, in a way that other religions and beliefs are not, regardless of what those religions and beliefs are. Religion and belief do not matter to human rights law because of the social or spiritual contribution they make, but because of their contribution to individual personality and as an expression of individual freedom.

Human rights law cannot judge the merits of individual beliefs, but it can uphold the value of pluralism by striving to ensure that all individuals equally enjoy freedom of religion and belief. Any bias towards one religion or belief over another cannot be justified on the basis of their content, viability, popularity, durability or influence. The particular vulnerability of atheists would be an argument for elevating their position in such a hierarchy above less vulnerable rights-holders, but this too is an undesirable outcome in a bid for neutrality and equality. An individual's freedom of religion and belief should not be qualified on the basis of his religion or belief, any more than his right to hold opinions should be qualified on the basis of the opinions he holds. A non-discriminatory approach must be taken to uphold the universality of human rights attaching to all humans on the basis of their humanity. Humans – not their beliefs – are the common denominator in equality of freedom of religion and belief.[13]

1.2. Relevance of religion or belief in social life

An alternative argument to justify the pro-religious bias of international human rights law could be found by looking to the impact that religions and beliefs have on society, beyond their intrinsic value to the individual. Religion can determine how an individual spends his or her time, who he or she associates with or even marries, or even how he or she earns and spends money. Put another way, some would posit that religion or belief determines how we are to live. Parameters for measuring the relevance of religion and belief in social life are the extent of its influence, the extent to which it benefits society, and the extent to which religion and belief unite rights-holders into a discernible group or 'minority'.

13 Heiner Bielefeldt, Nazila Ghanea and Michael Weiner, *Freedom of Religion and Belief: An International Law Commentary* (Oxford, 2016) 25.

Extent to which religion or belief influences community

Article 18 speaks explicitly of the enjoyment of freedom of religion and belief "either individually or in community with others". Certainly some religions have had more influence on community than others. As Anthony Bradney comments, "[t]he most vibrant examples of belonging to a religion occur where the religion is both a religious resource and also a significant social resource for its members."[14] Therefore, an argument in favour of elevating established religions over others is that they integrate people into a religious community and regulate and organise social relationships between them. This rationale would point to the significant impact that major religions have on social life including in practices that bring communities together for key occasions such as births, deaths and marriages. Diwali, Ramadan and Christmas are social, cultural and familial highlights of the year for many members of society, often irrespective of whether they are adherents of those religions or not; some key religious events are observed even in states that have no official religion, or in states that officially adopt another religion.[15]

Major religions have also made significant contributions to the way societies are governed, adding ingredients and principles to law. The application of Sharia in some states is evidence of the far-reaching and long-standing influence of Islam, which has shown that it can govern societies, punish transgressions and mediate disputes that may arise in human relationships. Similarly, the continuance of canon law in some Church communities speaks to the organisational capacity of Catholicism, and the fact that some communities choose to adhere to Jewish law (the *halakhah*) underscores the enduring role of major religions in social life. Accordingly, the higher place that these three Abrahamic religions occupy on the hierarchy could be justified by the fact that precepts from each continue to influence governance in several countries in ways that cannot yet be said for other religions.[16] A history of Europe, for instance, cannot be separated from the history of Christianity, nor the Middle East from the history of Islam.[17] Some states have even organised themselves into communities on the basis of religion, most notably, the 57 member state Organisation of Islamic Cooperation (OIC).[18] Hinduism and Buddhism also influence legal systems in some countries (including India and Bhutan respectively).[19] In contrast, newer religions have not yet proved that they can underpin viable and enduring societies.

14 Anthony Bradney, *Law and Faith in a Sceptical Age* (Routledge-Cavendish, 2009) 22.

15 For instance, Christmas is widely celebrated in secular Australia, and streets are festively decorated to mark that event in the streets of Buddhist Thailand.

16 See, however, Micheline R. Ishay, *The Human Rights Reader* (2nd edn, Routledge, 2007) 23–38 in which the influence of several other religions on the development of human rights law is discussed.

17 See Peter Cumper and Tom Lewis, *Religion, Rights and Secular Society: European Perspectives* (Edward Elgar Publishing, 2012) 5.

18 See Organisation of Islamic Cooperation website, accessed 22 March 2017, http://www.oic-oci.org/home/?lan=en.

19 However, as mentioned Chapter 1, section 2, few other religions determine the legal system in a state.

Yet the weight these considerations are given at the international level must be justified by clear criteria. A religion may play a significant role in one country and only a minor role elsewhere. Dangers of relativity arise in determining the point at which a religion or belief can be considered to have had adequate social influence to claim a high place in the hierarchy. It also must be asked whether a prescribed number of societies, or individuals within them, is necessary to affirm that a religion has earned or lost its position. Such questions would likely elicit relativist and inconsistent answers depending on who is required to respond to them.

Furthermore, the above examples speak largely to the breadth of influence through time and across the globe, not necessarily to its depth. The continued celebration of Christmas by non-Christians in secular countries may point to the continued influence of Christianity or be conversely tendered as evidence of its dilution. Some new religious movements may have achieved a higher level of influence in particular communities, albeit on a smaller scale: some polygamist sects in the United States for instance, or the Sea Org faction of the Church of Scientology, or communes of 'The Family', could on face value be considered to have absolutely permeated every aspect of the social life of those communities. Confronting implications of establishing criteria on these grounds emerge; the paradoxical result of ranking one religion above another on the basis of the depth of its influence may be to value religions that are detrimental to human rights over those that are rights-supportive. Religions that now bind people together are often the result of religious wars and conflict marked by extreme violence and untold casualties. It is inappropriate for human rights law to privilege the victorious religion for having 'triumphed' over a community and forcing individuals within it to surrender their beliefs through violence, terror or other aggression. Doing so would be to pit people against each other and neglect the plight of minorities within society. It is therefore wholly inappropriate to equate the influence a religion wields with its entitlement to respect in human rights law.

Extent to which religion or belief benefits society or its members

In asserting that the societal benefits of a religion are relevant to determining its place on the hierarchy of religion and belief, it must be asked how such benefit is to be determined. Should the measure of such benefits be taken within the religious community or in society at large? Is it even fair to rate a religion for its service to society where its aims are spiritual? Again issues of relativity and subjectivity arise: what is considered by some to advance societies, to others would be to degenerate it and what is considered to be a social 'good' may for others represent a social 'ill'. Judging which is which from a rights perspective could perhaps be achieved by considering which religions and beliefs advance human rights enjoyment in society. But even where the bar is set as low as being the absence of detriment to rights enjoyment, the criterion remains problematic.

Taken on face value, Scientology may ascend up the hierarchy in light of the fact that its founder explicitly included support for human rights in the Code of

Scientologists.[20] Meanwhile, some major religions may fall down, where some religious states fail to ratify international human rights instruments or make reservations to the obligations prescribed therein on religious grounds. The Holy See's prohibition of female leadership could justify demoting the standing of Catholicism and some interpretations of Sharia law could be criticised for the individual rights violations perpetrated in its implementation. Similarly, the high degree of influence wielded by less mainstream religions may reduce the rights enjoyment of adherents. An example is the Hindu practice of Chhaupadi that results in isolation and mistreatment of menstruating girls and women.[21] The pervasive influence of some new religious movements on members of their community may also have the effect of isolating them from wider society.[22]

Affording rights-holders more or less respect on the basis of the beneficial or detrimental influence their religion or belief has on society, cannot be supportable from a human rights perspective. Such an approach would imply that a person who adheres to an 'intolerant' religion or interpretation thereof (where the measure of 'intolerance' itself may be contested), would have a lesser claim to freedom of religion and belief than a person who adheres to a more pro-rights religion.[23]

Extent to which religion or belief unite people into a 'group' or 'minority'

The hierarchy of religion and belief could be justified by the extent to which religions and beliefs unite people into groups who accordingly have access to group rights. Article 27 of the ICCPR reads:

> In those States in which ethnic, religious or linguistic minorities exist, persons belonging to such minorities shall not be denied the right, in community with the other members of their group, to enjoy their own culture, to profess and practice their own religion, or to use their own language.

General Comment 23 on article 27 defines a minority as "those who belong to a group and share in common a culture, a religion and/or a language".[24] The UN Declaration on Rights of Persons Belonging to National or Ethnic, Religious and

20 See: http://www.scientology.org/how-we-help/human-rights.html accessed 22 March 2017.

21 See: 'Nepal police investigate death of girl banished for menstruating', *BBC*, 20 December 2016, accessed 21 December 2016, http://www.bbc.com/news/world-asia-38384889.

22 The controversial death in 1995 of Lisa McPherson in Clearwater, Florida in the custody of a branch of the Church of Scientology is often pointed to in highlighting concerns about the Church discouraging followers from seeking mainstream treatment for mental health problems. See Wright, above n 12.

23 See for instance Malcolm Evans, *Religious Liberty and International Law in Europe* (Cambridge University Press, 1997) 260.

24 Human Rights Committee, *General Comment 23: The rights of minorities* (Article 27), UN Doc CCPR/C/21/Rev.1/Add.5, (4 August 1994) [5.1].

Linguistic Minorities[25] grants persons belonging to religious minorities the right to profess and practise their own religion and effectively participate in religious life, as well as to establish and maintain associations and contact with other members of the group. However, the Declaration does not explain what religious minorities are.[26] And notably absent, are those groups who are bound by their non-religious 'belief'.

Natan Lerner has noted that "[r]eligion is based on faith, and faith is, of course, an individual phenomenon. But religious rights are also collective rights and encompass the rights of an entire group or community."[27] Perhaps a justification for some religions and beliefs being 'higher' than others is therefore found in their relative ability to maintain a group or community unified by it. The text of article 27 does not alter the fact that rights attach to individuals, yet individuals depend on the ability of the group to maintain culture, language or religion.[28]

Against this criterion, the bias may be somewhat justified. Dominant religious groups have clearly succeeded in creating cohesive group identities for the purposes of article 27. Newer religious groups have been less successful in doing so, so far, at least. But it is questionable whether non-believers and atheists could constitute a minority group; article 27 and the declaration omit 'belief' groups alongside national, ethnic, religious and linguistic groups. It is perhaps for this reason that the disadvantaged position of atheists vis-à-vis freedom of religion and belief can be explained. Though there are humanist and rationalist associations, there are few traditions or practices that unite atheists into a discernible 'group'.[29] Indeed, in surveys that track belief, atheists may simply be classified along with others including agnostics or those who do not identify with a particular religion, as 'none' or even as 'unaffiliated'.[30] Atheists do not congregate with any enduring regularity (with some exceptions including the recently founded 'Sunday Assembly').[31] Unlike members of religions, atheists may stand solo in beliefs they do not share with a cohesive 'group' of others. As former Special Rapporteur Jahangir noted, this circumstance could largely be due to the fact that atheistic or non-theistic beliefs often imply personal approaches that cannot unite individuals into a community in the same way that religious beliefs can.[32]

25 *United Nations Declaration of the Rights of Persons Belonging to National or Ethnic, Religious and Linguistic Minorities*, adopted and proclaimed by United Nations General Assembly Resolution 47/135 on December 18, 1992.
26 Lerner, above n 10, 35. Also see Natan Lerner, *Religion, Secularism and Human Rights* (2nd edn, Martinus Nijhoff Publishers, 2012) 45–46.
27 Lerner, above n 10, 120. Also see Lerner, above n 26, 15.
28 *General Comment 23*, UN Doc CCPR/C/21/Rev.1/Add.5 [6.2].
29 On the challenge of non-religious people forming communities and achieving recognition also see Lois Lee, *Recognizing the Non-religious: Reimagining the Secular* (Oxford, 2015) 98.
30 See for instance Pew Forum on Religion and Public Life, above n 6, 233.
31 The Sunday Assembly, http://sundayassembly.com accessed 22 March 2017.
32 It also noted that the lack of organisation among atheists is not necessarily due to their weakness in numbers. As Tom Flynn points out, "If atheists are lonely and downtrodden, we have only ourselves to blame. Numerically, we are strong. Let's start

By way of example, an ongoing struggle of Scientologists is for recognition of their status as a 'religion', which has been achieved in several countries. Such a status will never be accorded to, nor requested by atheists. As a result, it is unlikely that atheists will be eligible for tax exemptions in the way that Scientologists are in some countries. While a Scientologist may consider himself (and be considered by others) as 'religious' and part of an organisation, an atheist is by his own and by others' definition, 'irreligious', often defined by what he does not believe rather than by what he does. The logical conclusion is that although access to and enjoyment of human rights should not be conditional on the religion or belief of rights-holders, individuals who eschew religion have less recourse to religious rights than their religious counterparts do.

However, the fact that atheists are excluded from article 27 protection does not justify their low position as far as article 18 is concerned. Indeed, if any conclusion is to be reached on the basis of their lack of access to group rights, it should be the necessity of guaranteeing their enjoyment of the individual rights afforded to them by article 18 of the ICCPR.

Bias is unjustified

Emphasising the social elements of religion and belief in defending a hierarchy of respect at international law is ultimately equivalent to subverting the rights of individuals to the rights of groups, thereby exacerbating the vulnerability of persons who do not belong to them. Another point to consider is that religious or belief communities may not treat all members of their group equally, but privilege some over others (for example men over women, or full members over others).[33] As a result, there is a risk that the 'group' can be used to disguise the plight of individuals within it.

Rather than attempting to justify why different religions and beliefs are respected differently at international law, there is more value to be gained in understanding the nature of the respect that should be accorded to religion and belief. Former Special Rapporteur Bielefeldt offers salient advice in this regard, when he notes that such respect

> does not primarily refer to this or that concrete religion or belief which still we may consider wrong or unreasonable. Rather, respect is due for the ***underlying ability of human beings to have and develop deep convictions in the first place***.[34]

Here, the particular challenge of being an atheist in some parts of the world speaks to the respect they are entitled to. The conclusions reached point to the value of

punching our weight." 'Secularism's breakthrough moment' (2006) 26(3) *Free Inquiry* 16–17.

33 Nazila Ghanea, 'Religion, Equality, and Non-Discrimination', in John Witte Jr and Christian M. Green, *Religion and Human Rights: An Introduction* (Oxford University Press, 2012) 213. Also see Peter Edge, *Religion and Law: An Introduction* (Ashgate, 2006) 8.

34 Heiner Bielefeldt, 'Freedom of Religion or Belief – a Human Right under pressure' (2012) 1 *Oxford Journal of Law and Religion* 1, 3.

the pluralism asserted at the outset of this thesis. Only by respecting all religions and beliefs equally can rights-holders be considered to meaningfully enjoy freedom of religion and belief. Anything less would dilute a rights-based approach. International human rights decision-makers cannot determine the merits of an individual's religion or belief but they can assert her right to practise it, subject to permissible limitations set out in article 18(3) of the ICCPR. This approach can only be effective where it is made in full respect for pluralism that demands equal respect for all rights-holders across denominations and also within them. Those on the lowest rung of the hierarchy of religion and belief, being atheists and non-theists, clearly fall within the ambit of article 18, which protects theistic, non-theistic and atheistic beliefs, as well as the right not to profess any religion or belief.[35] This being the case, the hierarchy that is evident in the practice of international human rights law is not one that is justified on the basis of it.

2. Freedom *from* religion as the measure of religious freedom

The hierarchy of religion and belief is not justifiable from a rights perspective. The key question then becomes: how can the playing field be levelled in a way that does not discriminate between or depend on the religion or belief of the rights-holders concerned?

2.1. Pluralism as the guiding principle

Questions of when to limit manifestations or not should be driven by consideration of how freedom of religion and belief can be most enhanced, not how religion or belief itself can be. Decision-makers must ensure that they do not inadvertently impose a hierarchy of religion and belief, by testing their decisions against the extent to which they support pluralism. And perhaps most tellingly, tendencies to support the dominant faith over other religions and beliefs must be kept in check by testing whether decisions also serve to protect the rights of non-believers, including atheists, to be free from that dominant faith. In short, the human right to freedom of religion and belief can be defended against the harms of unequally applied horizontality through properly realising and meaningfully protecting freedom *from* religion alongside freedom *of* religion.

In his 2016 foreword to the International Humanist and Ethical Union report on discrimination against humanists, atheists and non-believers, Special Rapporteur Ahmed Shaheed restated that

> international human rights law protects both the freedom of religion and its corollary, the freedom from religion, for without the latter, the former has no practical meaning at all.[36]

35 *General Comment 22*, UN Doc CCPR/C/21/Rev.1/Add.4 [2].
36 Ahmed Shaheed, United Nations Special Rapporteur for Freedom of Religion or Belief, http://freethoughtreport.com/foreword-to-the-2016-edition/.

Freedom *from* religion, then, is not a new right but a well-established and vital component of a non-derogable right. Natan Lerner explains that freedom from religion is implicitly incorporated in freedom of religion, though its implementation is neglected given the focus of article 18 has been primarily on the rights of believers rather than non-believers.[37] Indeed, there have been few international cases that have contended with the right to be free *from* the religion of others.[38] Here a need is identified: the apparatus of human rights law must be presented and promoted as accessible to those whose freedom *from* religion is trespassed upon.

To remedy this gap in protection, Lerner asserts that a detailed catalogue of the specific rights and freedoms involved is necessary to ensure the principle of equality in matters of religion and belief.[39] In outlining the content of the right to freedom of and *from* religion, Lerner sets out the following rights:

a) To have or not to have a religion or a belief and not to be coerced to belong to a religious community, church, or faith;
b) To opt out from any religious community, church, or faith which one does not want to identify with or be a member of;
c) To be excluded from any official register identifying persons by religion or belief;
d) Not to be coerced to perform any ceremony or act of a religious nature;
e) Not to be obliged to take an oath related to religion;
f) Not to be exposed to religious indoctrination or mandatory religious instruction against one's will or the will of the parents or legal guardians of a minor;
g) Not to be buried in a religious ceremony;
h) Not to be coerced to reveal one's religion or belief in official documents;
i) Not to be exposed to religious propaganda, indoctrination or proselytism when forming part of a captive audience.[40]

37 Lerner, above n 26, 60.
38 See *Leirvåg et al v Norway*, Human Rights Committee, Communication No. 931/00, UN Doc CCPR/C/82/D/1155/2003 (2004), [14.2–14.7]. At the European level, see the similar case of *Folgerø and Others v Norway*, European Court of Human Rights, Grand Chamber Judgment, Application No. 15472/02 (29 June 2007) in which the Court found a violation of Article 2 of Protocol No. 1 on the right to education, on similar facts. The case of *Hasan and Eylem Zengin v Turkey*, European Court of Human Rights, Application No 1448/04 concerned parents of the Alevist branch of Islam, which also resulted in the finding of a violation of Article 2 of Protocol No. 1. The case of *Grzelak v Poland*, European Court of Human Rights, Application No 7710/02, involved agnostic parents; the Court found a violation of Article 14 taken together with Article 9 given the stigmatising absence of a mark in school reports for the religion/ethics subject. Among European cases are *Eweida*, European Court of Human Rights, Application Nos. 48420/10, 59842/10, 51671/10 and 36516/10 (15 January 2013); *Dahlab v Switzerland*, European Court of Human Rights, Judgment, Application No. 42393/98, 15 February 2001, and *Leyla Şahin v Turkey*, European Court of Human Rights, Judgment, Application No. 44774/98 (10 November 2005).
39 Ibid 61.
40 Ibid 60–61.

In acknowledging the rights of individuals who do not wish to practise religion alongside those who do, Lerner's approach is grounded in the principle of pluralism. Indeed, this list of rights reveals something fundamental to that principle: these are rights not only that atheists need to meaningfully enjoy their freedoms, but are also essential for religious rights-holders to enjoy theirs.

David Robertson, speaking in the domestic UK context, makes a point that could equally be applied at the international level when he says that taking pluralism seriously, requires that all people – whether Christian, Muslim, Hindu, Sikh or atheist, agnostic or humanist – "need to see a shared interest in tackling religious inequity".[41] This is the true meaning of equality in pluralism: it requires that any entrenched advantage of one religion or belief over another be challenged on the basis of the equal rights of all rights-holders. It means emphasising the common value of religious and belief freedoms for both religious and non-religious communities.[42] In short, pluralism must be valued over fundamentalism of all types, so that international law does not succumb to notions of superiority of one religion over another, or one version of a religion over others. Pluralism is essential to recognising that it is as much in the interests of atheists to support the religious and belief rights of theists, as it is in the interests of theists to support the religious and belief rights of atheists. At the very least, it requires that any action that undermines these freedoms be limited only where human rights are violated, not where religions or belief are challenged. When holders of different religions or beliefs conflict on the basis of their religions and beliefs, the principle of pluralism determines that the correct response is not to repress one or the other in a bid to remove the cause of conflict, but rather to assert their equal entitlements in a bid to increase tolerance and parity between them.[43]

In concluding his *Study on Discrimination*, Krishnaswami noted with approval the trend of greater acceptance across and between faiths, and the benign attitude of the public towards 'dissenters'. However, he also prophetically cautioned that a reversal of these trends could not be ruled out in the future. More than half a century later, when religion and belief permeates the lives not only of those who adhere to and hold those religions and beliefs, but also affects others who do not, we are wise to take note of his concluding words:

> It is the duty of the United Nations to see to it not only that all types of discrimination – whether they are remnants of the past or something new – are eradicated, but also that in the future no one should be subjected to treatment likely to impair his right to freedom of thought, conscience and religion.

41 David Robertson, 'Neutrality between Religions or Neutrality between Religion and Non-Religion?' in Peter W. Edge and Graham Harvey (eds), *Law and Religion in Contemporary Society* (Ashgate, 2000) 67.

42 Peter Cumper, 'The Accommodation of "Uncontroversial" Religious Practices' in M. L. P. Loenen & J. E. Goldschmidt (eds) *Religious Pluralism and Human Rights in Europe: Where to Draw the Line?* (Intersentia, 2007) 209.

43 Ibid 155.

> In short, its duty is to ensure that the trend towards equality should become both universal and permanent.[44]

The United Nations system itself must be at the forefront of non-discrimination; in protecting freedom of religion and belief, it must urgently and courageously defend dissenters irrespective of their religion and belief, or that of those who threaten their rights. In order to afford such equality, and to level the existing 'hierarchy' that skews it, the individuals charged with fulfilling the United Nations' mandate to protect religious and belief freedom should consider the extent to which freedom *from* religion is protected alongside freedom of religion.

This monograph stands on the belief that religious freedom entails choice. That choice is only valuable where it can extend to any religion or belief including the choice to have no religion and to manifest atheism. Only when people are also free to enjoy freedom *from* the religions of others do they meaningfully enjoy freedom of religion and belief. Balancing conflicting rights in respect of that choice, then, would mean that an adult would be allowed to refuse a blood transfusion, but would not be entitled to refuse that same life-saving treatment on behalf of a child.[45] Boys would be free to grow into men who can choose to be circumcised in accordance with their own religion or belief, or not, rather than be subject to the religious choices of their parents. And where a person is not free to leave a religious group, whether it is a new religious movement led by a new prophet, or the established, major religion of her community, interventions are justified on the basis of her right to be free from that religion, as an essential corollary of the freedom to practise that religion in the first place.

2.2. Freedom from *religion as the litmus test*

Distinctly asserting freedom *from* religion as a means of upholding freedom of religion and belief is not to suggest that the hierarchy be inverted so that non-religious rights-holders are elevated above their religious counterparts. Rather, it is a check of religious and belief freedoms across the spectrum of worldviews in the same way that religious and belief freedom is itself a check on other freedoms. Indeed, freedom *from* religion can serve as an indicator of the health of all human rights: the International Humanist and Ethical Union comments that countries with the worst records on article 18 freedom of thought, conscience and religion, also have the worst records on all human rights, nothing that "[t]his is no coincidence: when thought is a crime, no other freedom can long survive."[46]

As stressed above, freedom from religion is not a new right; it is a protected component of freedom of religion and belief but, thus far, a neglected one, particularly as far as atheists and non-believers are concerned. Natan Lerner, in offering the rights of freedom *from* religion that were set out above, notes:

44 Arcot Krishnaswami, *Study of Discrimination in the matter of Religious Rights and Practices*, UN Doc. E/CN.4/Sub.2/200/Rev.1 (1960), UN Pub. No 60.XIV.2, 60.
45 Nowak and Vospernik, above n 2, 163–164.
46 International Humanists and Ethical Union, above n 36, 12.

> One of the neglected ingredients of freedom of religion or belief is the right to be a secular person, not to be coerced to believe, to practice a religion, to behave according to some religious precepts, to identify with a particular faith, to belong to a religious community, organization or association, or to be registered in official documents, *volens non volens*, as a member of a religion, faith, church or any form of institution related to religion.[47]

Bielefeldt reminds us that in honouring the diversity of religion and belief we must have equal concern for 'positive' freedom and 'negative' freedom, as two sides of the same coin, for "one is not free to do something unless he is also free to not do it."[48] For this reason, Bielefeldt explains that religious and belief freedom also entails the 'negative' dimension, including the freedom *not* to profess or practise a religion. He emphasises that there is no hierarchy between these positive and negative freedoms but that they are inextricable; any attempt to isolate or elevate either would undermine "the liberating essence of freedom of religion and belief in general".[49] Added to this, though, is an essential, positive dimension of freedom *from* religion, being the right to manifest non-theism or atheism.

Accordingly, the freedom *from* religion rights that Lerner outlines (as noted above) should be enhanced. The freedoms he sets out in his non-exhaustive list are phrased negatively, but it is submitted here that that list should go a crucial step further to not only exempt rights-holders from the religion around them, but also to explicitly capture their positive right to manifest and profess their rejection of it – namely:

> j) Freedom to manifest non-religion or atheism.

Accordingly, freedom *from* religion should not be comprised only of a negative right to not participate in religion, but also entail a positive right to manifest atheism, subject only to proportionate limitations prescribed by law, as with other components of freedom of religion and belief.

Freedom *from* religion, then, can thus be understood as the litmus test of freedom of religion and belief. Freedom of religion and belief includes a set of rights and freedoms that a person has to manifest his or her religion or belief, as well as to *not* be coerced by the state or non-state actors to submit to a particular religion or version of it. Meaningful enjoyment of this right requires that the state refrain from imposing precepts or enforcing practices, and also that it fulfils its horizontal obligations to actively protect rights-holders from such imposition by non-state actors. But more than this it also entails positive obligations of the state to protect the rights of individuals to manifest atheism. The litmus test of religious and belief freedom is the extent to which a person enjoys the positive freedom to profess no religion or even to profess atheism.

47 Lerner, above n 26, 57.
48 Heiner Bielefeldt, 'Misconceptions of Freedom of Religion or Belief' (2013) 35 *Human Rights Quarterly* 33, 49–50. Also see Bielefeldt, above n 34, 8.
49 Bielefeldt, above n 34, 8.

Explicit recognition of the right to manifest atheism will be an unwelcome approach in many states that favour particular religions or beliefs. But this fact speaks only to the enormous challenges of implementing this right; it does not mean that the right does not exist or that it should not be pursued. Indeed, those challenges go to the very heart of the value to be offered by such a test and underscore its urgency; it is in light of them that the extent to which a person is meaningfully free *from* religion becomes a key measure of freedom of religion and belief for all rights-holders. Freedom from religion empowers a religious person to develop and defend his faith against dated and dogmatic interpretations and manifestations of it, and it empowers an atheist to openly engage in discussion with others about the fact of his non-belief. Freedom *from* religion is a vital right for all rights-holders, irrespective of their religion or belief.

Bibliography

Books, articles and chapters

Ahdar, Rex J., 'Children's Religious Freedom, Devout Parents and the State' in Peter W. Edge and Graham Harvey (eds), *Law and Religion in Contemporary Society* (Ashgate, 2000) 93–114

Ahdar, Rex and Leigh, Ian, *Religious Freedom in the Liberal State* (Oxford University Press, 2013)

Ali, Ayaan Hirsi, 'How (and Why) I Became an Infidel' in Christopher Hitchens (ed.), *The Portable Atheist* (Da Capo Press, 2007) 477–480

Amor, Abdelfattah, Special Rapporteur, Implementation of the Declaration on the Elimination of all forms of intolerance and of discrimination based on religion or belief, UN Doc E/CN.4/1998/6/Add.2 (22 December 1997) [105]

Amor, Abdelfattah, Special Rapporteur, Implementation of the Declaration on the Elimination of all forms of intolerance and of discrimination based on religion or belief, UN Doc E/CN.4/1998/6 (22 January 1998)

An-Na'im, Abdullahi A., 'Islamic Foundations of Religious Human Rights' in Johan van der Vyver and John Witte (eds), *Religious Human Rights in Global Perspective: Religious Perspectives* (Martinus Nijhoff Publishers, 1996) 337–360

An-Na'im, Abdullahi A., 'Islam and Human Rights' in John Witte Jr and M Christian Green, *Religion and Human Rights: An Introduction* (Oxford University Press, 2012) 56–70

Bader, Viet, 'Religious Pluralism and Democratic Institutional Pluralism' (2003) 31 *Political Theory* 265

Bader, Viet, 'Taking Religious Pluralism Seriously, Arguing for an Institutional Turn' (2003) 6 *Religious Pluralism, Politics and the State* 3

Baderin, Mashood, *International Human Rights and Islamic Law* (Oxford University Press, 2003)

Baderin, Mashood A., 'Islam and the Realisation of Human Rights in the Muslim World: a Reflection on Two Essential Approaches and Two Divergent Perspectives' (2007) 4 *Muslim World Journal of Human Rights* 5

Barker, Eileen, 'Why the Cults? New Religious Movements and Freedom of Religion or Belief' in T. Lindholm, W. Cole Durham and B. G. Tahzib-Lie, *Facilitating of Freedom of Religion or Belief: A Deskbook* (Martinus Nijhoff, 2004) 571–594

Beck-Peccoz, Roberta Aluffi, 'Proselytism and the Right to Change Religion in Islam' in Silvio Ferrari and Rinaldo Cristofori, *Law and Religion in the 21st Century* (Ashgate, 2010) 253–260

Behar, Richard, 'The Thriving Cult of Greed and Power', *Time Magazine* 6 May 1991

Bielefeldt, Heiner, 'Freedom of Religion or Belief – a Human Right Under Pressure' (2012) 1 *Oxford Journal of Law and Religion* 1

Bielefeldt, Heiner, 'Misconceptions about Freedom of Religion and Belief' (2013) 35 *Human Rights Quarterly* 33

Bielefeldt, Heiner, Ghanea, Nazila and Weiner, Michael, *Freedom of Religion and Belief: An International Law Commentary* (Oxford University Press, 2016)

Bishop, Kaci, 'Politics before Policy: The Bush Administration, International Family Planning, and Foreign Policy' (2003–2004) 29 *North Carolina Journal of International and Commercial Law Regulation* 521

Bollinger, D., and Howe, R. Van, 'Alexithymia and Circumcision Trauma: A Preliminary Investigation' (2011) 10 *International Journal of Men's Health* 184–195

Bossuyt, Marc J., *Guide to the Travaux Préparatoires' of the International Covenant on Civil and Political Rights* (Martinus Nijhoff Publishers, 1987)

Boswell, John, *Christianity, Social Tolerance, and Homosexuality: Gay People in Western Europe from the Beginning of the Christian Era to the Fourteenth Century* (University of Chicago Press, 1980)

Bowker, John (ed.), *The Concise Oxford Dictionary of World Religions* (Oxford University Press, 2005)

Bradney, Anthony, *Islam and European Legal Systems* (Ashgate, 2000)

Bradney, Anthony, *Law and Faith in a Sceptical Age* (Routledge-Cavendish, 2009)

Brems, Eva, 'Article 14: The Right to Freedom of Thought, Conscience and Religion' in A. Allen, J. Vande Lanotte, E. Verhellen, F. Ang, E. Berghams and M. Verheyde (eds), *A Commentary on the United Nations Convention on the Rights of the Child* (Martinus Nijhoff Publishers, 2006)

Brown, Wendy, *Regulating Aversion: Tolerance in the Age of Identity and Empire* (Princeton University Press, 2006)

Cismas, Ioana, *Religious Actors and International Law* (Oxford University Press, 2014)

Cumper, Peter, 'Religious Liberty in the United Kingdom' in Johan Van der Vyver and John Witte (eds), *Religious Human Rights in Global Perspective: Legal Perspective* (Martinus Nijhoff Publishers, 1996) 205–242

Cumper, Peter, 'The Rights of Religious Minorities: The Legal Regulation of New Religious Movements' in Peter Cumper and Steven Wheatley (eds), *Minority Rights in the 'New Europe'* (Kluwer Law International, 1999) 165–184

Cumper, Peter, 'Inciting Religious Hatred: Balancing Free Speech and Religious Sensibilities in a Multi-Faith Society' in Nazila Ghanea, Alan Stephens and Raphael Walden (eds), *Does God Believe in Human Rights?* (Martinus Nijhoff Publishers, 2007) 233–258

Cumper, Peter, 'The Accommodation of "Uncontroversial" Religious Practices' in M. L. P. Loenen and J. E. Goldschmidt (eds), *Religious Pluralism and Human Rights in Europe: Where to Draw the Line?* (Intersentia, 2007) 195–210

Cumper, Peter and Lewis, Tom, *Religion, Rights and Secular Society: European Perspectives* (Edward Elgar Publishing, 2012)

Danchin, Peter G., 'Of Prophets and Proselytes: Freedom of Religion and the Conflict of Rights in International Law' (2008) 49 *Harvard International Law Review* 249

Darby, Robert and Svboda, J. Seven, 'A Rose by Any Other Name: Rethinking the Similarities and Differences between Male and Female Genital Cutting' (2007) 21 *Medical Anthropology Quarterly* 301–323

Davis, Derek H., 'The Evolution of Religious Freedom as a Universal Human Right: Examining the Role of the 1981 United Nations Declaration of the Elimination of all

forms of Intolerance and of Discrimination based on Religion or Belief' (2002) *Brigham Young University Law Review* 217
Dawkins, Richard, *The God Delusion* (Bantam Press, 2006)
Day, Abby, *Believing in Belonging* (Oxford University Press, 2011)
de Jong, Cornelis D., *The Freedom of Thought, Conscience and Religion or Belief in the United Nations (1946–1992)* (Intersentia, 2000)
De Jong, Dennis, 'Freedom of Religion in Light of Recent Challenges' in Nazila Ghanea, Alan Stephens and Raphael Walden (eds), *Does God Believe in Human Rights?* (Martinus Nijhoff Publishers, 2007) 181–206
Dickson, Brice, 'The United Nations and Freedom of Religion' (1995) 44 *International and Comparative Law Quarterly* 327
Dillard, Annie, *Pilgrim at Tinker Creek* (1st Perennial Classics ed., 2007)
Edge, Peter, *Legal Responses to Religious Difference* (Kluwer, 2002)
Edge, Peter, *Religion and Law: An Introduction* (Ashgate, 2006)
Einstein, Albert, 'Selected Writings on Religion' in Christopher Hitchens, *The Portable Atheist* (De Capo Press, 2007) 155–165
Evans, Carolyn, *Freedom of Religion under the European Convention on Human Rights* (Oxford, 2001)
Evans, Malcolm, *Religious Liberty and International Law in Europe* (Cambridge University Press, 1997)
Fateh-Moghadam, Bijan, 'Criminalizing Male Circumcision? Case Note: Landgericht Cologne, Judgment of 7 May 2012 – No. 151 Ns 169/11' (2012) 13 *German Law Journal* 1131
Feinberg, Joel, 'The Child's Right to an Open Future' in William Aiken and Hugh LaFollette (eds), *Whose Child? Children's Rights, Parental Authority, and State Power* (Rowman and Littlefield, 1980)
Fernandes, Phil, *The Atheist Delusion: A Christian Response to Christopher Hitchens and Richard Dawkins* (Xulon Press, 2009)
Gewirth, Alan, *Human Rights: Essays on Justification and Applications* (University of Chicago Press, 1982)
Ghanea, Nazila, 'Religion, Equality, and Non-Discrimination' in John Witte Jr and Christian M. Green, *Religion and Human Rights: An Introduction* (Oxford University Press, 2012) 204–217
Goldman, R., 'The Psychological Impact of Circumcision' (1999) 83(S1) *British Journal of Urology International* 93 http://www.cirp.org/library/psych/goldman1/ accessed 22 March 2017
Gozdecka, Dorota Anna, *Rights, Religious Pluralism and the Recognition of Difference* (Routledge, 2016)
Grim, Brian J. and Finke, Roger, *The Price of Freedom Denied: Religious Persecution and Conflict in the Twenty-first Century* (Cambridge University Press, 2011)
Guiora, Amos N., *Freedom from Religion* (Oxford University Press, 2009)
Gunn, Jeremy, 'Adjudicating Rights of Conscience under the European Convention on Human Rights' in Johan van der Vyver and John Witte (eds), *Religious Human Rights in Global Perspective: Legal Perspectives* (Martinus Nijhoff Publishers, 1996) 305–330
Gunn, Jeremy T., 'The Complexity of Religion and the Definition of "Religion" in International Law' (2003) 189 *Harvard Human Rights Journal* 16
Günzel, Angelika, 'Nationalisation of Religious Parental Education? The German Circumcision Case' (2013) 2 *Oxford Journal of Law and Religion* 206

Hackett, Rosalind I. J., 'Traditional, African, Religious, Freedom?' in Elizabeth A. Castelli et al (eds), *Politics of Religious Freedom* (University of Chicago Press, 2015)

Hashemi, Kamran, *Religious Legal Traditions, International Human Rights Law and Muslim States* (Martinus Nijhoff Publishers, 2008)

Hinchley, Geoff, 'Head to Head: Is Infant Male Circumcision an Abuse of the Rights of the Child?' (2007) 335 *British Medical Journal* 1180

Hitchens, Christopher, *The Missionary Position: Mother Teresa in Theory and Practice* (Verso, 1995)

Hitchens, Christopher, *God is not Great* (Allen & Unwin, 2007)

Hunsberger, Bruce and Jackson, Lynne M., 'Religion, Meaning and Prejudice' (2005) 61 *Journal of Social Issues* 807

Hunter-Henin, Myriam, 'Law, Religion and the School' in Silvio Ferrari (ed.), *Routledge Handbook of Law and Religion* (Routledge, 2015) 259–270

Huntington, Samuel P., *The Clash of Civilisations and the Remaking of World Order* (Simon & Schuster, 1996)

Ishay, Micheline R., *The Human Rights Reader* (Routledge, 2nd edn, 2007)

Jackson, Lynne M. and Hunsberger, Bruce, 'An Intergroup Perspective on Religion and Prejudice' (1999) 38 *Journal for Scientific Study of Religion* 509

Jamal, Arif A., 'The Impact of Definitional Issues on the Right of Freedom of Religion and Belief' in Silvio Ferrari (ed.), *Routledge Handbook of Law and Religion* (Routledge, 2015) 91–102

Joseph, Sarah, 'Toonen v Australia: Gay Rights under the ICCPR' (1994) 13 *University of Tasmania Law Review* 392

Joseph, Sarah, 'Human Rights Committee: Recent Cases' (2001) 1 *Human Rights Law Review* 83

Joseph, Sarah, 'Human Rights Committee: General Comment 29' (2002) 2(1) *Human Rights Law Review* 81

Joseph, Sarah, Schultz, Jenny and Castan, Melissa, *The International Covenant on Civil and Political Rights: Cases, Materials, and Commentary* (Oxford University Press, 2nd edn, 2004)

Khadduri, Majid, *War and Peace in the Law of Islam* (The Lawbook Exchange, 2006)

Kilkelly, Ursula, 'The Child's Right to Religious Freedom in International Law: The Search for Meaning' in Martha Alberson Fineman and Karen Worthington (eds), *What is Right for Children? The Competing Paradigms in Religion and Human Rights* (Ashgate, 2009) 243–268

Kraybill, Donald B. (ed.), *The Amish and the State* (Johns Hopkins University Press, 2nd edn, 2003)

Langlaude, Sylvie, *The Right of the Child to Religious Freedom in International Law* (Martinus Nijhoff Publishers, 2007)

Langlaude, Sylvie, 'Children and Religion under Article 14 UNCRC: A Critical Analysis' (2008) 16 *International Journal of Children's Rights* 475

Lee, Lois, *Recognizing the Non-religious: Reimagining the Secular* (Oxford, 2015)

Lerner, Natan, *Religion, Beliefs and International Human Rights* (Orbis Books, 2000)

Lerner, Natan, *Religion, Secularism and Human Rights* (Martinus Nijhoff Publishers, 2nd ed., 2012)

Linford, Orma, 'Mormons, the Law, and the Territory of Utah' (1979) 23 *American Journal of Legal History* 213

Luchenitser, Alex J., '"InnerChange": Conversion as the Price of Freedom and Comfort – A Cautionary Tale about the Pitfalls of Faith-based Prison Units' (2007) 6 *Ave Maria Law Review* 445
Mandela, Nelson, *Long Walk to Freedom* (Abacus, 1994)
Maoz, Asher, 'Proselytism and the Right to Change Religion' in Silvio Ferrari and Rinaldo Cristofori, *Law and Religion in the 21st Century* (Ashgate, 2010) 243–252
Mason, Christine, 'Exorcising Excision: Medico-legal Issues Arising from Male and Female Genital Surgery in Australia' (2001) 9 *Journal of Law and Medicine* 58
Mayer, Ann Elizabeth, 'Universal versus Islamic Human Rights; a Clash of Cultures or a Clash with a Construct?' (1994) 15 *Michigan Journal of International Law* 307
Mayer, Ann Elizabeth, *Human Rights and Islam: Tradition and Politics* (Westview Press, 5th edn, 2013)
Mayer, Ann Elizabeth, *Islam and Human Rights* (Westview Press, 2013)
McGoldrick, Dominic, 'Multiculturalism and its Discontents' (2005) 1 *Human Rights Law Review* 5
Merritt, Deborah Jones and Merritt, Daniel C., 'The Future of Religious Pluralism: Justice O'Connor and the Establishment Clause' (2007) 39 *Arizona State Law Journal* 895
Milne, Elijah L., 'Blaine Amendments and Polygamy Laws: The Constitutionality of Anti-Polygamy Laws Targeting Religion' (2006) 28 *Western New England Law Review* 257
Mkandawire-Valhmu, L. et al., 'Marriage as a Risk Factor for HIV: Learning from the Experiences of HIV-infected women in Malawi' (2013) 8 *Global Public Health* 187
Moon, Dawne, 'Beyond the Dichotomy: Six Religious Views of Homosexuality' (2014) 61 *Journal of Homosexuality* 1215
Mutua, Makau, 'Returning to my Roots: African "Religions" and the State' in Abdullahi Ahmed An-Na'im, *Proselytisation and Communal Self-Development in Africa* (Orbis Books, 1999) 169–190
Mutua, Makau, *Human Rights: A Political and Cultural Critique* (University of Pennsylvia Press, 2008)
Mutua, Makau, 'Human Rights, Religion and Proselytism' in Philip Alston and Ryan Goodman, *International Human Rights* (Oxford University Press, 2013) 622–625
Narulla, Ranipul, 'Circumscribing Circumcision: Traversing the Moral and Legal Ground around a Hidden Human Rights Violation' (2007) 12 *Australian Journal of Human Rights* 89
Nowak, Manfred, *CCPR Commentary* (NP Engel Kehl, 2nd edn, 2005)
Nowak, Manfred and Vospernik, Tanja, 'Permissible Restrictions on Freedom of Religion or Belief' in T. Lindholm, W. Cole Durham and B. G. Tahzib-Lie, *Facilitating of Freedom of Religion or Belief: A Deskbook* (Martinus Nijhoff, 2004) 147–172
Partsch, K. J., 'Freedom of Conscience and Expression, and Political Freedoms' in L. Henkin (ed.), *The International Bill of Rights: The Covenant on Civil and Political Rights* (Columbia University Press, 1981) 209–245
Patrick, Kirsten, 'Head to Head: Is Infant Male Circumcision an Abuse of the Rights of the Child?' (2007) 335 *British Medical Journal* 1181
Pérez-Peña, Richard and Vega, Tanzina, 'Brandeis Cancels Plan to Give Honorary Degree to Ayaan Hirsi Ali, a Critic of Islam' *New York Times*, 8 April 2014
Rawls, John, *Political Liberalism* (Columbia University Press, 1996)
Rehman, Javaid and Polymenopoulou, Eleni, 'Is Green a Part of the Rainbow? Sharia, Homosexuality, and LGBT Rights in the Muslim World' (2013–2014) 27 *Fordham International Law Journal* 1

Richardson, James T. and Lukes, Valerie A., 'Legal Considerations Concerning New Religious Movements in the "New Europe"', in Peter Cumper and Tom Lewis, *Religion, Rights and Secular Society: European Perspectives* (Edward Elgar Publishing, 2012) 293–322

Robertson, David, 'Neutrality between Religions or Neutrality between Religion and Non-Religion?', in Peter W. Edge and Graham Harvey (eds), *Law and Religion in Contemporary Society* (Ashgate, 2000) 31–52

Robertson QC, Geoffrey, *The Case of the Pope: Vatican Accountability for Human Rights Abuse* (Penguin, 2010)

Robertson QC, Geoffrey, *Crimes against Humanity* (The New Press, 4th edn, 2013)

Sachedina, Abdulaziz, *Islam and the Challenge of Human Rights* (Oxford University Press, 2009)

Sánchez, Juan O., *Religion and the Ku Klux Klan: Biblical Appropriation in their Literature and Song* (McFarland and Company, 2016)

Scharffs, Brett G., 'International Law and the Defamation of Religion Conundrum' (2013) 11 *The Review of Faith and International Affairs* 66

Schwartz, Shalom H. and Huismans, Sipke, 'Value Priorities and Religiosity in Four Western Religions' (1995) 58 *Social Psychology Quarterly* 88

Sharma, Arvind, *Problematizing Religious Freedom* (Springer, 2011)

Specter, Michael, 'Political Science' *New Yorker*, 13 March 2006

Stahnke, Tad, 'Proselytism and the Freedom to Change Religion in International Human Rights Law' (1999) 1 *Brigham Young University Law Review* 251

Stahnke, Tad, 'Proselytism' in Silvio Ferrari (ed.), *Routledge Handbook of Law and Religion* (Routledge, 2015) 395–413

Sullivan, Donna, 'Advancing the Freedom of Religion or Belief through the UN Declaration on the Elimination of Religious Intolerance and Discrimination' (1988) 82 *American Journal of International Law* 487

Sullivan, Winnifred Fallers, *The Impossibility of Religious Freedom* (Princeton University Press, 2011)

Taylor, Paul, *Freedom of Religion: UN and European Human Rights Law and Practice* (Cambridge University Press, 2005)

Taylor, Paul M., 'Religion and Freedom of Choice' in John Witte Jr and M. Christian Green, *Religion and Human Rights: An Introduction* (Oxford University Press, 2012) 170–187

Temperman, Jeroen, 'Blasphemy, Defamation of Religion, Religious Hate Speech' in Silvio Ferrari (ed.), *Routledge Handbook of Law and Religion* (Routledge, 2015) 381–394

Temperman, Jeroen, *Religious Hatred and International Law: the Prohibition of Incitement to Violence or Discrimination* (Cambridge University Press, 2016)

Theriot, Esq., Kevin H., 'Prince or Pauper? Religious Proselytising and the First Amendment' (2009) 3 *University of St. Thomas Journal of Law & Public Policy* 46

Thornberry, Patrick, *International Law and the Rights of Minorities* (Clarendon Press, 1991)

Tobin, John, 'The International Obligation to Abolish Traditional Practices Harmful to Children's Health: What Does it Mean and Require of States?' (2009) 9 *Human Rights Law Review* 272

Trigg, Roger, *Equality, Freedom and Religion* (Oxford University Press, 2012)

Van Bueren, Geraldine, 'The Right to be the Same, The Right to be Different: Children and Religion' in T. Lindholm, W. Cole Durham and B. G. Tahzib-Lie, *Facilitating of Freedom of Religion or Belief: A Deskbook* (Martinus Nijhoff, 2004) 561–570

van der Vyver, Johan D., 'Limitations on Freedom of Religion or Belief: International Law Perspectives' (2005) 19 *Emory International Law Review* 499

Wilkinson, Philip, *Religions* (Dorling Kindersley, 2008)

Witte, John Jr and Green, M. Christian, 'Religious Freedom, Democracy, and International Human Rights' (2009) 23 *Emory International Law Review* 583

United Nations Documents

Allegation Letter G/SO 214(78–15) G/SO 214(56–23) USA 4/2011 (24 March 2011)

Allegation Letter G/SO 214(67–17) G/SO 214(56–23) G/SO 214(107–9) BGD 2/2013 (18 January 2013)

Amor, Abdelfattah, *Report of the Special Rapporteur on the implementation of the Declaration on the Elimination of all Forms of Intolerance and of Discrimination based on Religion or Belief*, UN Doc E/CN.4/1995/91 (22 December 1994)

Amor, Abdelfattah, *Report submitted in accordance with Commission on Human Rights Resolution 1999/39*, UN Doc E/CN.4/2000/65 (15 February 2000)

Baderin, Mashood A., *Report of the Independent Expert on the situation of human rights in the Sudan*, UN Doc A/HRC/27/69 (4 September 2014)

Bielefeldt, Heiner, *Interim report of the Special Rapporteur on freedom of religion or belief*, UN Doc A/69/261 (5 August 2014)

Bielefeldt, Heiner, *Interim report of Special Rapporteur on freedom of religion or belief*, UN Doc A/70/286 (5 August 2015)

Bielefeldt, Heiner, *Interim report of the Special Rapporteur on freedom of religion or belief, Elimination of all forms of religious intolerance*, UN Doc A/71/269 (2 August 2016)

Bielefeldt, Heiner, *Report of the Special Rapporteur on freedom of religion or belief*, UN Doc A/HRC/16/53 (15 December 2010)

Bielefeldt, Heiner, *Report of the Special Rapporteur on freedom of religion or belief*, UN Doc A/HRC/16/53/Add.1 (14 February 2011)

Bielefeldt, Heiner, *Report of the Special Rapporteur on freedom of religion or belief*, UN Doc A/HRC/19/60/Add.2 (27 January 2012)

Bielefeldt, Heiner, *Report of the Special Rapporteur on freedom of religion or belief*, UN Doc A/HRC/25/58 (26 December 2013)

Bielefeldt, Heiner, *Report of the Special Rapporteur on freedom of religion or belief*, UN Doc A/HRC/28/66 (29 December 2014)

Bielefeldt, Heiner, *Report of the Special Rapporteur on freedom of religion or belief*, UN Doc A/HRC/31/18 (23 December 2015)

Bielefeldt, Heiner, *Report of the Special Rapporteur on freedom of religion or belief on his mission to Bangladesh*, UN Doc A/HRC/31/18/Add.2 (22 January 2016)

Combating Defamation of Religions, GA Res 65/224, § III.A, UN Doc A/RES/65/224 (11 April 2011)

Commission on Human Rights, *Resolution 2005/40 on Elimination of all forms of Intolerance and of Discrimination based on Religion or Belief*, UN Doc E/CN.4/RES/2005/40 (19 April 2005)

Commission on Human Rights, *Siracusa Principles on the Limitation and Derogation Provisions in the International Covenant on Civil and Political Rights*, UN Doc E/CN.4/1985/4 (28 September 1984)

Commission on Human Rights, *Tolerance and pluralism as indivisible elements in the promotion and protection of human rights*, E/CN.4/RES/1998/21 (9 April 1998)

Committee on Economic, Cultural and Social Rights, *Summary Record of the 7th meeting: Iran (Islamic Republic of)*, UN Doc E/C.12/1993/SR.7 (3 June 1993)
Committee on Economic, Cultural and Social Rights, *Summary Record of the 8th meeting: Morocco 11/05/94*, UN Doc E/C.12/1994/SR.8 (11 May 1994)
Committee on the Elimination of Racial Discrimination, *Eleventh Periodic Reports of States Parties due in 1992: Morocco*, UN Doc CERD/C/225/Add.1. (12 May 1993)
Committee on the Elimination of Racial Discrimination, *Summary Record of the 1020th meeting: Morocco*, UN Doc CERD/C/SR.1020 (29 July 1996)
Committee on the Elimination of Racial Discrimination, *Summary Record of the 1021st meeting: Morocco*, UN Doc CERD/C/SR.1021 (10 March 1994)
Committee on the Rights of the Child, *Concluding Observations on China (including Hong Kong and Macau Special Administrative Regions)*, 40th sess., UN Doc CRC/C/CHN/CO/2 (24 November 2005)
Committee on the Rights of the Child, *Concluding observations on the second periodic report of the Holy See*, UN Doc CRC/C/VAT/CO/2 (25 February 2014)
Committee on the Rights of the Child, *General Comment 1, The aims of education*, UN Doc CRC/GC/2001/1 (17 April 2001)
Committee on the Rights of the Child, *General Comment 13, The right of the child to freedom from all forms of violence*, UN Doc E/C.12/1999/10 (8 December 1999)
Concluding observations of the Committee on the Elimination of Racial Discrimination: Islamic Republic of Iran, 26th sess., No.18, UN Doc CERD/A/8418 (1971)
Concluding observations of the Human Rights Committee: Colombia, UN Doc CCPR/A/35/40 (1980)
Concluding observations of the Human Rights Committee: Iraq, UN Doc CCPR A/35/40 (1980)
Concluding observations on the initial report of the Holy See, UN Doc CAT/C/VAT/CO/1 (17 June 2014)
Concluding observations on the specific periodic report of the Holy See, Committee on the Rights of the Child, UN Doc. CRC/C/VAT/CO/2 (25 February 2014)
Consideration of Reports submitted by states parties under article 40 of the Covenant, Initial report of States parties due in 1993, Addendum, Israel, UN Doc CCPR/C/81/Add.13 (9 April 1998)
Convention on the Rights of the Child, opened for signature 20 November 1989, 1577 UNTS 5 (entered into force 2 September 1990)
Declaration of the Rights of Persons Belonging to National or Ethnic, Religious and Linguistic Minorities, adopted and proclaimed by United Nations General Assembly Resolution 47/135 (18 December 1992)
Declaration on the Elimination of All Forms of Intolerance and of Discrimination Based on Religion or Belief, UN GAOR, UN Doc A/Res/36/55 (25 November 1981)
Discriminatory Laws and Practices and Acts of Violence against Individuals Based on Their Sexual Orientation and Gender Identity: Report of the United Nations High Commissioner for Human Rights, UN Doc A/HRC/19/41 (17 November 2011)
General Assembly, *Elimination of all forms of religious intolerance, 7st session, item 69(b) of provision agenda*, UN Doc A/71/269 (2 August 2016)
General Assembly, *Elimination of all forms of religious intolerance*, UN Doc A/67/303 (13 August 2012)
General Assembly Resolution 65/244, UN Doc A/RES/65/244 (11 April 2011)
General Assembly Resolution 66/167, UN Doc A/RES/66/167 (27 March 2012)
General Assembly Resolution 66/168, UN Doc A/Res/66/168 (11 April 2012)

Human Rights Committee, *Consideration of reports submitted by States Parties under article 40 of the Covenant*, UN Doc CCPR/CO/82/POL, 82nd Sess. (2 December 2004)
Human Rights Committee, *Consideration of reports submitted by States Parties under article 40 of the Covenant*, UN Doc CCPR/C/USA/CO/3, 87th Sess. (10–28 July 2006)
Human Rights Committee, *Consideration of reports submitted by States Parties under article 40 of the Covenant*, UN Doc CCPR/C/SWE/CO/6, 95th Sess. (7 May 2009)
Human Rights Committee, *Consideration of reports submitted by States Parties under article 40 of the Covenant*, UN Doc CCPR/C/CHE/CO/3, 97th Sess. (3 November 2009)
Human Rights Committee, *Consideration of reports submitted by States Parties under article 40 of the Covenant*, UN Doc CCRP/C/RUS/C/6, 97th Sess. (24 November 2009)
Human Rights Committee, *Consideration of reports submitted by States Parties under article 40 of the Covenant, Concluding Observations of the Human Rights Committee*, UN Doc CCPR/C/POL/CO/6, 100th Sess. (15 November 2010)
Human Rights Committee, *General Comment 17: Article 24 (Rights of the Child)*, CCPR 35th Session (7 April 1989)
Human Rights Committee, *General Comment 22: The right to freedom of thought, conscience and religion (Article 18)*, UN Doc CCPR/C/21/Rev.1/Add.4 (27 September 1993)
Human Rights Committee, *General Comment 23: The rights of minorities (Article 27)*, UN Doc CCPR/C/21/Rev.1/Add.5 (4 August 1994)
Human Rights Committee, *General Comment 24: Issues relating to reservations made upon ratification or accession to the Covenant or the Optional Protocols thereto, or in relation to declarations under article 41 of the Covenant*, UN Doc CCPR/C/21/Rev.1/Add.6 (11 April 1994)
Human Rights Committee, *General Comment 29: Article 4: Derogations during a State of Emergency*, UN Doc CCPR/C/21/Rev.1/Add.11 (31 August 2001)
Human Rights Committee, *General Comment 34: Freedom of Opinion and Expression (Art 19)*, UN Doc CCPR/C/GC/34 (29 June 1983)
Human Rights Committee, *Report of the Human Rights Committee*, UN GAOR, 56th sess., UN Doc A/56/40 (Vol. II, 2000)
Human Rights Committee, *Summary Record of the first part (public) of the 1553rd meeting: Germany*, 58th sess., 1553rd mtg., UN Doc CCPR/C/SR.1553 (23 January 1997)
Human Rights Committee, *Summary Record of the 1600th meeting: France*, 60th sess., 1600th mtg., UN Doc CCPR/C/SR.1600, (11 November 1997)
Human Rights Committee, *Summary Record of the 1683rd meeting: Algeria*, UN Doc CCPR/C/SR.1683 (28 July 1998)
Human Rights Committee, *Summary Record of the 1847th meeting of the Human Rights Committee: Ireland*, 69th sess., 1847th mtg., UN Doc CCPR/C/SR.1847 (12 November 2001)
Human Rights Council Resolution 6/37, *Elimination of All Forms of intolerance and discrimination based on religion and belief* (14 December 2007)
Human Rights Council Resolution 17/19, Rep. of the Human Rights Council, 17th Sess., May 31–June 17, 2011, UN Doc A/HRC/17/L.9/Rev.1 (15 June 2011)
Human Rights Council Resolution 32/2, Rep. of the Human Rights Council, 27th Session, UN Doc A/HRC/RES/27/32 (2 October 2014)
Human Rights Council Resolution 32/2, Rep. of the Human Rights Council, 32nd Sess., 30 June 2016, UN Doc A/HRC/RES/32/2 (15 July 2016)

Human Rights Council, *Freedom of Religion or Belief*, UN GAOR, 16th Session, Agenda Item 3, UN Doc A/HRC/16/L.14 (18 March 2011)

International Covenant on Civil and Political Rights, opened for signature 16 December 1966, 999 UNTS 171 (entered into force 23 March 1976)

Jahangir, Asma, *Elimination of all forms of religion intolerance: interim report of the Special Rapporteur on freedom of religion or belief*, UN Doc A/62/280 (20 August 2007)

Jahangir, Asma, *Report of the Special Rapporteur on freedom of religion and belief*, UN Doc E/CN.4/2005/61 (20 December 2004)

Jahangir, Asma, *Report of the Special Rapporteur on freedom of religion or belief to the Human Rights Council*, UN Doc A/HRC/4/21 (26 December 2006)

Jahangir, Asma, *Report of the Special Rapporteur on freedom of religion or belief*, UN Doc A/HRC/6/5 (20 July 2007)

Jahangir, Asma, *Report of the Special Rapporteur on freedom of religion or belief*, UN Doc A/HRC/13/40 (29 December 2009)

Kiai, Maina, *Report of the Special Rapporteur on the rights to freedom of peaceful assembly and of association*, UN Doc A/HRC/20/27 (21 May 2012)

Krishnaswami, Arcot, *Study of Discrimination in the matter of Religious Rights and Practices*, UN Doc E/CN.4/Sub.2/200/Rev.1(1960), UN. Pub. No 60.XIV.2

Ligabo, Ambeyi, *Report of the Special Rapporteur on the promotion and protection of the right to freedom of opinion and expression*, UN Doc A/HRC/7/14 (28 February 2008)

Optional Protocol to the International Covenant on Economic, Social and Cultural Rights, opened for signature on 24 September 2009, GA Resolution A/RES/63/117, entered into force on 5 May 2013

Rabat Plan of Action on the prohibition of advocacy of national, racial or religious hatred that constitutes incitement to discrimination, hostility or violence, UN Doc A/HRC/22/17/Add.4, annex, appendix (11 January 2013)

Report of the Human Rights Council, HRC Res 16/18, UN Doc A/66/53 (24 March 2011)

Report of the Special Rapporteur on freedom of religion or belief, Asma Jahangir, and the Special Rapporteur on contemporary forms of racism, racial discrimination, xenophobia and related intolerance, Doudou Diène, further to Human Rights Council decision 1/107 on incitement to racial and religious hatred and the promotion of tolerance, UN Doc A/HRC/2/3 (20 September 2006)

Secretary General, *Annotations on the text of the draft International Covenants on Human Rights*, UN GAOR, 10th Session, Agenda Item 28, Part II, Annexes, UN Doc A/2929 (1 July 1955)

Secretary General, *Elimination of all forms of religious intolerance*, UN GAOR, 55th sess., UN Doc A/55/280/Add.2 (9 August 2000)

Security Council Resolution 1373, Adopted by the Security Council at its 4385th Meeting, on 28 September 2001, UN Doc S/RES/1373(2001)

Security Council Resolution 1624, Adopted by the Security Council at its 5261st Meeting, on 14 September 2005, UN Doc S/RES/1624(2005)

Security Council Resolution 2199, Adopted by the Security Council at its 7379th Meeting, on 12 February 2015, UN Doc S/RES/2199(2015)

Security Council Resolution 2249, Adopted by the Security Council at its 7565th Meeting, on 20 November 2015, UN Doc S/RES/2249(2015)

Security Council Resolution 2253, Adopted by the Security Council at its 7587th Meeting, on 17 December 2015, UN Doc S/RES/2253(2015)

Security Council Resolution 2255, Adopted by the Security Council at its 7590th Meeting, on 21 December 2015, UN Doc S/RES/2255(2015)

Security Council Resolution 2354, Adopted by the Security Council at its 7949th Meeting, UN Doc S/RES/2354 (24 May 2017)

Treaty Series (Online), *Declarations and Reservations to the International Covenant on Civil and Political Rights*, 1197 UNTS 411, available at https://treaties.un.org/Pages/ViewDetails.aspx?src=IND&mtdsg_no=IV-4&chapter=4&clang=_en#EndDec accessed 22 March 2017

Universal Declaration of Human Rights, GA Res 217A(III), UN GAOR, 3rd sess., 183rd plen. mtg., UN Doc A/810 (10 December 1948)

Urgent Appeal G/SO 218/2 G/SO 214(56–23) G/SO 214 (3–3-16) G/SO 214(53–24) EGY 13/2012 (3 October 2012)

Urgent Appeal G/SO 218/2 G/SO 214(67–17) Health (2002–7) G/SO 214(107–9) G/SO 214 (3–3-16) G/SO 214(53–24) G/SO 214(56–23) KAZ 4/2013 (22 August 2013)

Vienna Declaration on the Alliance of Civilizations, 27 February 2013, accessed 22 March 2017, http://www.vienna5unaoc.org/fileadmin/user_upload/documents/Vienna_Declaration.pdf

Jurisprudence

Human Rights Committee

Andersen v Denmark, Communication No. 1868/09, UN Doc CCPR/C/99/D/1868/2009 (7 September 2010)

Arenz v Germany, Communication No. 1138/2002, UN Doc CCPR/C/80/D/1138/2002 (24 March 2004)

Atasoy and Sartuk v Turkey, Communication Nos 1853/2008 and 1854/2008, UN Doc CCPR/C/104/D/1853–1854/2008 (29 March 2012)

Boodoo v Trinidad and Tobago, Communication No. 721/1996, UN Doc CCPR/C/74/D/721/1996 (2 April 2002)

Coeriel et al v The Netherlands, Communication No. 453/1991, UN Doc CCPR/C/52/D/453/1991 (31 October 1994)

Delgado-Paez v Colombia, Communication No. 195/1985, UN Doc CCPR/C/39/D/195/1985 (12 July 1990)

Ernst Zündel v Canada, Communication No. 953/2000, UN Doc CCPR/C/78/D/953/2000 (27 July 2003)

Faurisson v France, Communication No. 550/1993, UN Doc CCPR/C/58/D/550/1993 (8 November 1996)

Goyet v France, Communication No. 1746/2008, UN Doc. CCPR/C/94/D/1746/2008 (30 October 2008)

Hartikainen et al v Finland, Communication No. 40/1978, UN Doc CCPR/C/12/D/40/1978 (9 April 1981)

Hertzberg et al v Finland, Communication No. 61/1979, UN Doc CCPR/C/OP/1 (2 April 1982)

Hudoyberganova v Uzbekistan, Communication No. 931/2000, UN Doc CCPR/C/82/D/931/2000 (5 November 2004)

J.R.T. and the W.G. Party v Canada, Communication No. 104/1981, UN Doc CCPR/C/OP/2 at 25 (6 April 1983)

Kasem Said Ahmad and Asmaa Adol-Hamid v Denmark, Communication No. 1487/2006, UN Doc CCPR/C/92/D/1487/2006 (18 April 2008)

Leirvåg et al v Norway, Communication No. 931/00, UN Doc CCPR/C/82/D/1155/2003 (3 November 2004)

M.A. v Italy, Communication No. 117/1981, UN Doc Supp No 40 (A/39/40) 190 (10 April 1984)

MAB and ors v Canada, Admissibility, Communication No. 570/1993, UN Doc CCPR/C/50/D/570/1993 (8 April 1994)

Malakhovsky and Pikul v Belarus, Communication No. 1207/2003, UN Doc CCPR/C/84/D/1207/2003 (26 July 2005)

Mavlonov and Sa'id v Uzbekistan, Communication No. 1334/2004, UN Doc CCPR/C/95/D/1334/2004 (19 March 2009)

Prince v South Africa, Merits, Communication No. 1474/2006, UN Doc CCPR/C/91/D/1474/2006 (31 October 2007)

Ross v Canada, Communication No. 736/1997, UN Doc CCPR/C/70/D/736/1997 (26 October 2000)

Singh Bhinder v Canada, Communication No. 208/1986, UN DOC CCPR/C/37/D/208/1986 (1989)

Sister Immaculate v Sri Lanka, Communication No. 1249/2004, UN Doc CCPR/C/85/D/1249/2004 (21 October 2005)

Toonen v Australia, Communication No. 488/1992, UN Doc CCPR/C/5/D/488/1992 (31 March 1994)

X v Colombia, Communication No. 1361/2005, UN Doc CCPR/C/89/D/1361/2005 (30 March 2007)

Young v Australia, Communication No. 941/2000, UN Doc. CCPR/C/78/D/941/2000 (6 August 2003)

European Court of Human Rights

Angelini v Sweden, Application No. 10491/83 (1988)

Appel-Irrgang v Germany, Application No. 45206/07 (6 October 2009)

Campbell and Cosans v. The United Kingdom, Application Nos. 7511/76, 7743/76 (25 February 1982)

Church of Scientology Moscow v Russia, Application No. 18147/02 (5 April 2007)

Çiftçi v. Turkey, Application No. 71860/01 (17 June 2004)

Dahlab v Switzerland, Application No. 42393/98 (15 February 2001)

Eweida and Others v The United Kingdom, Application Nos 48420/10, 59842/10, 51671/10 and 36516/10 (15 January 2013)

Folgerø and Others v Norway, Grand Chamber Judgment, Application No. 15472/02 (29 June 2007)

Grzelak v Poland, Application No. 7710/02 (15 June 2010)

Hasan and Eylem Zengin v Turkey, Application No. 1448/04 (9 October 2007)

Hoffmann v Austria, Application No. 12875/87 (23 June 1993)

Ismailova v Russia, Application No. 37614/02 (8 November 2007)

Kokkinakis v Greece, Application No. 14307/88 (5 June 1993)

Larissis and Others v Greece, Application Nos 23372/94, 26377/94 and 26378/94 (24 February 1999)

Lautsi and others v Italy, Application No. 30814/06 (3 November 2009)

Leyla Şahin v Turkey, Application No. 44774/98 (10 November 2005)

Palau-Martinez v France, Application No. 64927/01 (16 December 2003)

Vojnity v Hungary, Application No. 29617/07 (12 February 2013)

Wingrove v the United Kingdom, Application No. 17419/90 (26 November 1996)
X and Church of Scientology v Sweden, Application No. 7805/77 (5 May 1979)

Other

Abdullah-Zentrum eröffnet, ORF News, 26 November 2012, accessed 15 February 2013, http://wien.orf.at/news/stories/2560515/

Actus Formalis Defectionis ab ecclesia Catholica, Pontifical Council for Legislative Texts, Vatican City, 13 March 2016, accessed 22 March 2017, http://www.vatican.va/roman_curia/pontifical_councils/intrptxt/documents/rc_pc_intrptxt_doc_20060313_actus-formalis_en.html

'African family values', *BBC News*, 27 June 2004, accessed 22 March 2017, http://news.bbc.co.uk/2/hi/programmes/panorama/3844959.stm

Aitkenhead, Decca, 'AC Grayling: 'How can you be a militant atheist? It's like sleeping furiously', *Guardian*, 3 April 2011, accessed 22 March 2017, https://www.theguardian.com/books/2011/apr/03/grayling-good-book-atheism-philosophy

Amnesty International Report 2015/16 (Amnesty International, 2016)

'Atheists hit back at clergy for criticism of non-belief', *Sydney Morning Herald*, 2 April 2010, accessed March 2017, http://www.smh.com.au/national/atheists-hit-back-at-clergy-criticism-of-nonbelief-20100402-rjmr.html

Auden, W. H., 'Port and nuts with the Eliots' (on 'Notes towards the definition of culture' by T. S. Eliot)', *New Yorker*, 17 July 1948

'Aust Muslim calls for beheading: report', *SBS*, 4 September 2010, updated 24 February 2015, accessed 22 March 2017, http://www.sbs.com.au/news/article/2010/09/04/aust-muslim-calls-beheading-report

'Baby bleeds to death after circumcision', *Miami Herald*, 26 June 1993

Baldas, Tresa, 'Religious Defense planned in landmark Detroit genital mutilation case', *Detroit Free Press*, 21 May 2017, accessed 26 May 2017, http://www.freep.com/story/news/2017/05/21/female-genital-mutilation-religious-freedom/319911001/

'Bangladesh blogger Niloy Neel hacked to death in Dhaka', *BBC*, 7 August 2015, accessed 22 March 2017, http://www.bbc.com/news/world-asia-33819032

'Bangladeshi professor Shafiul Islam hacked to death', *news.com.au*, 17 November 2014, accessed 22 March 2017, http://www.news.com.au/world/asia/bangladeshi-professor-shafiul-islam-hacked-to-death/news-story/ea9038ef36d7a2ca82dd6f2ffadb9b0e

'The Battle of the Books', *The Economist*, 19 December 2007, accessed 22 March 2017, http://www.economist.com/world/international/displaystory.cfm?story_id=10311317

'BBC Profile: Shoko Asaraha', *BBC*, 27 February 2004, accessed 22 March 2017, http://news.bbc.co.uk/2/hi/asia-pacific/3504237.stm

'B. C. parents lobby against circumcision', *CBC News*, accessed 22 March 2017, http://www.cbc.ca/news/canada/b-c-parents-lobby-against-circumcision-1.513363

Benito, Elizabeth Odio, *Elimination of all Forms of Intolerance and Discrimination based on Religion or Belief* (United Nations Centre for Human Rights, 1989)

Boyle, Kevin, and Sheen, Juliet, *Freedom of Religion and Belief: A World Report* (Routledge, 1997)

Brennan, Frank, 'Frank Brennan answers atheist manifestos', *Eureka Street*, 5 June 2007, accessed 22 March 2017, http://www.eurekastreet.com.au/article.aspx?aeid=2955

'Bush accused of Aids damage to Africa', *Guardian*, 30 August 2005, accessed 22 March 2017, http://www.guardian.co.uk/world/2005/aug/30/usa.aids

Carroll, James, 'The New Morality of Pope Francis', *New Yorker*, 8 April 2016, accessed 22 March 2017, http://www.newyorker.com/news/news-desk/new-morality-of-pope-francis-joy-of-love

Catch the Fire Ministries Inc & Ors v Islamic Council of Victoria Inc [2006] VSCA 284 (14 December 2006)

Chapman, Paul, 'Why a tribe in Vanuatu believes their god Prince Philip is set to visit', *Telegraph*, 25 April 2015, accessed 2 May 2017, http://www.telegraph.co.uk/news/worldnews/australiaandthepacific/vanuatu/11563091/Why-a-tribe-in-Vanuatu-believes-their-god-Prince-Philip-is-set-to-visit.html

Chee, Foo Yun, 'Dutch Protest against Islam critic's Koran protest', *Reuters*, 22 March 2008, accessed 22 March 2017, http://uk.reuters.com/article/idUKL2243365220080322

Cherry, Matt, 'An interview with Christopher Hitchens on Mother Teresa', *Free Inquiry Magazine*, Volume 16, Number 4

Claburn, Thomas, 'Anti-Islamic Film Taken Offline Following Threats', *InformationWeek*, 28 March 2008, accessed 11 November 2009, http://www.informationweek.com/news/internet/showArticle.jhtml?articleID=207000505

Combating trafficking in persons in accordance with the principles of Islamic law (UNODC, 2010)

Conference Summary: Freedom of Religion and Belief and Sexuality, Organized by the United Nations Special Rapporteur on Freedom of Religion or Belief and Muslims for Progressive Values (Muslims for Progressive Values, 2016)

'Convictions show society won't tolerate homophobia', *Derby Telegraph*, 21 January 2012, accessed 22 March 2017, http://www.derbytelegraph.co.uk/convictions-society-won-t-tolerate-homophobia/story-14994895-detail/story.html

Decety, J., et al., 'The Negative Association between Religiousness and Children's Altruism across the world' (November 2015) 25 *Current Biology* 2951, accessed 22 March 2017, http://www.cell.com/current-biology/pdf/S0960-9822(15)01167-7.pdf

de Klerk, Piet, Ambassador at Large of the Netherlands on Human Rights (Speech delivered at the 25th Anniversary Commemoration of the adoption of the 1981 Declaration on the elimination of intolerance and discrimination based on religion or belief, Prague, 25 November 2006), accessed 22 March 2017, http://www.tolerance95.cz/1981declaration/download.php

'Derby men guilty over gay hate leaflets', *BBC News*, 20 January 2012, accessed 22 March 2017, http://www.bbc.co.uk/news/uk-england-derbyshire-16656679

The Devil's Playground, film, directed by Lucy Walker, Stick Figure Productions, 2002

Early Marriage, A Harmful Traditional Practice (UNICEF, 2005)

'Egypt girl's death puts spotlight on genital mutilation', *BBC News*, 19 June 2013, accessed 22 March 2017, http://www.bbc.co.uk/news/world-middle-east-22975400

Ellen, Barbara, 'If condoms are OK for Zika, why not Aids, Pope Francis?' *Guardian*, 21 February 2016, accessed 22 March 2017, https://www.theguardian.com/commentisfree/2016/feb/21/pope-francis-zika-virus-contraception

Ewing, Jack, 'Some Religious Leaders See a Threat as Europe Grows More Secular', *New York Times*, 19 September 2012, accessed 22 March 2017, http://www.nytimes.com/2012/09/20/world/europe/circumcision-debate-in-europe-reflects-deeper-tensions.html?pagewanted=all&_r=0

Flynn, Tom, 'Secularism's breakthrough moment', 200626(3) *Free Inquiry* 16

The Freedom of Thought Report (International Humanist and Ethical Union, 2016) http://freethoughtreport.com/foreword-to-the-2016-edition/

Freedom of Thought 2012: A Global Report on Discrimination against Humanists, Atheists and the Non-Religious (International Humanists and Ethical Union, 2012)
'Gay men told they would burn in hell by preacher', *BBC News*, 9 February 2012, accessed 22 March 2017, http://www.bbc.co.uk/news/uk-england-somerset-16967037
'Germany imposes ban on Tom Cruise', *BBC*, 26 June 2007, accessed 22 March 2017, http://news.bbc.co.uk/2/hi/6240312.stm?lsm
Godfrey, Miles, 'Atheists are believers who hate god, says Anglican Archbishop Peter Jensen', *News*, 3 April 2010, accessed 22 March 2017, http://www.news.com.au/national/atheists-are-believers-who-hate-god-says-anglican-archbishop-peter-jensen/story-e6frfkvr-1225848927144?from=igoogle+gadget+compact+news_rss
Gold, Jennifer, 'Catholic condom ban is helping Aids spread in Latin America: UN', *Christian Today*, 23 October 2007
Goldberg, Michelle, 'Donald Trump, the Religious Right's Trojan Horse', *New York Times*, 27 January 2017, accessed 22 March 2017, https://www.nytimes.com/2017/01/27/opinion/sunday/donald-trump-the-religious-rights-trojan-horse.html?_r=0
Hasan, Nasra, 'An Arsenal of Believers', *New Yorker*, 19 November 2001, accessed 22 March 2017, http://www.newyorker.com/magazine/2001/11/19/an-arsenal-of-believers
Hitchens, Christopher, 'Letter to the Editor', *New York Review of Books*, 19 December 1996, accessed 22 March 2017, http://www.nybooks.com/articles/archives/1996/dec/19/mother-teresa/
Hobby Lobby Stores, Inc. v Sebelius, 723 F.3d 1114(2013); *Burwell v Hobby Lobby Stores, Inc.* 573 US__ (2014); *Burwell v Hobby Lobby Stores, Inc.* 134 S Ct 2751(2014)
Hoffman v Custodian of the Western Wall, H.C.J. 257/89, 2410/90, 48(2) P.D. 265
Holligan, Anna, 'Dutch Jews and Muslims fight for circumcision right', *BBC News*, 3 November 2011, accessed 22 March 2017, http://www.bbc.co.uk/news/world-europe-15486834
Human Rights and Equal Opportunity Commission, *'Article 18 Freedom of Religion and Belief'* (Commonwealth of Australia, 1998)
Human Rights Report: Germany, US Department of State 2008 (25 February 2009), accessed 22 March 2017, http://www.state.gov/g/drl/rls/hrrpt/2008/eur/119081.htm
Human Rights Watch, 'Africa: Bush's Trip highlights flaws in US HIV/AIDS policy', 14 February 2008, accessed 22 March 2017, http://www.hrw.org/en/news/2008/02/14/africa-bush-s-trip-highlights-flaws-us-hivaids-policy
'Indonesia: "Restrictive bill threatens freedoms of association, expression and religion," warn UN rights experts', OHCHR, 14 February 2013, accessed 22 March 2017, http://newsarchive.ohchr.org/en/NewsEvents/Pages/DisplayNews.aspx?NewsID=12989
International NGO Council on Violence against Women, *Violating Children's Rights: Harmful practices based on tradition, culture, religion or superstition* (CRIN, 2012)
International Religious Freedom Report for 2015, US Department of State, 2015, accessed 22 March 2017, http://www.state.gov/j/drl/rls/irf/religiousfreedom/index.htm#wrapper
Jackson, Robert, *Signposts – Policy and Practice for teaching about religions and non-religious worldviews in intercultural education* (Council of Europe, 2014)
Jahangir, Asma, Speech delivered at the 25th Anniversary Commemoration of the adoption of the 1981 Declaration on the elimination of intolerance and discrimination based on religion or belief, Prague, 25 November 2006, accessed 22 March 2017, http://www.tolerance95.cz/1981declaration/download.php

Jones, Jeffrey M., 'Atheists, Muslims see most Bias as Presidential Candidates', *Gallup*, 21 June 2012, accessed 22 March 2017, http://www.gallup.com/poll/155285/atheists-muslims-bias-presidential-candidates.aspx

Kearney, Marianne, 'Religious groups are exploiting Aceh chaos', *Telegraph*, 14 January 2005, accessed 22 March 2017, http://www.telegraph.co.uk/news/worldnews/1481197/Religious-groups-are-exploiting-Aceh-chaos.html

Khazan, Olga, 'Why some women choose to get circumcised', *Atlantic*, 8 April 2015, accessed 22 March 2017, https://www.theatlantic.com/international/archive/2015/04/female-genital-mutilation-cutting-anthropologist/389640/

'Knife attack kills Bangladeshi blogger Washiqur Rahman', *BBC*, 30 March 2015, accessed 22 March 2017, http://www.bbc.com/news/world-asia-32112433

'Lally Weymouth interviews Australian Prime Minister Julia Gillard', *Washington Post*, 8 March 2013, accessed 22 March 2017, https://www.washingtonpost.com/opinions/lally-weymouth-interviews-australian-prime-minister-julia-gillard/2013/03/08/9d0035c0-8733-11e2-999e-5f8e0410cb9d_story.html?utm_term=.3dc6ee019749

Landgericht Köln, Beschneidung, Judgment of Monday, 7 May 2012, No. 151, Ns 169/11, Neue Juristische Wochenschrift (NJW), http://www.justiz.nrw.de/nrwe/lgs/koeln/lg_koeln/j2012/151_Ns_169_11_Urteil_20120507.html in German. An unofficial translation is available at http://www.scribd.com/doc/98810698/Cologne-Circumcision-Decision-Translated-6-12

Macnair, Trisha, 'Female Genital Mutilation', *BBC*, January 2011, accessed 4 May 2011, http://www.bbc.co.uk/health/physical_health/conditions/female_genital_mutilation.shtml

Madrid, Carolina, 'Jews, Muslims sue to block referendum on circumcision', *Reuters*, 22 June 2011, accessed 22 March 2017, http://www.reuters.com/article/2011/06/23/us-circumcision-sanfrancisco-idUSTRE75M05120110623

Male Circumcision: Global trends and determinants of prevalence, safety and acceptability (World Health Organization and Joint United Nations Programme on HIV/AIDS, 2007)

Manual for early infant circumcision under local anaesthesia (World Health Organization, 2010)

Markel, Howard, 'Circumcision, Religious Freedom, and Herpes Infections in New York City', *Medscape*, 17 October 2006, accessed 22 March 2017, http://www.medscape.com/viewarticle/545756

Marr, David, 'Gillard's bizarre act of faith leaves vulnerable unprotected', *The Age*, 14 January 2013, accessed 22 March 2017, http://www.theage.com.au/opinion/politics/gillards-bizarre-act-of-faith-leaves-vulnerable-unprotected-20130113-2cnf0.html

Mason, Paul, Commissioner for Children, Hobart, Tasmania, Australia, 'Letter to the Editor', *Sydney Morning Herald*, 6 June 2009, accessed 22 March 2017, http://www.smh.com.au/national/letters/stopping-circumcision-a-matter-of-human-rights-20090605-byf4.html?page=6

'Michael Overd cleared of verbally abusing gay men in Taunton', *BBC News*, 10 February 2012, accessed 22 March 2017, http://www.bbc.co.uk/news/uk-england-somerset-16984133

'Moldova fails to adequately protect lesbian, gay, bisexual, transgender and intersex (LGBTI) individuals from discrimination' (Amnesty International Public Statement, 29 March 2011), accessed 22 March 2017, http://www.amnesty.org/en/library/info/EUR59/004/2012/en

Mrs. Yulitha Hyde And Ors vs State Of Orissa And Ors, 1973 A.I.R. 116 (Ori) 121 (24 October 1972)

'Muslim guilty of inciting racial hatred', *BBC*, 3 May 2002, accessed 22 March 2017, http://news.bbc.co.uk/2/hi/uk_news/england/1966839.stm

Naraghi, Arash, 'The Quran and Human Rights of Sexual Minorities' in *Lesbian, Gay, Bisexual and Transgender Rights in Iran* (International Gay and Lesbian Rights Commission, 2015) 27–55

'National Action Plan to tackle child abuse linked to religion or belief' (The UK National Working Group on Child Abuse linked to Religion or Belief, 2012)

'Navy approves first ever Satanist', *BBC News*, 24 October 2004, accessed 15 February 2013, http://news.bbc.co.uk/2/hi/uk/3948329.stm

'Nepal police investigate death of girl banished for menstruating', *BBC*, 20 December 2016, accessed 22 March 2017, http://www.bbc.com/news/world-asia-38384889

Newman, Andy, 'City Questions Circumcision Ritual after Baby Dies', *New York Times*, 26 August 2005, accessed 22 March 2017, http://www.nytimes.com/2005/08/26/nyregion/26circumcise.html

Ngo, Thoai D. and Obhai, George, Marie Stopes International, *At the Cutting Edge: Delivering Male Circumcision through Marie Stopes' Reproductive Health Mobile Outreach Programmes in Kenya* (2009)

OHCHR, *Fact Sheet 23, Harmful traditional practices affecting the health of women and children*, accessed 22 March 2017, http://www.ohchr.org/Documents/Publications/FactSheet23en.pdf

Organisation of Islamic Conference (OIC), *Cairo Declaration on Human Rights in Islam*, 5 August 1990

Parliamentary Assembly of the Council of Europe, *Resolution 1805 on Blasphemy, religious insults and hate speech against persons on grounds of their religion*, 27th sitting (29 June 2007)

Paul Holdengraber interview with Christopher Hitchens (in conversation at the New York Public Library), 4 June 2010

Pew Forum on Religion and Public Life, 'The Future of World Religions: Population Growth Projections, 2010–2050', April 2015

Pew Forum on Religion and Public Life, 'The Global Religious Landscape; A report on the size and distribution of the world's major religious groups as of 2010', December 2012

Pew Research Center, 'Faith and the 2016 Campaign', January 2016

'Pope Francis: better to be an atheist than a hypocritical Catholic', *Guardian*, 23 February 2017, accessed 22 March 2017, https://www.theguardian.com/world/2017/feb/23/pope-francis-better-to-be-atheist-than-hypocritical-catholic

Pope Paul VI, 'Humanae Vitae', *Encyclical on the Regulation of Birth Control* (1968)

Prohibiting incitement to discrimination, hostility of violence: Policy Brief (ARTICLE 19, December 2012)

Prosecutor General v Green (Supreme Court, Sweden) Appeal Judgment, Case No B, 1050–1005, ILDC 200 (SE 2005) (29 November 2005)

'Rev. Sun Myung Moon, Self-proclaimed messiah who built religious movement, dies at 92', *New York Times*, 2 September 2012, accessed 22 March 2017, http://www.nytimes.com/2012/09/03/world/asia/rev-sun-myung-moon-founder-of-unification-church-dies-at-92.html?pagewanted=all&_r=0

Rich, Frank, 'Show me the money', *New York Times*, 25 January 1997, accessed 22 March 2017, http://www.nytimes.com/1997/01/25/opinion/show-me-the-money.html?ref=scientology

Riman, Iman, 'Muslim Women protest Australian visit of anti-Islam activist Ayaan Hirsi Ali', 20 March 2017, sbs.com.au, accessed 28 April 2017, http://www.sbs.com.au/yourlanguage/arabic/en/article/2017/03/20/muslim-women-protest-australian-visit-anti-islam-activist-ayaan-hirsi-ali

Roberts, Amos, 'Waiting for Philip', *Dateline Report* (SBS Australia), 8 August 2010, accessed 2 May 2017, http://www.sbs.com.au/dateline/story/about/id/600662/n/Waiting-for-Philip

Sampathkumar, Mythili, 'Donald Trump defunding of UN's women's health service will cause "millions to suffer"', *Independent*, 4 April 2017, accessed 27 April 2017, http://www.independent.co.uk/news/world/americas/us-politics/donald-trump-abortion-defunding-global-mexico-city-rule-un-population-fund-a7666916.html

Saner, Emine, 'Germany 1, Scientology 0', *Guardian*, 27 June 2007, accessed 22 March 2017, http://www.guardian.co.uk/world/2007/jun/27/germany.features11

'San Francisco circumcision ban struck from ballot', *BBC News*, 28 July 2011, accessed 22 March 2017, http://www.bbc.co.uk/news/world-us-canada-14335715

Saslow, Laura, et al., 'My Brother's Keeper? Compassion Predicts Generosity More among Less Religious Individuals', *Social Psychology and Personality Science*, 26 April 2012, accessed 22 March 2017, http://journals.sagepub.com/doi/abs/10.1177/1948550612444137?journalCode=sppa

Saudi Arabia Country Report, *Freedom of Thought Report* (International Humanist and Ethical Union, 2016), accessed 2 February 2017, http://freethoughtreport.com/countries/asia-western-asia/saudi-arabia/

'Saudi Arabia: Writer Faces Apostasy Trial', *Human Rights Watch*, 13 February 2012, accessed 22 March 2017, https://www.hrw.org/news/2012/02/13/saudi-arabia-writer-faces-apostasy-trial

'Saudi blogger Raif Badawai faces further round of flogging, supporters say', *Guardian*, 18 October 2016, accessed 22 March 2017, https://www.theguardian.com/world/2016/oct/18/saudi-blogger-raif-badawi-faces-further-flogging

'Saudi rights activist faces apostasy charge', *Middle East Online*, 17 December 2012, accessed 22 March 2017, http://www.middle-east-online.com/english/?id=56110

Second Vatican Ecumenical Council, *Dignitatis Humanae: Declaration on Religious Freedom* (1965)

Secretary General Statement, 'No Justification for Hate Speech or Incitement, says Secretary-General in strong condemnation of Anti-Islamic Film', 28 March 2008, accessed 22 March 2017, http://www.un.org/News/Press/docs/2008/sgsm11483.doc.htm

'Secular activist who criticised Islamism killed in Dhaka', *Guardian*, 7 April 2016, accessed 22 March 2017, https://www.theguardian.com/world/2016/apr/07/secular-activist-who-criticised-islamism-hacked-to-death-in-bangladesh

Sherwood, Harriet, 'No baptism, no school: Irish parents fight for equal access to education', *Guardian*, 21 October 2015, accessed 2 February 2016, https://www.theguardian.com/world/2015/oct/21/no-baptism-no-school-irish-parents-fight-for-equal-access-to-education

Siegal, Nina, 'Geert Wilders, Dutch Far-Right Leader, Is Convicted of Inciting Discrimination', *New York Times*, 9 December 2016, accessed 7 March 2017, https://www.nytimes.com/2016/12/09/world/europe/geert-wilders-netherlands-trial.html?_r=0

Southwestern Baptist Theological Seminary, accessed 22 March 2017, http://catalog.swbts.edu/school-of-evangelism/master-of-arts-islamic-studies/

Statement by UN High Commissioner for Human Rights Navi Pillay to the Panel on ending violence, discrimination against people because of their sexual orientation,

Geneva, 7 March 2012, accessed 22 March 2017, http://acnudh.org/en/pillay-presents-groundbreaking-un-study-on-violence-discrimination-against-people-because-of-their-sexual-orientation/

'Statement of interpretation of the Holy See on the Adoption of the Declaration of Commitment on HIV/AIDS', *Vatican*, 27 June 2001, accessed 22 March 2017, http://www.vatican.va/roman_curia/secretariat_state/documents/rc_seg-st_doc_20010627_declaration-aids_en.html

Statement of the Holy See in Explanation of its Position on the Resolution 'Women, the child and HIV/AIDs' (E/CN.6/2011/L.3), 55th Session of the Commission on the Status of Women of the ECOSOC, New York, 4 March 2011

Tan, Yvette, 'Why female genital mutilation still exists in modern Singapore', *BBC News*, 21 November 2016, accessed 22 March 2017, http://www.bbc.com/news/world-asia-37819753

Taylor, Sue, Church of Scientology, International, 'Scientology' (paper presented at the International Coalition for Religious Freedom Conference on 'Religious Freedom in Latin America and the New Millennium', Sheraton Mofarrej Hotel, Sao Paolo, Brazil, October 10–12, 1998)

Tempest, Matthew, 'Religious hatred bill "will not harm free speech"', *Guardian*, 31 January 2006, accessed 22 March 2017, http://www.guardian.co.uk/politics/2006/jan/31/immigrationpolicy.religion1?INTCMP=ILCNETTXT3487

Theodorou, Angelina E., *Which countries still outlaw apostasy and blasphemy?*, Pew Research Centre's Forum on Religion and Public Life, 29 July 2016, accessed 22 March 2017, http://www.pewresearch.org/fact-tank/2016/07/29/which-countries-still-outlaw-apostasy-and-blasphemy/

Toledo Guiding Principles on Teaching about Religions and Beliefs in Public Schools (OSCE, 2007)

Toynbee, Polly, 'What's at stake is the right to insult and cause offence', *Guardian*, 31 January 2006, accessed 22 March 2017, http://www.guardian.co.uk/politics/2006/jan/31/religion.politicalcolumnists?INTCMP=ILCNETTXT3487

Trends in Global Restrictions on Religion (Pew Research Center, 2016)

UNAIDS, 'Empowering women to protect themselves: Promoting the Female Condom in Zimbabwe', 1 July 2010, accessed 22 March 2017, http://www.unfpa.org/news/empowering-women-protect-themselves-promoting-female-condom-zimbabwe

UNAIDS, *HIV Transmission in Intimate Partner Relationships in India* (2009), accessed 22 March 2017, http://www.aidsdatahub.org/sites/default/files/documents/HIVTransmission_Intimate_Partner_Relationships_India.pdf

US v Kuch, 288 F Supp 439(1968)

'Using the CRC and Protocols for Children', UNICEF, 22 March 2017, www.unicef.org/crc/index_using.html

'Vatican rejects criticism over its anti-condom stance', *Earth Times*, 25 July 2008, accessed 2 January 2009, www.wwrn.org

Vine, Jeremy, and Sweeny, John, 'Scientology and me' for BBC Panorama, 14 May 2007

Warhurst, John, 'Reflections on Gillard's atheism', *Eureka Street*, 16 October 2011, accessed 22 March 2017, http://www.eurekastreet.com.au/article.aspx?aeid=28547

The White House, 'Innovations in Compassion, The Faith-Based and Community Initiative: A Final Report to the Armies of Compassion', December 2008

'Why do Jews circumcise their children? Dossier of the Central Council of Jews in Germany on the issue of circumcision', Zentralrat der Juden in Deutschland, 10 July 2012, accessed 22 March 2017, http://www.zentralratdjuden.de/en/article/3734.html

World Council of Churches, Pontifical Council for Interreligious Dialogue, World Evangelical Alliance, 'Christian Witness in a Multi-Religious World: Recommendations for Conduct' (2011) 35 *International Bulletin of Missionary Research* 194

'The World from Berlin: Circumcision Ruling is a 'Shameful farce for Germany', *Spiegel*, 13 July 2012, accessed 22 March 2017, http://www.spiegel.de/international/germany/german-press-review-on-outlash-against-court-s-circumcision-ruling-a-844271.html

World Health Organization, *Fact Sheet: Female Genital Mutilation*, February 2017, accessed 22 March 2017, http://www.who.int/mediacentre/factsheets/fs241/en/

World Health Organization, *Male circumcision for HIV prevention*, accessed 22 March 2017, http://www.who.int/hiv/topics/malecircumcision/en/

World Report 2016 (Human Rights Watch, 2015)

World Report 2017 (Human Rights Watch, 2016)

Wright, Lawrence, 'The Apostate: Paul Haggis v the Church of Scientology', *New Yorker*, 14 February 2011, accessed 22 March 2017, http://www.newyorker.com/reporting/2011/02/14/110214fa_fact_wright

Index

For Product Safety Concerns and Information please contact our EU representative GPSR@taylorandfrancis.com
Taylor & Francis Verlag GmbH, Kaufingerstraße 24, 80331 München, Germany

www.ingramcontent.com/pod-product-compliance
Ingram Content Group UK Ltd.
Pitfield, Milton Keynes, MK11 3LW, UK
UKHW022125190926
475702UK00013B/1654
9780367886677